KIDDING OURSELVES

KIDDING OURSELVES

Breadwinning, Babies, and Bargaining Power

RHONA MAHONY

BasicBooks
A Division of HarperCollins*Publishers*

Copyright © 1995 by Rhona Mahony.
Published by BasicBooks, A Division of HarperCollins Publishers, Inc.

Library of Congress Cataloging-in-Publication Data
Mahony, Rhona.
Kidding ourselves : breadwinning, babies, and bargaining power /
Rhona Mahony.
p.   cm.
Includes bibliographical references and index.
ISBN 0–465–08593–8
1. Parenting.   2. Dual-career families.   3. Sexual division of
labor.   4. Working mothers.   I. Title.
HQ755.8.M34   1995
306.872—dc20   95–5761
                                                      CIP
95 96 97 98 ◆/RRD 9 8 7 6 5 4 3 2 1

To Mom, Dad, and Karin

Contents

Preface

HUNDREDS OF PEOPLE HELPED ME WRITE THIS BOOK, SOME ACCIdentally but most of them on purpose. They include just about everyone over the age of twelve I have met in the last three years. At dinners with my cousins and my in-laws, at picnics, and at neighborhood Halloween parties, I quizzed everyone who could stand it, and many who couldn't, about their views on the sexual division of labor at home. A wide network of friends, acquaintances, and strangers told me about couples who were sharing child raising and about househusbands. So many people helped, in so many ways, often without my even knowing, that I find it impossible to thank them all individually.

A few people will find themselves mentioned in the text, and many will see their names listed in the endnotes. Others I'd like to give special thanks to here: George Akerlof, Ian Ayres, George Baker, Gary Becker, Jennifer Brown, Victor Fuchs, Claudia Goldin, Gillian Hadfield, Lauren Jennings, David Kreps, Alan Krueger, and Peter Menell. Thanks also to my very energetic agent, Susan Golomb, and my editor, Susan Rabiner, who not only saw a good book hiding in my murky proposal but also organized the book sensibly.

Warm thanks also to Paulette Caldwell, Beth Conway, and Ruth Hakim, who helped take care of our daughter so that my husband and I could spend time at our other jobs. Finally, inexpressible thanks to Jeremy, who even now is slapping his forehead and telling his friends, "Can you believe that I supported Rhona for two and a half years so she could become an expert on how to negotiate with your husband?!"

For mistakes, omissions, and adamantine optimism herein, I take full responsibility.

November 1994

Introduction

CHERYL AND DEAN HAVE TWO CHILDREN WHO ARE NOW EIGHTEEN and twelve years old. When the children were small, both parents worked full-time. Cheryl worked at a computer center, giving technical help to people on-line. Dean ran the shipping and receiving department of a medical equipment company. Cheryl brought the children to and from the babysitter and the day care center. She stayed home when they were sick. At night, after she came home from work, she took care of the children, cleaned the house, cooked dinner, washed dishes, washed clothes, and ironed. When Dean came home, he felt he had earned the right to relax for a few hours. In the late 1970s and early 1980s, that arrangement made a rough sort of sense to both Cheryl and Dean. He earned $11 an hour; she earned $8 an hour. Dean's own mother had taken meticulous care of him and his eight siblings. Cheryl's mother had kept the house spotless while raising her and her brother. The big difference, which Cheryl and Dean never discussed because they simply didn't see it, was that neither of their mothers had held a paying job while she was raising her children.

Thanks to the sociologist Arlie Hochschild (1989), we have a name for Cheryl's predicament: the second shift. Many people now realize how exhausting and unfair it is for a mother with a full-time job to do all the housework and child raising while her husband does none. Even Cheryl and Dean see that now; Dean does more at home than he used to. However, few people see that the assignment of chores at home has broad consequences. More is at stake than women's fatigue or unfairness in millions of families. What is at stake is the subject of this book: women's centuries-old struggle to achieve real economic equality with men.

Chores at home are tied to women's equality because there are only twenty-four hours in a day. While women are cleaning, cooking, and raising children, what are men doing? They are earning money, taking part in community groups, unions, or professional associations, running for public office, inventing widgets in the garage, playing sports, or resting. They are doing things that women don't get a chance to do.

Chores at home are also tied to women's equality because people act on their expectations. Girls who grow up believing the spoken or unspoken assumption that a big chunk of their adult life will be devoted to child raising don't take the hard courses in school that lead to high-paying jobs: trigonometry, calculus, or physics. Their brothers do. They expect that they will be responsible for supporting their wives and children.

Chores at home also matter because young women who believe that they will devote a big chunk of their adult lives to child raising don't go into challenging, nontraditional jobs. They don't choose jobs that require travel, lots of overtime, or inflexible or unpredictable hours. They rule out thousands of jobs in business, science, law enforcement, and the military. Or they never even consider them, because they conflict with that big job at home.

Chores at home also matter because they don't pay. No matter what else we say, reform, or re-engineer, people who do thousands of hours of unpaid work each year are going to have less money than people who work only for pay. Money isn't everything. However, it does matter. The lower a wife's income, the more likely she is to suffer real hardship if she and her husband separate. Also, the more likely she is to suffer battering by her husband while she stays with him.

Finally, chores at home matter because women get surprised by them, particularly by child raising. They get surprised by how much time and energy it consumes, by how wonderful it is, and by how hard it is to hire someone who will take care of their children in just the ways they want, which they want with surprising intensity. As a result, many mothers scale back their paying work much further than they ever expected. Some are happy to. Others don't understand why they can't get their husbands to share more in the effort and rewards of taking care of the children. That difficulty surprises them, too.

My argument in this book is that who does what at home matters a lot outside the home. It shapes the whole economy. Because women and only women raise children, they are scarce in whole swaths of occupations and in the top echelons of business, politics, art, science, technology, and religious organizations.

Social scientists call who does what at home the division of labor. Because our division of labor hinges on whether people are male or female, social scientists say that we have a sexual division of labor. For us to understand women's struggle to achieve economic equality with men, we need a much, much better understanding of the sexual division of labor in the home.

Most of the research that I draw on here was published during the 1980s.

Until now, though, no one has assembled the puzzle pieces to make this particular picture. I think that no one assembled this picture for two reasons. First, feminists have mainly focused their energies on big and important evils outside the home. They have been working to end discrimination against women, racial minorities, and disabled people, sexual harassment, and the glass ceiling. They have also been working to make schools safer and fairer for girls. Those efforts are valuable. The catch is, this is not enough.

Second, it is hard for people to imagine an alternative to the sexual division of labor in the home. Sure, men should do more. But who, really and truly, is going to stay home when Junior is sick, read him *The Lorax* eight times, and make blackberry tea with honey just the way he likes it? Because many women—even many clever, devoted feminists—found it hard to imagine an alternative to millions of mothers staying home to read *The Lorax,* they didn't subject the sexual division of labor in the home to the searching scrutiny it deserves.

In fact, instead of searching and scrutinizing, I'm afraid that many women have been kidding themselves. We kidded ourselves when we thought that government subsidies to child care centers would eliminate the second shift. We kidded ourselves when we thought about our own futures. "Oh, it won't happen to me," we said. "I have lots of energy and my husband will help." Or: "My mother will babysit and I'll be office manager in no time." We were kidding ourselves when we said those things because we weren't facing up to some basic arithmetic. There are 24 hours in a day. There are 7 days in a week. That means that there are 168 hours in a week. If Grandma or the child care center or a babysitter takes the children for, say, 50 hours a week, that still leaves 118 hours. Our kids need us for a surprising, appalling, delightful number of those 118 hours. If all those hours are women's work, then women's lives are going to look very different from men's—even after we have eliminated discrimination, sexual harassment, the glass ceiling, and unfair schools.

But what about the women who said, "My husband will help"? Surely they weren't kidding themselves. These are the 1990s, after all. Fathers are spending more time with their small children than ever before, right? Surely a woman could tell before she had children whether her boyfriend or husband was the type of guy who would keep his promise to share the responsibility for child raising.

Wrong. Women kid themselves about that, too. Both before and after the birth of the first child, they don't see the real obstacles that prevent fathers from getting involved in child raising. *Before* the baby, it is almost impossible to peep over the threshold and see what your life will be like afterward. You and your husband may have an arrangement: he buys groceries, you cook dinner. That seems fair. You expect that he'll do a lot of child raising, and so does he. Neither of you realizes that, after the baby arrives, the workload at home will increase by a factor of 20. It's nearly inconceivable.

After the baby is born, women don't see the real obstacles because the atmosphere at home is very emotionally charged. That charged field of emotion—and the fatigue of brand-new parents—makes it much harder for you and your partner to talk in an articulate or insightful way about who should do what at home.

Also, women don't see the real obstacles because they created lots of the obstacles themselves, many years before. Suddenly, decisions they made in high school and in their twenties start to have consequences they never foresaw. Many women don't see the consequences even as they unfold in their own homes. The truth is that from an early age, many women shape themselves into becoming primary parents. Unwittingly, they lock themselves into child raising and lock their husbands out. They are not as free to choose what their families will be like as they think, or as their husbands think.

So, will women ever achieve real equality with men? I propose that the answer to that question is another question: Can a father raise babies and can a woman let him do it?

That is the key question, because in order for women to achieve economic equality with men, *men will have to do half the work of raising children.* Whether or not that happens depends on whether men can be tender and competent hands-on parents and whether women will let them do it.

What does it mean for men to do half the work of raising children? It does *not* mean that in every couple the man and the woman will each do half the child raising. It does *not* mean that parents will split responsibility toward their children according to their incomes, as in, You earn one-third of the income so you should do two-thirds of the child raising. Nor does it mean that a few more fathers will be househusbands.

None of those formulas would bring real equality within women's reach. More to the point, we couldn't pull off those formulas even if we wanted to. The typical woman on the brink of having her first child does *not* get to pick what percentage of child raising she will do. She has already made decisions that lock her into a traditional motherly role.

Instead, I propose a revolution in people's attitudes toward the sexual division of labor in the home. I propose that we throw away the stereotypes that say men cannot be tender and competent as hands-on parents. I propose that we also throw away the stereotypes about what makes a woman a good mother. A woman who earns most of her family's income while her partner does most of the child raising is a caring, loving, good mother, too.

The stereotypes stand in women's way. They make it impossible for men to do half the work of raising children. For that to happen, women and men will have to see each other differently. Millions of women will have to give up the search for a man who will take care of them financially. Millions of men will have to give up the search for a woman who will reflect their glory. Mothers and fathers will also have to ask their sons to do much more work at home and their daughters to set high earnings goals.

When the sexual division of labor in the home has melted away, the link between people's sex and their work will be severed. Women will be as likely as men to be surgeons and pilots, on average. They will be as likely as men to work for pay full-time their entire lives, on average. Men will be as likely as women to shift into part-time work when their first baby is born, or to quit paying work entirely. When there are roughly as many househusbands as housewives and roughly as many female breadwinners as male breadwinners, then men will really be doing half the child care. That scenario is the prerequisite of women's equality. It is the *only* scenario in which women will finally and really achieve economic equality with men.

The key to understanding how that scenario might come about is *negotiation*. The division of labor in the home—who does what chores—is the result of negotiation between the people who live together. That negotiation can be full of talk or it can be silent. It can be planned or accidental. It can be conscious or unconscious. Most important of all, by the time the sun sets on the typical woman's wedding day (or, if she hasn't married, on the day she conceives her first baby), *she has already done nearly all the negotiating over chores and child care that she will ever do.* How can that be? This book says that the decisions women make about school, about jobs, and about who their romantic partners will be put them, years later, into a particular negotiating position. Usually, that position is weak. Usually, it makes it hard for women to reach their goals, even when their goals are mainly to cherish their children and husbands as they think best.

In this book, readers will learn how to assess the strengths and weaknesses of people's negotiating positions, including their own. They will learn how women can improve their negotiating position. As we'll see, that is easi-est for young women, but possible for all women. We'll look at what steps women can take singly, and what steps can be taken only by lots of people working together. Throughout, I will emphasize that every word of this analysis applies with full force to working-class and poor women, to African-American and Latino women, and to women in developing countries. Taken as a group, of course, they make up the biggest proportion of women in the world and those for whom real equality will bring the sweetest fruits.

The view of negotiation I take in this book is based in economics and game theory. You may know that economics is the study of how people deal with scarcity. Time is scarce, money is scarce, and energy is scarce, so we have to make decisions about how we spend those things. You may not have heard where the word *economics* comes from. Long ago, someone on the shores of the Mediterranean wrote a manuscript called "Ta Oikonomika." Some people think that it may even have been Aristotle. The manuscript was about how to manage a household. (*Oikos* is classical Greek for "house"; *nomos* means "managing.") Since then, economists have figured out a lot of things, but until this book no one thought to apply them to the nitty-gritty details of who does what at home and what difference it makes. (But see the trailblazing theorists McElroy and Horney, 1981; and Manser and Brown, 1980.) As we will see, the difference it makes is the difference between equality and second-class citizenship for the two and a half billion people in the world who happen to be female.

You may also know about game theory, especially since the 1994 Nobel Prize in Economics went to three pioneers in the field. Game theory is the study of how people behave in situations in which other people are going to react to their decisions and those reactions matter. So everyone tries to look ahead. Lucky for us, we can delve deeply and thoroughly into our topic—the negotiations that create, sustain, or melt away the sexual division of labor in the home—using simple ideas from game theory. If you can play checkers, you can follow every bit of the analysis in this book (even if you usually lose!).

So this book brings some good news and some bad news. The good news is that the dream of real, practical equality between women and men isn't a dream anymore. Women can make it happen. The bad news is that it's up to women themselves. It isn't coming on any silver platter. Then again, maybe that's good news, too.

I

The Elements of Negotiation

I

Women's Predicament

All women become like their mothers. That is their tragedy. No man does. That's his.

—Oscar Wilde, *The Importance of Being Earnest*

L ONG AGO, MOST PEOPLE HAD LOTS OF CHILDREN. ALL OVER THE world—among farmers in the Andes, colonial settlers in North America, hunter-gatherers in Southeast Asia—people wanted three or four children to work alongside them as soon as they were able and to support them in their old age. That wasn't easy to manage. Death rates were so high that a woman had to have seven or eight children just to make sure that three or four of them would survive.

Because people didn't have good alternatives to breastfeeding in those days, children kept women very busy. A woman who had seven children and breastfed them all spent up to 63 months being pregnant and between 35 and 168 months breastfeeding—that is, between eight and nineteen years of pregnancy and nursing combined.

Until very recently, nearly everyone in the world followed this way of life. In many poor countries today, people still face the same ancient constraints. For such people, a sexual division of labor may make sense. That is, it makes sense for most girls to grow up expecting to specialize in baby care and in tasks that are compatible with baby care. Those tasks might include farming patches of land close to home, processing food, and settling disputes. All the tasks necessary to sustain the community that are *incompatible* with baby care will have to be performed by someone else: by men, and by those few women who plan to have no children. People will train their boys, and maybe a few tomboys, to go on long-distance hunting trips and to ambush enemies with axes.

No one knows for sure why people really first invented a sexual division of labor. The story I just told is an economic one. Psychologists, anthropologists, biologists, and theologians have all told other stories. In this book I am asking a different question, which is more urgent: Why do we still have a sexual division of labor today, in the United States? Given that the practical circumstances of our lives have changed completely, I find it remarkable that we still do. Families are small and few mothers nurse for more than a few months. Yet women still do nearly all the child care. The glaciers have receded and mammoths are extinct, but this relic of the Pleistocene still slouches across our living rooms. Mom raises the kids.

This fossilized social life that we seem to be inhabiting is not just a curiosity. It matters a great deal, because it puts us and keeps us in a nasty predicament. The thesis of this book is that babies are now what prevent American women from achieving economic equality with men.

What do I mean by "economic equality"? From the outset, I want to emphasize that "economic" refers to much more than monetary income or wealth saved up in the form of stocks and bonds. It refers to *all the good things in life as each person defines those things for herself or himself.* Those might include a roomy and safe place to live; dignified work with a chance to learn and to exercise responsibility; freedom from fear of violence, homelessness, and illness; leisure time to relax, make music, play sports, or visit with relatives; respect from people who know you and a presumption of respect from people who haven't met you yet; a chance to participate in local and national politics; and frills that give life zest, like snowboarding and chocolate sundaes.

Babies are what now stand between women and an opportunity equal to men's opportunity to enjoy those good things. Why am I picking on babies? They are just a shorthand way of saying "the sexual division of labor."

What about discrimination against women and sexual harassment in the workplace? Of course they are intolerable and illegal. We have to work hard—individually and collectively—to eliminate them. However, even eliminating them completely would not, in itself, close the gap in economic well-being between women and men, for two reasons.

First, discrimination and harassment aren't the only forces keeping women from entering some traditionally male jobs. Their responsibility for taking care of babies and children creates big obstacles because it affects their self-conceptions, and therefore the training they get when they are young. It also sets up serious practical constraints when they are older.

Second, discrimination in the labor market and sexual harassment do much of their dirty work by *reinforcing* the sexual division of labor. They make paying work pay less than it would otherwise and make the workplace unpleasant or dangerous. Thus, they make staying at home more attractive—that is, artificially attractive—to women.

Discrimination and sexual harassment are like Bigfoot. Bigfoot's footprints don't cover the whole terrain, but wherever it walks, the footprints are deep. The terrain is the sexual division of labor.

In this chapter, we are going to take a fresh look at six important areas of women's experience: women's education and earnings; their segregation into a small number of jobs; battering; their vulnerability upon separation or divorce; an unpleasant fact of life I call the beauty problem; and statistical discrimination. Together, these six factors have a huge impact on women's economic well-being, especially their economic well-being relative to men. As we will see, they are all connected to women's nearly sole responsibility for raising children.

Education and Earnings

As the newspapers announce cheerily every week or so, American women have come a long way in the last thirty years. Forty-three percent of new lawyers and 38 percent of new doctors are women (*Review of Legal Education,* 1992; Association of American Medical Colleges, 1994, table B-8). Women are also more highly educated than at any time in the past. In 1970, only 8 percent of white American women and 5 percent of black American women twenty-five years old and over were college graduates; the comparable figures today are 19 percent and 12 percent (*Current Population Reports,* 1991, table 29; *Statistical Abstract,* 1993, table 231).

These shifts have all improved women's economic well-being. However, during those years less privileged women—especially those with only a high school education or less—suffered setbacks. Also, most significant for the purposes of this section, men's economic welfare increased a great deal. In spite of the improvement in women's position, then, we are left with a very important question: Have women closed the historic gap between themselves and men? If so, by how much? If not, why not?

Let's note from the beginning that comparing women's progress to men's progress is not an exercise in envy. Most Americans agree that rough social equality and equality of opportunity are good things. Women's *relative* standing has a big impact on their social status, their influence in the political process, the contribution they can make to their communities, and the degree to which their tastes and priorities are reflected in their families, their workplaces, on television, and throughout popular culture. Women can't hold up half the sky until their stance is as firm and their reach as high as those of the average man.

Looking closely at women's progress relative to men's will give us important clues about the obstacles holding back women's progress in the absolute sense. Millions of women don't waste time envying rich male professionals; they're just looking for a way out of the quagmire of poverty, violence, and dead-end jobs.

To review the basics:

Women still earn less than men. In 1991, among people twenty-five to thirty-four years old who worked full-time, year-round, women's median income was $21,022 and men's was $26,100. Of course, we need to compare people with the same level of education. Among all full-time, year-round workers who were twenty-five to thirty-four years old *and* who had a bachelor's degree or more, men's median income was $32,430 and women's was $26,281. The men made about 23 percent more (*Current Population Reports,* 1991, table 29).

Race has a significant impact on earnings in the United States. It also has an impact on the gender gap in earnings. Young, college-educated black women who worked full-time, year-round, had incomes very close to their white female peers': $23,396. That represents a remarkable increase in black women's earning power. Their black male peers earned only a little more: $26,944. For this group of black workers, then, men's incomes were 15 percent higher than women's. The gender gap is much smaller among blacks than among whites.

Also, women still have less schooling than men, despite the increase in the percentage of women who have graduated from college in the last thirty years. Among people who were twenty-five to sixty-four years old in 1991, the proportion of male professionals was almost three times that of females, and the proportion of male Ph.D.s was over two and a half times that of females (*Current Population Reports,* 1991, table 29, my calculations).

However, young women are staying in school longer than their mothers did, so figures that lump all age groups together are misleading. In fact, a higher percentage of young women than young men are now graduating from college. However, among whites who were twenty-five to thirty-four years old in 1991, the proportion of male professionals was still almost 40 percent higher than that of females, and the proportion of male Ph.D.s was one-third again as high as that of females. A higher percentage of young white men than young white women also held master's degrees. (The story is a little different for black and Hispanic women who were twenty-five to thirty-four years old in 1991. They had graduated from college at a higher rate than black and Hispanic men. Young black women were *more* likely to hold Ph.D.s than young black men but much less likely to hold a professional degree. The opposite was true for Hispanics. A slightly *higher* percentage of young Hispanic women than men held professional degrees, but a much lower percentage of young Hispanic women than men held Ph.D.s.)

American women, then, have completely closed the gap between themselves and men in college attendance and college graduation, but not in graduate or professional education. They go on to earn much less money.

Consider one other set of basic numbers. In an important sense, the income figures given here for well-educated young people understate the difference between women and men since they included only full-time, year-round workers. Women—even young women—are still much less likely than men to work for pay. What is particularly interesting is what marriage and having young children do to men's and women's tendency to work for pay.

In 1992, among people twenty-five to thirty-four years old who were single, 89.8 percent of men and 80.5 percent of women were in the labor force. Among those who were married and living with their spouse, 96.6 percent of men and 70.9 percent of women were in the labor force (*Statistical Abstract,* 1993, table 631). In essence, then, marriage has a seesaw effect. Married men are more likely to work for pay than single men. Married women are less likely to than single women.

Looking more closely at the impact of children clarifies the picture. In 1992, among married women living with their husbands who had children six to thirteen years old, 74.9 percent were in the labor force. Among those with children under six years old, only 59.9 percent were (*Statistical Abstract,* 1993, table 634). What about men? Unfortunately, it is hard to say. The Census Bureau does not even tabulate figures on men's labor force participation rate broken down by how many children they have.[1]

Nonetheless, it is clear that getting married and having children greatly reduce the average woman's earnings. Moreover, with each child she has, her earnings drop even lower (Fuchs, 1988). In contrast, men's income rises with children. Married fathers living with their children work longer hours and seek promotions. There is also some evidence that bosses give new fathers raises (see *The Economist,* 1993, p. 26).

Another reason for the seesaw pattern is that men and women take different approaches to part-time work. Men hardly ever resort to it. Women rely on it. For example, in 1986, among women twenty-five to sixty-four years old who held a job, 20 percent were working fewer than thirty hours a week. That is one standard definition of working part-time. Among employed men in that age group, only 7 percent worked fewer than thirty hours a week. It is largely marriage and children—and what they mean to women today—that cause the difference. Only 13 percent of unmarried women worked part-time in 1986, but 25 percent of married women did. (Note that married black women are more likely to continue to work full-time. That may be because black husbands' earnings are lower on average than white husbands'.) Only 19 percent of employed women who had no preschool children (under six years old) worked part-time, but 29 percent of employed women with a preschool child did (Fuchs, 1988). That pattern greatly reduces women's earnings, job experience, and likelihood of promotion relative to men's.

One fact that makes this point dramatically is that among the self-employed, women are twice as likely to work part-time as men. Self-employed women are also much more likely to work part-time if they have children (Devine, 1991).

The Pink-Collar Ghetto

As recently as the 1970s, newspapers ran two separate sections of classified advertisements for job openings, one for men, one for women. Very few people thought that division was strange. Earlier in the century, there had been a strong public consensus that it was good to separate men and women at work (Goldin, 1990). That way, women wouldn't distract men or pull down their wages. Men wouldn't spatter women with tobacco juice or harass them. It was all quite tidy. These days, however, separate sections of job advertisements would offend most people's sensibilities. Even so, the labor market itself is still divided tidily.

That tidiness costs women a lot. One important factor contributing to the gender gap is that for every hour the average woman works, she earns much less than the average man. The main reason for that difference is that nearly all working women are crowded into a few occupations.[2] Economists call that crowding "occupational segregation by sex."

Everyone knows that American men and women work in very different sorts of jobs, but the numbers can be surprising. Women make up 99 percent of dental hygienists; over 98 percent of secretaries, typists, and kindergarten teachers; and over 90 percent of registered nurses, speech therapists, and billing clerks. Men make up 99 percent of auto mechanics; over 97 percent of airplane pilots and firefighters; and over 90 percent of precision metal workers, surveying technicians, and sewage plant operators (*Employment and Earnings,* 1993, table 22).

The crowding of women into a few occupations is so pronounced that in order for men and women to be evenly distributed across the Census Bureau's 503 occupational categories, 60 percent of women in the labor force would have to change occupations (Sorenson, 1989). Is women's work an example of separate but equal? Not at all. Their crowding into a few fields lowers their wages a lot.

Why? Imagine that every person who graduates from college this year decides to go into the ice-cream business. They will mix vats of ice cream at plants all around the country. They are stubborn. They will not be turned away. Would you expect wages in that occupation to be higher than last year, the same, or lower? Economists would expect the wages to be lower. Ice-cream plants need only so many workers. Because young people are competing with each other for a small number of jobs, employers will be able to offer lower wages than they otherwise would.

American women have acted out that scenario, as have women in Italy, France, and other European countries (Jenson, Hagen, and Reddy, 1988). They have stampeded one small part of the economy, mainly low-skill jobs in the service sector.

Male and female college graduates also still differ significantly in their choice of majors. In 1984, 57 percent of those men had majored in law, medicine, dentistry, science, mathematics, business, economics, or engineering. Only 28 percent of the women had (*Current Population Reports,* 1987). Women and men still work in separate economies. Men have the big, roomy one. Women have the little, cramped one. It costs them money.

What makes this issue dramatic is that those figures actually *understate* the real amount of segregation by sex in people's jobs. The problem is that the job categories the Census Bureau and the Bureau of Labor Statistics use are too wide. Consider the category "waiters and waitresses." In 1992, it was

80 percent female (*Employment and Earnings,* 1993, table 22). But think about the fanciest restaurants you have been to or have seen in the movies. The servers there are waiters, not waitresses. Bookkeeping, retail sales, and many other service jobs are the same way (Fuchs, 1988).

The underlying causes of occupational segregation are complex. Prejudiced bosses, co-workers, and customers cause part of it. Some male bosses and employees enforce their notion of masculinity—and their desire to work with people like them, as they define "like them"—by refusing to hire women, treating them rudely, or sexually harassing them. Such mistreatment, or fear of it, reinforces segregation (see evidence in England, 1992, p. 21). That is why sexual harassment is an economic issue, not only an insult to dignity and to psychological well-being. (See chapter 9 on what governments and employers can do about it.)

The pattern that occupational segregation takes, however, suggests that such bigotry can't be the whole reason. Most women still work in jobs that are located near residential areas; are open to part-time workers; are easy to start, drop, and start again; and don't require skills that get stale with disuse. Prime examples are selling cosmetics in a suburban department store, cutting hair in a beauty salon, teaching at the local elementary school, and working as a secretary. Those jobs are perfect for people who either have or expect to have primary responsibility for taking care of babies and young children. They are perfect for people whose main career is homemaking. It is no coincidence that it is women who raise children and women who crowd into low-skill service jobs. In fact, the pink-collar ghetto is a baby ghetto.

However, highly educated women are much more evenly spread across job categories than less educated women. They have successfully staked their claim on the best turf that men have. They have broken out of the baby ghetto but they are still having babies (though fewer and later than in the past). That suggests that education—especially in medical, technical, and managerial fields—is a way out of the trap of occupational segregation. Also, women who are unable or disinclined to stay in school in their twenties are much more likely to make a decent income if they avoid the pink-collar ghetto. That means working full-time, year-round, in their own small businesses, joining the military, or working their way up the ladder in a big firm.

One final note. Many scholars and activists have proposed comparable-worth rules—also called pay equity—as a remedy for the meager paychecks that women in female-dominated occupations bring home. In a comparable-worth scheme, members of a commission rate the jobs within a company or organization according to inherent difficulty, responsibility, or value, as they perceive it (England, 1992; Hill and Killingsworth, 1989). Managers then raise the pay of people in female-dominated jobs to take those factors into account. The net result is that, overall, women's wages rise relative to men's (since that was the goal of the re-evaluation). Comparable-worth advocates scored dramatic victories when the governments of Washington state and the province of Ontario adopted such rules for their employees.

Is comparable worth a good thing? Consider this question: What if white people paid black people living in Harlem, South Central Los Angeles, the South Side of Chicago, and all the other historically black, poor urban neighborhoods to stay exactly the heck where they were? Black people who got checks in the mail would be pleased. But would it be a good thing?

In 1961, James Baldwin wrote, "A ghetto can be improved in one way only: out of existence" (p. 65). Ghettoes are ghettoes. Let's have done with them.

Battering

Violence within families is distressingly common. The National Family Violence Resurvey of 1985 found that in 116 out of each 1,000 couples, husbands physically attacked their wives at least once. In 34 out of each 1,000 couples, the attack included punching, choking, or some other "severely violent" abuse (Strauss and Gelles, 1990, p. 96).

Activists who have campaigned against battering emphasize that women at all economic levels get beaten. That's true, but it's only part of the truth. A woman who is poor or economically dependent on her partner is much more likely to get beaten by him. That means that battering is connected to the sexual division of labor in the home.

A 1991 study of data from the National Crime Survey (NCS), run by the U.S. Department of Justice, discovered that family income is strongly correlated with battering.[3] For example, for an employed, white, married woman with no children, an average educational background, and an average family income, a 20 percent increase in that income would decrease her relative probability of being abused by 34 percent (Sandberg, 1991). ("Relative probability" means that if her basic odds were 10 percent, the increase in family income would lower them by roughly one-third, to 6.6 percent.)

The NCS does not ask people about their incomes as individuals, but it does ask about their level of education. A person's education gives us a pretty good idea of his or her earnings potential. According to the NCS data, holding a woman's employment status and family income constant, an increase in her own educational attainment significantly *reduces* the odds that she will be battered (Sandberg, 1991, p. 44). For an employed white woman who is married, has no children, and lives in an urban area, increasing her schooling from dropout to high school graduate would reduce her relative odds of being abused by 30 percent.

One reason for this effect is that a woman who has higher earnings potential can walk out on a violent man more easily. Or she can more credibly threaten that she'll walk out.

Another finding suggests that this reasoning may be correct. It turns out that children have a big effect on the rate of battering. Theoretically, the presence of a child might make a man less likely to abuse his female partner, since he would be worse off if she walked out and left him with the children. On the other hand, theoretically, he might be more likely to abuse her, if the children made her more dependent on him and so more likely to stay even if he did beat her. What actually happens in the real world? Holding other things constant, the presence of one child under age twelve increases the relative probability that a woman will be battered by 50 percent.

That is a large increase. It suggests to me that children make the typical woman much more dependent on her male partner. It is women's primary responsibility for child raising—and their resulting drop in earnings—that create that extra dependency. For some women, that dependency leads to serious injury; for a few, even death.

Separation and Divorce

A married woman who is a full-time homemaker makes herself very vulnerable. If she separates from her husband, she separates from most of her income. (That is less true in some other countries. See chapter 9.) The sociologist Lenore Weitzman made that fact famous in her 1985 book, *The Divorce Revolution*. She concluded that divorce lowered women's standard of living by 73 percent but raised men's by 42 percent. That news electrified readers all over the country. It has become part of folk wisdom.

Since then, other researchers have looked at the economic consequences of divorce. Greg Duncan and Saul Hoffman used data from the Panel Study on Income Dynamics (PSID), a large, nationally representative sample of people throughout the United States. The PSID data are likely to give a more reliable answer than Weitzman's data, since she interviewed only 228 people in one state who weren't chosen randomly.[4]

Duncan and Hoffman studied people who had separated or divorced between 1969 and 1975. They found that one year after the breakup, the standard of living of women who hadn't remarried was 13 percent lower than it had been just before their marriage broke up.[5] African-American women were hit especially hard. Their standard of living fell 29 percent. Men—including those who had remarried—experienced a 13 percent increase in their standard of living (Duncan and Hoffman, 1985, p. 491).

Duncan and Hoffman then asked another question: What happens *after* the first year? They found that most of the divorced women in the sample remarried soon. *Their* family income was the same as that of women who had never gotten divorced. It was as though they had jumped off an escalator, then gotten back, later, onto the same rising step. They not only climbed back up to where they had been before the divorce, but caught up with the years of income growth that intact couples had experienced in the meantime. So, looking at the incomes of women only one year after their marriages break up does not give an accurate picture of the economic effects of divorce.

Only half the women in the sample remarried within five years, however. The other half had it bad. Nor is it the case that if they had remarried, they could have had it easy: the unmarried men in the sample, who would have been their likely husbands, had very low incomes.

Other studies have reached similar conclusions.[6] What this body of research shows is that divorce means something completely different for women and men. That should not be surprising, since marriage means something completely different for women and men. The sexual division of labor in the home means that women almost always do much more unpaid work than men. They either work longer hours in total, or do less paid work. If they do less paid work—no matter how much they love their families and enjoy their daily accomplishments—they live in a state of permanent economic peril.

The Beauty Problem

There is even more bad news. Women's economic peril is not only permanent; it gets *worse* over time. As the years go by, divorced women have a harder and harder time remarrying (Cohen, 1987). Divorced men not only remarry more quickly than divorced women but, as they get older, the difference in age between them and their wives increases. Another way of putting it is that, over time, a woman is perceived as less and less attractive as a new marital partner compared to a man her age.

Why? Consider, first of all, what a young woman and a young man bring to a traditional marriage. She brings homemaking skills. He brings earning ability. They also bring their fertility, physical attractiveness, commitment, and, in some cultures, love.

Now look ahead. Women's fertility falls considerably after age thirty-five, but men's doesn't. Men's earnings rise steadily with age. Women's homemaking skills improve, too, but probably by a much smaller percentage. At age forty, then, a man who divorces is near the peak of his earnings. His ex-wife is usually encumbered by teenage children, who make her look like a more complicated prospective partner.

What about physical attractiveness? In fact, the typical husband looks older than his wife. If he is forty, she is probably thirty-seven or so because most women marry a man who is a few years older than they are. However, physical appearance just doesn't seem to matter as much for men. I think of this unpleasant conundrum as the beauty problem.

It is real. Teenage girls spend much more time grooming themselves than teenage boys do (Timmer, Eccles, and O'Brien, 1985, pp. 366–67). Women also spend more money on clothes than men do, even after they are married (Lazear and Michael, 1988). The cosmetics and dieting industries, and purported antidotes to them such as the feminist theorist Naomi Wolf's book *The Beauty Myth,* target mainly women.

Why do women spend so much more time and money on their looks than men do? In fact, serious things are at stake for women. We have strong evidence that appearance affects women's economic well-being much more than men's. Researchers have found that obesity hurts women's income much more than men's income. That is mainly because obese women marry men with much lower earnings than nonobese women do. The process of finding a marriage partner is, in part, competitive. Low-earning men and obese women tend to get picked last. Then they are left with each other. (This is mainly a white problem. African-American women pay only a small penalty in the marriage market for obesity.) (Averett and Korenman, 1993.)

Over the years, I've heard many informal explanations for women's preoccupation with makeup, clothes, and dieting. I've heard that women have an innate desire to preen for men and that men just naturally care more about their mate's appearance than women do. My research, though, has led me to this conclusion: that's baloney. The beauty problem is epiphenomenal. It is not a prime moving force. It is just a carbuncle on the ugly back of the sexual division of labor.

I suspect that traditional women care more about their looks than men care about theirs because beauty constitutes a higher fraction of women's total assets than men's. Young men of marriageable age have accumulated training and connections that will determine their earnings. Men's earnings have a much wider range than women's domestic skills, their counterpart asset. For that reason, a man's earnings can have a more dramatic impact on his family's well-being than a woman's domestic skills can. A multimillionaire husband puts his family in a mansion. A wife who is a championship baker keeps her family in desserts. Salary counts for so much as an asset that a man's other assets, such as physical appearance, are a less important part of his bundle.

Moreover, as the years pass, because their earnings (and power) can increase significantly over time, men's beauty as a *fraction* of their total assets actually falls. It becomes less and less of an issue in the world of romance and remarriage.

To make this explanation of the beauty problem more vivid, do the following thought experiment. Imagine that men who are under 5' 9" are completely barred from paying work. How will they make a living? Many will hope to find a wife, or male partner, who earns a good income and is otherwise appealing. How do they distinguish themselves from rival shorties looking for a good partner? They try to be kind and witty, and learn to run a household. They polish ornamental accomplishments, such as stunt water-skiing or a B.A. from a prestigious college (as women did in the 1950s). They also pay much more attention to their looks than tall men do.

Outlandish? Not at all. Consider this. Black men in the United States earn much less than white men, on average. Nearly half of all black men between the ages of twenty and fifty may be out of the labor force altogether. Racism, poor schooling, and limited skills keep their earnings low. What is the consequence? Several sociological studies have found that black women rate the physical appearance of black men as more important in their overall attractiveness than white women do for white men (Staples and Johnson, 1993, pp. 111–12).

If those findings are accurate, they suggest that many black women don't expect black men to earn lots of money. The men have to compete for a female partner *using every other means* available to them. So their looks represent a higher fraction of their total personal assets than is the case for white men.

Obviously, the beauty problem has implications that extend far beyond the economic consequences of divorce. One friend of mine, a law professor in San Francisco, received a letter from the school's administrators in 1992 telling her how to dress for her initial job interview. They told her to wear pumps or heels and makeup. Men got no instructions about their appearance. My friend got the job in spite of her failure to comply. Still, her fellow professors are warning her now that she should dress more like a corporate lawyer. She describes the problem as "a tax on women."

Much more taxing, of course, is the toll on women who accept the standards but believe they do not meet them. Think of eating disorders and cosmetic surgery. The beauty problem—and its toll on women's consciousnesses, time, energy, and health—will stay with us as long as appearance continues to matter economically for women. When the sexual division of labor in the home melts away, so will the beauty problem.

Statistical Discrimination

Most people can tell when they look at a woman that she *is* a woman. They feel that conveys some information about her. That's why they get so nervous when they can't tell.

This is so clear and commonplace that it hardly seems worth mentioning. However, it is actually the answer to a good question some critics of this book may ask: "Why do we have to end the sexual division of labor for everybody? Those few women who want househusbands can go out and find one. Everybody else can stick with tradition. Then we'll all be happy."

Unfortunately, it's not that easy. When people believe that the fact that Gerry is a woman conveys some information about her, they believe that, on average, women behave, think, and feel in ways that are distinctive and roughly predictable. They use everything they've ever seen or heard about women to build a picture in their minds about women on average. That picture influences their expectations about *particular* women.

Those expectations have one consequence that is crucial for the analysis in this book. If most women stay in charge of children, their behavior will always hurt the opportunities of those women who want to dedicate themselves to a paying career. That will happen even if we completely eliminate prejudice and bigotry. Economists call this phenomenon statistical discrimination (Phelps, 1972).

Statistical discrimination affects women because employers can't find out a lot of things they would like to know about each job applicant's abilities, temperament, and plans for the future. Some things just don't show up on interviews and written records. So, in some cases, employers supplement what the applicant tells them with things they know about the average members of that applicant's group. The group might be immigrants from China, members of the National Rifle Association, or women. What if the information is true about average group members, but not about that particular person? Then the group's characteristics hurt, or help, that person's chances.

Historically, women have been more likely than men to drop out of the labor market, have had fewer years on the job with their current employer, have been less willing to travel, and have been less willing to work overtime, especially on an unpredictable schedule (*Current Population Reports,* 1987, p. 1). Continuity on the job, travel, and overtime were inconsistent with the heavy demands the average woman had to answer to at home—mainly, the work of raising children.

So, even in a world free of prejudice against women, employers will hesitate before hiring a woman for certain sorts of jobs. Those include jobs with tremendous amounts of training paid for by the employer (such as astronauts) and jobs that require precise, delicate skills that go stale quickly with disuse (certain kinds of surgery). Those employers want someone who will stay on the job continuously. Some jobs also require lots of travel or crushing amounts of overtime every year at certain seasons (April and December for tax accountants) or at unpredictable times unpredictably often (such as insurance adjusters who traipse after floods and hurricanes).

In order to get hired, highly career-committed women try to signal that they are nontraditional. They buy expensive tools, suits, and credentials. They are saying, "Would I spend this money if I didn't expect to work long, hard, and continuously to recoup *my* investment?"

Still, consider the employer's point of view again. Some applicants fib; they don't expect to work long, hard, or continuously, but would like five or eight years of high pay. Others expect to, but change their minds and leave the labor market to devote themselves to unpaid work.

That means that statistical discrimination excludes highly career-committed women from many jobs that they would do very well. It makes it much harder for them to become pilots, surgeons, tax accountants, soldiers, insurance adjusters, store managers, and business executives. These are mostly high-skill, high-wage, high-status, and highly satisfying jobs. Those women lose big. Their bosses lose excellent employees. Society also loses whatever special contribution those women could have made.

The only way to counter statistical discrimination against women is to end the sexual division of labor. When there are no differences, on average, between men and women in their propensity to stop working for pay or in their willingness to chase tornadoes, well-meaning but profit-minded bosses will have no reason—and no way—to statistically discriminate. Then, the qualified woman will get the job. Her househusband will be grateful.

Children's Well-Being

So far, we have been looking at women's economic status. We also need to consider children. They need us and, alarmingly soon, we will need them. How we treat them, as parents and as a society, forms the best, easy measure of how we wield our power and how we treat the powerless.

According to that measure, how are we doing? Not well. Part of the predicament we are now stuck in is that, in some ways, children have never had it better but, in other ways, their lives are very painful.

In some ways, for example, American children have never been healthier. However, rates of obesity in children six to eleven years old rose from 18 percent to 27 percent during the 1960s and 1970s (Fuchs, 1990). During the 1980s, children's obesity rates increased further (Burros, 1994). It may be a disorder that only children living in rich countries have the opportunity to suffer. Even so, it increases the risk of high blood pressure, respiratory disease, and diabetes.

Children's performance in school is also mixed. Scores on the Scholastic Aptitude Test (SAT), which colleges use to gauge high school students' academic skills, dropped sharply in the 1960s and 1970s. The average math score dropped 36 points and the average verbal score dropped 54 points. In the early 1980s, SAT scores leveled off; they have even risen a little since.

However, they still haven't come close to the scores that students achieved thirty years ago. We do know that many more youngsters with grades and family incomes that are lower than average have begun taking the test. That is good news, even though it has lowered average scores. However, today's *top scorers* don't perform as well as the top scorers did thirty years ago. For example, between 1966–67 and 1979–80, the number of students who scored 700 or over on the math test fell from 55,500 to 38,900. The number of students who scored 700 or over on the verbal test fell from 33,200 to 12,300. That decline took place even though *more* students took the test in 1979–80 (Zill and Rogers, 1988, pp. 64–65). During the 1980s, the math scores of top students recovered a bit, but not their verbal scores (Herrnstein and Murray, 1992). That is bad news.

Also, the changes in young people's suicide rates since 1960 are stunning. Among teenagers fifteen to nineteen years old, between 1960 and 1984 the suicide rate rose from 3.6 per 100,000 to 9 per 100,000 (Zill and Rogers, 1988, p. 87). One possible explanation for this change is that now more children have access to guns.

As we all know, the rates of children's homicide, pregnancy, and HIV infection have also risen a lot. Most American parents today don't have to worry about polio, but they still have a lot to worry about.

Political conservatives have claimed for decades that mothers' movement into paid jobs has been bad for children. Lots of researchers have looked at that question (for a review article, see Furstenberg and Condran, 1988). On balance, the studies do *not* show a convincing link between mothers' work, divorce rates, or births outside of marriage and changes in children's educational performance, crime rates, rates of pregnancy outside marriage, or drug use (Furstenberg and Condran, 1988).

In a subtle way, though, part of children's troubles does come from the sexual division of labor in the home. Some observers think it has been hard to build a social movement to advocate for children because children are seen as women's work and women lack status.[7] I suspect that when more men raise their children, children's advocates will be more successful. Highly involved fathers are more likely to think that playgrounds, public libraries, the foster care system, Aid to Families with Dependent Children, and school enrichment programs are important. More men will push for improvements in the child support system, because the left-behind, needy spouse will more often be a man. (See, for example, these sympathetic articles on single and divorced fathers raising children: *Business Week,* 1992, and Johnson, 1993.) Of course, when that day comes, more city councillors, state legislators, and U.S. senators will be women.

We also have to remember that many of the most important things that children need don't come from the government. A shift in people's attitudes away from materialism, selfishness, and racial prejudice, toward caring, faith in education, and a thirst for justice would benefit children, along with the rest of us, immeasurably.

2

How Women Negotiate

Love is blind:
But, soft! what light through yonder window breaks? It is the east, and Juliet is the sun!

—*Romeo and Juliet*

Love is calculating:
Girls marry merely to better themselves, *to borrow a significant vulgar phrase, and have such perfect power over their hearts not to permit themselves to* fall in love *till a man with a superior fortune offers.*

—Mary Wollstonecraft, *A Vindication of the Rights of Women*

WE HAVE SEEN HOW THE TRADITIONAL SEXUAL DIVISION OF labor in the home stands in the way of women's equality. Where does that division of labor come from? How does it find its way inside our houses?

Social scientists who have studied how people run their households find that how those people's parents lived and their cultural surroundings make a difference (for example, Goldscheider and Waite, 1991). Early experiences shape your expectations of the future, what you will do at home, and what your spouse and children will do.

However, you don't automatically get what you expect. The other grown-up in the couple has expectations, too. They might not be consistent with yours. Also, children have surprisingly stubborn minds of their own. Circumstances can foil expectations, too. They can take a turn for the better or the worse, or turn topsy-turvy. If you win the lottery, you suddenly have lots of money to spend. If the main earner in the family breaks both ankles and can't do his job, things will change at home, at least for a few months. If a tornado evicts you, or soldiers fighting a civil war chase your family from your home, your routine may be shattered for years.

We certainly don't do everything our ancestors did. Nor do we do everything we expected we'd do when we were young. So, how do people decide who does what chores at home?

What I see is people carrying on the traditions that make sense to them, or that are deeply ingrained, and acting on their expectations insofar as they mesh with the traditions and expectations of their spouses. Then they work out their differences. Sometimes they talk; more often they just try one thing after another. They may think ahead to imagine how their spouses will react to the things they try. Usually, couples find a pattern to settle into. The whole process may go on with one or both partners only dimly aware that it's happening. Or they may be keenly aware of their disagreements, shout, and throw dish towels around the kitchen. Either way, it may be happy or it may be miserable.

In this book, I call that process of having a notion of how things should be at home with one's spouse and then muddling about negotiation. In the next chapter, I will discuss negotiation in detail. Here, I'd like to make a few preliminary observations about women and negotiation.

Knowing But Not Knowing That You Know

My friend Linda is a good example of someone who knows, but doesn't know that she knows. She is the administrator of a geology department at a big university. She keeps the books, orders supplies, processes federal grant applications, oversees the payroll, pacifies egotistical professors, comforts miffed secretaries, and generally runs the place.

At lunch one afternoon, Linda mentioned to me that she was reading a book on how to reduce stress. She explained how she'd finished one chapter, turned to the next, and frozen: "The next chapter was about negotiation. I thought, Ack! I don't know anything about that. I can't do that! That's not me!"

Twenty minutes later, she was telling me about her week. As supervisor of a major remodeling of the geology department's building, she had to oversee contractors, subcontractors, deadlines, and the quality of work. To her horror, she had discovered that morning that workers had laid a garish pink carpet in the seminar room.

What did she do? She pointed out the mistake. They said that as far as they knew, it wasn't a mistake. She got the order forms, clarified ambiguities, persuaded, and cajoled. The workers ripped up the garish horror and laid down the serene blue-gray carpet she had asked for. Then, she told me with a grin, she suggested that the contractor call the carpet wholesaler, to see whether he could sell the carpet to some other customer at a discount, since it was, after all, used. Then she noticed that the rubberized borders they had installed at the bottom of the walls were brown, not gray as she had ordered. . . .

I suspect that a lot of people are like Linda. They know a lot about negotiation, but they don't know that they know it. Partly, that's because negotiation is just a fancy word for the everyday business of getting along with people.

I'm reminded of the man in a horse-drawn carriage on Martha's Vineyard who stopped early one morning to talk with another man, out for a stroll with a bulging knapsack.

Said the man in the carriage, "Circumambulating the island, eh?"

Said the man on foot, after looking the carriage up and down, "Rather walk, thank you."

We all circumambulate, even though we don't all know it. Likewise, we all negotiate.

High-Context Negotiating

Now, we know that Linda is good at negotiating. Why does she say "Ack! That's not me!"? One reason is that when she persuaded the construction workers to replace the carpet at their expense, she wasn't acting on her own behalf. She was acting for someone else, her employer. A lot of people (although not all) who are kind and generous feel inhibited about aggressively advocating for themselves. It feels a little selfish. Put them in charge of defending someone else's interests, though, and they're tigers.

I noticed that difference for the first time in law school. In my early twenties, I was quiet and shy. When I became a student lawyer, in my second year, I had clients to represent. They relied on me. Suddenly, I found myself saying things, inventing arguments, and feigning heat and outrage to win concessions for my clients in ways that amazed me.

For example, one of my clients wanted to continue living in his plywood cubicle, built in the basement of a rooming house, until he found a job. His alternative was homelessness. However, the Housing Department said that his cubicle violated the rules on basement dwellings because it was too far underground. At an informal hearing, in a flash of invention, I argued that we could correct the defect by digging a seven-inch trench all the way around the rooming house.

The hearing officers were shocked. So was I. Would I ever have proposed anything that ridiculous to defend my own interests? I would have been too embarrassed. In the end, although they rejected the trench idea, they did give my client extra time in his cubicle, in part, I think, because of the kooky tenacity of his young lawyer. In a few weeks he found a job and, soon thereafter, a decent place to live.

We are all familiar with the idea that lawyers negotiate. Union stewards, businesspeople, senators, and diplomats negotiate. But some of us are not familiar with the idea that in our ordinary lives, at home, in our families, and in our romantic relationships, we all negotiate. To some people—maybe especially to the kind, generous types who feel inhibited about asserting their own interests—it sounds cold at first.

That's understandable. After all, the family is a special setting. Many techniques that we consider fair in the workplace have no business appearing at the dinner table. In a family, people are committed to a long-term relationship with one another. They love one another. They have pledged to act on their highest moral feelings toward one another. They have helpless dependents.

The hesitaters are wrong, though—even the kindest and most giving of them—if they think they don't negotiate in their families. Or if they think they shouldn't. The mistake they are making is that they are confusing negotiation with some sort of Machiavellian pursuit of self-interest. That isn't the sort of negotiation we are discussing in this book. I will not describe how women can crush their husbands, or tyrannize them into doing all the housework, or manipulate them into begging, "Pretty, pretty please? Can I cook dinner *every* night?" (This may be the time to ask for a refund.)

Nor will I argue that savvy readers should take a second look at their romantic relationships and keep a running score of favors they've extended and favors that have been returned. That would be disastrous. In fact, psychologists have found that people who are very concerned with keeping score that way, especially in the short run, have trouble maintaining friendships and have unhappy marriages (Brown, 1986). They aren't trusting. Real love and rewarding friendship rest on trust.

Here is a final list of things this book will *not* argue: that millions of romantic partners handle their conflicts with a can-do, problem-solving attitude; that they always act, and assume the other is acting, instrumentally and rationally in pursuit of her or his own goals; or that they value material goals (money, leisure time, a new colossal multiscreen TV) over psychic rewards (love, respect, enjoyable cooperation). That would be psychologically unrealistic.

For one thing, in many parts of the world, not even diplomats and businesspeople carry out negotiations with a can-do, instrumentally rational, money-comes-first attitude. That negotiating style is peculiar to Americans and the British. It often irritates people in other places. In many societies, negotiators stress the long-term and emotional facets of their relationship with their negotiating counterpart. They care a lot about symbolism, status, and not losing face. They use subtle ways of communicating in order to avoid stark confrontations. Overarching principles and the history of the relationship, as opposed to nitty-gritty details, matter a lot. Many people aren't enthusiastic about explicit, formal agreements and go about things in a dilly-dally way. Researchers call that style "high-context negotiating" (Cohen, 1991).

If you think about your own family, you may recognize in *your* style of getting things done bits and pieces of high-context negotiating. I know that my family makes a specialty of highly refined communication strategies that avoid confrontation: hints, counterhints, body language, pauses, changing the subject, then, inaction. Presto—it's decided. I did not want to go to Catholic catechism class in the seventh grade; there was no way my eleventh-grade sister was going to a co-ed slumber party unsupervised by adults; and it was unthinkable that either of us would go to college outside New England. Confrontation? Can-do-ism? That wasn't our style. Still, all these points of contention got negotiated.

Now, some readers—especially those who majored in anthropology in college—may already have jumped to their feet shouting, "That's not negotiation. It's gift exchange!"

I invite them to sit down. It's true, as they say, that much of what happens in families is gift exchange, not negotiating. In some societies, people circulate nearly all their wealth in the form of gifts from clan to clan, from island to island, according to well-defined rules (Sahlins, 1972). The gifts knit people, clans, and regional groups together in a web of obligation and shared moral understandings. We see gift exchange in families all the time. For example, suppose Theo puts Morgan through nursing school by working double shifts at a photocopying store. Neither expects Theo to get compensated monetarily, plus interest, for those efforts. He is making a gift of that effort. The gift creates a special obligation in Morgan to reciprocate (not to pay back). It also creates deep feelings and a bond between them that can't be expressed in terms of money.

All true. My objection, though, is that family life is not all gifts and rose petals. Families are also places where power gets wielded. In some families, the yoke is as light as dandelion fluff. In others, there is no yoke at all. However, you don't have to be a social critic, a feminist, or a social scientist to see power at work in many families. We have all seen its heavy wheels in motion. The analysis I will use here draws on ideas about negotiation that were developed expressly to dissect, anatomize, and reveal the everyday mechanisms of power.

Of course, no one wants a theory that crushes what we are studying. We need an approach that admits that power is at work, but leaves room for the bubbly action of love. My goal in chapter 3 is to sketch out basic principles which, taken together, form a baggy, loose sort of theory that leaves room for both emotion and calculation, for both giving and taking, for both the heavy wheels and the sweetness that makes us glad to be alive.

Can Women Be Good Negotiators

In the Bible, Joshua becomes the leader of the Israelites after Moses dies. He sends two spies into the land of Canaan to scout out the terrain. They come to Jericho and ask to stay the night in the house of Rahab. Rahab knows that the king of Jericho will find out that she is sheltering strangers who mean to take over the country. However, she has heard that the god of the Israelites helps them win all their battles. She intends to side with the winners. How can she pull it off?

Rahab tells the spies to hide in her roof. When the king's messengers come, she tells them the spies have left already.

Then she says to the spies: "Now, since I have shown my loyalty to you . . . [p]rovide me with a reliable sign that you will spare the lives of my father and mother, my brothers and sisters, and all who belong to them, and save us from death" (Joshua 2:12–13).

She has just saved their lives, so the spies owe her. Also, they are vulnerable. If she were to shout, the king's messengers could come back and kill them. However, for all she knows, the spies are armed. They could kill her where she stands. She has a lot of courage.

The spies decide to accept her proposal. She tells them what route to take to escape the king's men. They tell her to gather her whole family together in her house and tie a red cord to the window, so the Israelite soldiers will know to pass over the house. Later, in the pitch of battle, the spies lead Rahab and all her relatives out of the city to safety (Brams, 1990).

That story was written over 2,500 years ago. Here is another, even older one.

The Ramayana, an epic poem of India, tells the story of the hero Rama, whose father, the king, plans to name him as his successor. Rama is dazzlingly virtuous, handsome, and intelligent. Everyone in the kingdom adores him. Everyone, that is, except the king's wife, Kaikeyi, who wants her son Bharata to become king. How can she persuade her husband to change his mind?

She goes to her room, dishevels her hair, and pretends to be desperately unhappy. When the king rushes to see what's wrong, she tells him two things. First, she reminds him that long ago she saved his life on the battlefield. In gratitude, he vowed to grant her two wishes in the future, no matter what they were. Second, she tells him that if he doesn't grant her wish, she will kill herself with poison. The king is appalled. He insists that she tell him her wish so that he can grant it. She tells him that she wants Bharata to be named king and Rama to be sent into the forest to live on roots and leaves for fourteen years. The king is stunned. He falls into a trance. Finally, Rama hears about the scene and gently urges everyone—even the reluctant Bharata—to respect Kaikeyi's wish.

Kaikeyi's goal seems less noble than Rahab's. So do her methods. Still, she used imagination and flair, and she succeeded. (Her apparent selfishness is actually part of a divinely ordained plan: Rama needs to live in the forest because his experiences there will further his heroic mission.) (Narayan, 1972.)

Stories like these about women negotiating for their families and in their families come to us from ancient times and recent times, from all over the world. For example, in "The Cloud Scraper," a comic Chinese story written by Li Yu in 1657, a clever servant girl maneuvers the upper-class young man who is courting her mistress into marrying her, too. She gets him to sign a contract in which he promises to call her by a respectful title, never to take a concubine, and never to take a third wife. It is an astonishing achievement. The threesome live happily ever after.

And in Laurence Sterne's *Tristram Shandy* (1759), Tristram's grandmother manages to negotiate a premarital contract with his grandfather in order to compensate her financially for the deficiency of his nose (we are told).[1]

This long history of storytelling about women who negotiate brings us to a question: Even if not all ordinary women can negotiate as well as the extraordinary women in these stories, is it something they can do roughly as well as ordinary men? Or does something in women's nature or upbringing make them less effective at it than men?

That question is important. Many psychologists and economists have worked on it for over twenty years. Some have reasoned that if, on average, women enjoy cooperation and dislike confrontation more than men do, they will lose lots of disagreements (Rose, 1992). Sometimes their male partners won't even know there has been a disagreement, because the women will cave in without mentioning that they'd rather do things differently.

Do women really like cooperation and dislike confrontation more than men do? The findings are inconclusive. Four laboratory studies have found that women cooperate more than men; three have found that men cooperate more than women; and several have found no particular difference at all (see citation in Orbell, Dawes, and Schwartz-Shea, 1994).

Maybe, though, we don't need strong evidence for the proposition that women like cooperation more than men do. Some scholars have put forward the argument that if people in general merely *believe* that women like to cooperate more, that belief, even if incorrect, will disadvantage women in their everyday negotiations (Rose, 1992).

You can imagine how the disadvantages might mount up. Parents might pay for less education for their daughters than their sons, because they believe women who go out into public life simply get suckered and wind up accomplishing nothing. Bankers might not like to lend money to women, because they believe businesswomen will get pushed around by far tougher businessmen (Rose, 1992). Women who speak up for themselves might provoke explosions of frothing disbelief from men who can't believe they're hearing backtalk from a female. Those women might lose arguments more often than men only because men rarely face such intimidating displays of temper.

We do have evidence that many people in the United States think women are more selfless and cooperative than men (see citation in Eagly and Steffen, 1984). It's a commonly held stereotype.

We also have interesting experimental evidence from the real world that shows how such a stereotype can disadvantage women in negotiating. Ian Ayres, a law professor at Yale, enlisted students to go to car dealers and pretend to be interested in buying a new car. In nearly all U.S. auto stores, buyers have to haggle with sellers over the price. Ayres wanted to see whether the dealers behaved differently toward buyers who were male or female, black or white. They did. On average, white women ended up paying $150 more than white men did for the same car. Black women ended up paying almost $900 more. Car dealers gave a much higher starting price to women than to men, and to blacks than to whites. Those buyers had to do lots of haggling just to make it down to the starting price offered to white men (Ayres, 1991).

Why do car dealers behave that way? They hold a stereotype that women and blacks are more likely than white men to accept the starting price as the *final* price, either because they don't know that car prices are negotiable or because they're shy about haggling. Dealers make lots of money by doing this; some make 50 percent of their profits from 10 percent of their sales.

Luckily, in many other settings, people do just the opposite. They purposely set aside their stereotypes and treat women as individuals.

Psychologists who have studied stereotypes about women have pinpointed why people probably believe one thing in general but behave differently when facing a specific individual woman. Researchers have found that many people believe that grown-ups who take care of children at home are more selfless and concerned about others than people who hold paying jobs are. They believe that grown-ups who hold paying jobs are more self-assertive and more motivated to master tasks than homemakers are.

For example, in experiments at Purdue University with a group of 140 people, both men and women believed that female *and male* homemakers were much more selfless and concerned with others than the average employed person. If they weren't told whether or not a particular woman being described to them held a paying job, they tended to assume that she was a homemaker.

Once the subjects learned more about an individual woman, however, they quickly used those facts. They rated women who held paying jobs as even more assertive than the typical employed man. Apparently, that was because they saw those women as having asserted themselves in making the choice to hold a job outside the home (Eagly and Steffen, 1984).

That experiment took place in 1984. A higher percentage of women in the United States now hold paying jobs. The same is true in Europe, Latin America, and east Asia. Since then, stereotypes about women being especially cooperative may have weakened. They are likely to weaken further in the future. As that happens, even the sharpest car dealers will change their behavior.

Despite what lingering stereotypes may suggest, I suspect that women are, on average, just as skillful at negotiating as men are. After all, we get lots of practice. We negotiate with our parents and teachers, with our friends, with our romantic partners, and, most of us, with our children (who really hone our skills!). The reason men seem to outnegotiate women in many situations—such as avoiding housework and child care when their wives would like them to contribute more—is not that women are less skillful but that they have fewer resources. On average, they have lower social status, lower earnings, less savings, and, in most places in the world, fewer years of education. As we shall see, those things matter a lot.

Negotiating Is What You Do, Not Just What You Say

The classic stories about Rahab, Kaikeyi, and their literary successors, and the experiments just cited, describe situations in which women know what is at stake, face the person they are trying to persuade, and do a lot of talking. However, negotiating—as I use the term here—takes place in many other kinds of situations. It takes place, for example, when girls make decisions about school and jobs without knowing what is at stake: the division of labor in their marriage twenty years in the future. It also takes place when no one is saying a word.

To me, those negotiating situations are more interesting than face-to-face conversations, because they are invisible, yet terribly influential. In fact, they determine the content of couples' face-to-face conversations ten, twenty, and thirty years later.

How can they do that? Think of Alice's adventures in *Through the Looking-Glass*. As she walked down the lanes, past the hedges, and across the fields of that familiar-looking landscape, she had no idea that she was really walking across a giant chessboard. Moves that people made on that chessboard mattered a lot (although in absurd ways). What they said about their moves mattered much less.

As we move across the landscape of our childhood, our adolescence, and our young adulthood, many of us have no clue that we are really making moves in a much larger game—a game in which we are negotiating who will do most of the unpaid work at home when we are grown up and who, instead, will do most of the paying work of running government, business, science, and the arts.

Let's turn now to the details of how we negotiate the division of labor in our very own families.

3

BATNAs, Babies, and Bedrock Facts

Woman and man were made for each other, but their mutual dependency is not the same. The men depend on the women only on account of their desires; the women on the men both on account of their desires and their necessities. We could subsist better without them than they without us.

—Jean-Jacques Rousseau, *Émile*

IN THIS BOOK, A NEGOTIATION IS ANY SITUATION IN WHICH TWO OR more people are interdependent, have some perceived conflict, can use strategic behavior, and have room for agreement (Lax and Sebenius, 1986).[1]

People are *interdependent* if they can't walk away from each other without thinking twice about it. To me, that seems like a fair description of romantic partners. They depend on each other for love and emotional support; for money and help in running the household; for cooperation in raising children and caring for sick and elderly relatives; and sometimes for their very identity as respected members of the community.

What about *conflict*? Is the perfect marriage entirely free of it? I doubt it. No one marries his or her identical twin, and even identical twins sometimes disagree. No two people have exactly the same tastes and priorities.

That brings us to *strategic behavior.* Checkers is a game of strategy because most of us try to think ahead one or two moves. Craps, on the other hand, is a game of chance. You just roll the dice and pray. In negotiating, acting strategically means thinking ahead. In particular, it means imagining how the other person is likely to react if you do A, B, or C, and choosing the option, the time, the setting, and the approach most likely to persuade her to go your way. For example, how many wives choose the middle of the Super

Bowl broadcast, or the World Cup soccer finals, to propose a weeklong family vacation to their mother's house? Those who do aren't acting strategically. Or they have unusual husbands (or unusual mothers).

Room for agreement means that there is overlap between what each person can tolerate. They can compromise. And, as a prelude to compromise, they can try to influence each other's tastes and priorities.

One way to picture that room for agreement is as a straight line (figure 3.1).

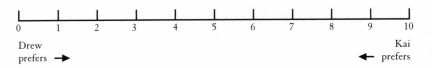

Figure 3.1. Room for Agreement

For example, Drew's ideal would be to eat Chinese food ten times a week. His wife, Kai, is not crazy about Chinese food and would prefer never to eat it. If Drew pushes hard, Kai might budge all the way up to ten. If Kai stonewalls, Drew might have to settle for zero. In reality, they will probably settle for something in between.

Cooperation and Competition

In every romantic partnership, two forces pull at each partner. Each person can compete against the other, in order to get a bigger slice of the pie, or each can cooperate and make the pie bigger. There is no way around that fundamental tension (Lax and Sebenius, 1986). Aggressive people may think that they never need to cooperate, or that cooperation is for sissies. However, that bullheadedness could cost them a lot. They are giving up an opportunity to share information with the other person, to concoct ideas together, and to invent solutions that would make both of them better off.

Altruists, on the other hand, may believe that competition has no place in their romantic relationships. However, complete selflessness is neither psychologically healthy nor easy to put into effect. Imagine that saintly Sue is reluctant to get her way when what she wants doesn't happen to be what her husband wants. The problem is that once she discloses what she prefers, she'll probably find that John wants to make her happy by going along with at least part of it, even if it's not what he prefers. If Sue clams up and doesn't disclose, she'll frustrate him.

I doubt that this book will persuade altruists to start looking out for number one. I can point out two things, though. First, remember the words of Hillel, the first-century rabbi revered for his compassion: "If I am not for myself, who is for me?" Second, if Sue is in the least bit activist in her saintliness, she will have opinions about what is best for the relationship and for John and, when John disagrees, she will strive honestly to prevail. She will be competing with John at those times *and* she will be acting altruistically.

Are there people who never compete, as I am using the word here? Who never have a conflicting opinion or never express one? Sure. For our purposes, though, they are not negotiators. They are doormats. In all likelihood, they are emotionally unbalanced or have been terrorized into abject submission.[2]

For the rest of us, cooperation and competition are inextricably entwined in all negotiations, including the negotiation of loving relationships.

Another way of saying this is to return to the metaphor of the pie. Two people come together to form a couple because they have more together than they have apart. That something more is like a pie. Will they split the pie equally? Will one get more than half? The time they spend maneuvering over who will buy groceries, clean, or work overtime so that they can afford a new couch is time spent competing. Each is maneuvering to protect his or her slice or to get a bigger slice.

Suppose, though, that they begin to reveal things to each other. Faruk actually enjoys grocery shopping at the neighborhood market, where everyone knows him by name. But he hates cleaning the bathroom. Zoe wouldn't mind working overtime next month, because her boss will be out of town and things will be relaxed at work. Moreover, now that she thinks about it, she just heard that her sister-in-law's neighbor is eager to do housecleaning for five dollars an hour. By pooling their information and thinking creatively, these two invent solutions that actually make their pie bigger. That is a wonderful achievement. Instead of simply claiming value, they are creating value.

However, now that the pie is bigger, they have to decide how to divide it up again. The housecleaner frees up two hours of time a week for them. Should Zoe use that time to do the home repairs she's been putting off? Or is her overtime paying for the housecleaner, and thus entitling her to more leisure when she's home? Decisions, decisions. And, as long as there is a difference of opinion, there will be some effort to claim value and, therefore, some competition.

This insight suggests a different way of picturing the room for agreement that negotiators face; see figure 3.2.

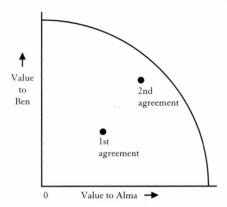

Figure 3.2. The Possibilities Frontier

Whenever Alma and Ben move closer to the curved line, they have created value for one of them. If they move toward it by moving northeast, they have created value for both of them at the same time. That is, they have made their pie bigger. If they move straight north, they made the pie bigger but Ben got all the new value. If they move straight east, Alma got all the new value. The curved line represents the very best they can do, if they share all their information and have their best, creative ideas, at this point in time. That line is called the *possibilities frontier.*

Note the point where the curved line meets the vertical line. At that point, Ben hogs all the value available and Alma has none. Ben might be a ruthless batterer or a ruthless psychological manipulator. Alma is a doormat. The converse is true at the point where the curved line meets the horizontal line. In contrast, a couple perched exactly midway down the curved line is brilliant and perfectly fair. Most of us muddle along somewhere inside the curved line, trying to think of ways to creep northeast.

Trade-offs

We all try to further our interests as we see them. In a marriage, of course, two people have individual interests and common interests, which are hard to separate.

Most people want to continue and improve their relationship with their spouse while staying true to certain cherished principles. They may also like a particular style of interaction between themselves and their spouse, such as emotional and loud or quiet and relaxed. They may avoid decisions that seem to set bad precedents. For example, if you let your husband make a recklessly extravagant purchase because, as he says, "It's on plastic—we have months to pay it off," you may see more recklessness in the future.

We can distinguish *interests,* which hang in the background like scenery, from *needs,* which stride across the stage and must be dealt with. Faruk and Zoe faced three needs simultaneously: food (someone to buy it), a hygienic bathroom (someone to clean it), and a new couch (someone to earn the money for it). We can also distinguish needs from *positions.* When Zoe insists that Faruk clean the bathroom, she is taking a position. If she sticks to it no matter what Faruk tells her about his preferences or their alternatives, she is being stubborn. People stick tight to claim value, but when they do they may miss opportunities, even ones that would benefit mainly themselves. (They may stick tight to further other interests, too, such as saving face or developing a reputation for persistence.)

These concepts are important because, when they are not sticking tight, people make trade-offs. They make trade-offs between interests, between needs, between positions, *and* among interests, needs, and positions. Faruk and Zoe gave up the immediate purchase of a new couch when they decided to hire a housecleaner. They traded off immediate beautification of their living room for more potential leisure time. They needed the free time more than a couch on which to spend it.

People can trade off interests for high-priority needs (plunking down $500 to bail out a friend, even though you're afraid it sets a bad precedent) and quickly jettison positions that are discovered to violate fundamental interests (Faruk gets excused from scrubbing the bathroom when he develops a severe respiratory allergy to chlorine cleanser). Those trade-offs are the everyday stuff of negotiation.

Differences Make Us Rich

Look again at the picture of the possibilities frontier. All the space bounded by the straight lines and the curved line represents value (good things as perceived by Alma and Ben), which Alma and Ben may discover and, when discovered, must divvy up. But where does value come from?

One source of value in a marriage, as in every negotiation, is that the partners are different. As we said before, no one marries his or her identical twin. In fact, though, people do tend to marry spouses who are very much like them in IQ scores, level of education, age, race, wealth, religion, ethnic background, height, place of origin, and even such puzzling characteristics as finger length and the distance between their eyes (Becker, 1991, p. 117; Brown, 1986, p. 111). Moreover, people who choose a spouse who is unlike them in religion, race, age, or level of education have a relatively high rate of divorce (Becker, p. 118).

What about the adage that opposites attract? I leave the answer to wizards of romance. Even the traits just listed, though, leave lots of room for difference.

Before listing the differences that can create value in couples, we need an illustration of how difference, in general, can create value. In the classic example, Iz and Oz each have one orange. Each wants two oranges. What can they do? Do they both need to go door-to-door, searching for someone who has oranges but doesn't want them? If Iz and Oz were suspicious and reticent, they'd have to search. But they're not. They talk. Iz says he wants the peel from two oranges to grate into his frosting. Oz says, "You're kidding! All I want is the flesh from two oranges to make juice." Delighting in their cleverness and good fortune, they peel the oranges and swap peel for flesh. Each is better off than he was before. They have created value.

Is the typical married couple like Iz and Oz? In many ways, yes. The husband and wife differ in certain traits, and those differences create complementarity. In a traditional society, of course, the biggest difference results in the biggest complementarity: the sexual division of labor. Girls grow up expecting to specialize in child care. Boys grow up expecting to specialize in warfare and deep-sea fishing, emetic rituals, or paying work in the market. Men and women need each other to complement their work and build a thriving family. Apart, neither can easily raise children. Together, they can do that and lots more; they create value.

Romantic partners can differ in other ways and invent arrangements that make their differences work for them (swapping peel for flesh) rather than against them (searching door-to-door). Sometimes differences in tastes are complementary. Rachel loves to cook but hates washing dishes; with Don it's vice versa. Some differences in ability are complementary. Rachel is great with paperwork and family finance; Don is good at home repair.

Partners can also have different criteria of success. Rachel wants to climb to the top of her profession; Don wants to be a good person and put energy into his personal relationships. Couples who respect that difference find that they complement each other, as in a traditional marriage.

Bargaining Power

What happens when spouses fail to agree? A pile of greasy dishes grows taller and taller in the sink; the telephone company threatens to cut off service; Zoe scrubs the bathtub because she can't stand it; a new mother signs up for Aid to Families with Dependent Children. Negotiation gurus call that outcome the best alternative to a negotiated agreement, or BATNA (Raiffa, 1982, p. 45). One partner might hate it. The other might not mind it. We say that the first has a lousy BATNA, the second a tolerable one.

Jean-Jacques Rousseau had a condescending attitude toward women. Still, he knew a BATNA when he saw one. In 1762 he wrote, "We [men] could subsist better without them than they [women] without us" (1979, p. 364). In the upper-middle-class French society that he knew, men faced a better alternative to (a negotiated agreement about) marriage than women did. They also faced a better alternative to staying in an unhappy marriage than women did. Single and separated men got on much better than single and separated women. That theme, and its many consequences, runs throughout literature. Take the novel *Jane Eyre* (1847), for example. For Rochester, singlehood meant loneliness; for Jane, it meant poverty. In Murasaki Shikibu's *Tale of Genji,* written in roughly 1010, being single for Prince Genji meant having one elegant affair after another. For those women, it meant hoping that he would be gentlemanly and support them as occasional mistresses. When they were disappointed, all they could do was cry and look for ways to live more frugally.

Both Rochester and Genji were rich, handsome, and intelligent. Those assets gave them good BATNAs. What's great about having a good BATNA is that you can be choosy. You can be patient. You can demand, or wait for, a very attractive offer. You can afford to turn down proposals that others might accept. We say that you have lots of bargaining power.

Rochester, for example, could afford to marry for love, physical attraction, or whatever he felt like. His first choice was unfortunate; she became mentally ill and violent. He locked her in the attic. What makes *Jane Eyre* a feminist novel for some readers, though, is that his second choice refused him (Rich, 1979). Jane was plain, orphaned, had to work as a governess to earn a meager living, and stood out only because of her honesty, kindness, and spirited insistence on autonomy. She accepted him at the end only because she had inherited an income that made her independent. At that point, he was blind and maimed. His bargaining power was shattered. Jane felt free to act on her love and marry him.

A person with a very good BATNA, such as Rochester in his youth, not only has leverage to enter a relationship on favorable terms but can credibly threaten to leave the relationship. Nowadays, this form of bargaining power is much more relevant than in the past. Americans and Europeans don't have dowries anymore. However, we divorce more than ever. In a society in which separated or divorced men get on much better than separated or divorced women, men can threaten to walk out of the relationship and be believed by their spouses more easily than women can. Men can threaten to walk out for trivial reasons, such as cold soup or sexual boredom. We say that their *threat point* is lower. In cases where men do the earning, women do unpaid work in the home, and alimony is low or poorly enforced, men's threat point is much, much lower than women's.

Because the husband and the wife have different threat points, the husband can often, if he presses, get his way when their opinions conflict. That is the ugly side of a traditional marriage. Affection, respect, morality, custom, pressure from relatives, and public opinion can restrain men from using that bargaining power. However, that restraint is sometimes imperfect, as male domination of family decision making, battering of wives, and marital rape make plain.

Threat point is an important concept for our purposes because *children change threat points*. In most male–female couples, the arrival of the first child raises the woman's threat point more than it raises the man's. That happens for two reasons. First, the woman's emotional attachment to the baby is often more intense than the man's. Second, she has probably reduced or stopped her paying work in order to care for the baby. She has made herself, at least temporarily, more economically dependent on her partner. The result is that a threat that she would walk out on both him and the baby is scarcely credible. It is remarkable how seldom that happens. Also, a threat that she would leave him and take the baby has little credibility because she would have to find someone else who would either earn money to support the two of them or take care of the baby while she earned money. In most places at most times, those things have been hard to find.

As we will see in the chapters that follow, the effect of babies on threat points has profound consequences. Just when the couple faces more unpaid household work than ever before, the woman's bargaining power—her ability to persuade her partner to do chores he might not otherwise volunteer to do—has dropped. That factor may explain why some men manage to contribute relatively little to the new chores, even when their female partners want them to. Of course, when a first baby arrives, many men work longer hours at their paying jobs to earn more money. Nonetheless, the change in threat points gives them the power to choose whether and how they will contribute to the new needs of their family.

If a new baby often worsens the woman's BATNA more than it worsens her partner's, is she stuck with the BATNA that fate has dealt her? Are people born with bargaining power or born without it? Not at all. Negotiators expend a lot of energy away from the table, as it were, to improve their bargaining power. Many decisions that young men and young women make improve the bargaining power they will have *in the future* with their romantic partners and with their employers. Likewise, some decisions they make hurt their future bargaining power.

Looking back at the picture of the possibilities frontier (figure 3.2) will make this point clearer. Alma can improve her situation relative to Ben in several ways. First, note that the space bounded by the straight lines and the curved line represents the value that Alma and Ben can create together. Apart—if they split up, for example—each falls back to the zero point. At that point, of course, they aren't stuck with zero total value, just zero value *from the relationship*. That fall-back point is, for each of them, their best alternative to staying in the relationship, or their BATNA. Let's say that Alma does something that makes that fall-back point more attractive for her. She takes a computer course that makes her more employable in the big city 100 miles away. She patches up her relationship with her parents. She lucks into a good investment, makes $2,000, and saves it. All those things improve her BATNA. Thereby, they increase her bargaining power.

Second, Alma can do things that worsen Ben's BATNA. That sounds mean. Alma might intend it to be mean, intend it to be beneficial, intend it but regret it as a necessary accompaniment to something she thinks is good, or not intend it at all. Whichever, it improves her bargaining power relative to Ben's. For example, suppose Ben has always imagined that if they broke up, he could go work as a lumberjack in his cousin's logging outfit in Oregon. One Thanksgiving, Alma divulges to the cousin that Ben suffers prodigious hay fever and survives exposure to outside air between April and

August only if he takes medication that makes him drowsy. Alma believes that she is acting in Ben's best interests. Nonetheless, she has torpedoed his lumberjack option. If that was by far his best alternative to the relationship, she has also torpedoed his BATNA.

Third, Alma may do things that make it look as though her BATNA has improved. She might be intentionally or unintentionally misleading. For example, if she takes the computer course but skips the final exam that would have earned her the valuable certificate and forgets to tell Ben, he may figure, incorrectly, that she is now much more employable. He may defer to her, subtly and unconsciously, in ways that he didn't before.

Finally, of course, she can do things that make it look as though his BATNA has fallen. That is a trickier maneuver. Consider the consequences in the lumberjack example if she had not divulged Ben's hay fever to the cousin, but told Ben that she had. Ben would then think that his BATNA had been ruined, even though it hadn't been. Alma would be gambling that Ben's embarrassment would prevent him from ever again mentioning his dream to his cousin. It would be a risky move for Alma. But it might influence how Ben behaves in the relationship.

Of course, making things look like something they aren't is always risky. There is a big difference between bluffing and really holding the cards. When Alma truly improves her BATNA—through education, improving other relationships, or saving money—or truly reduces Ben's BATNA, then she has improved her hand relative to his. *The bedrock facts that the couple faces have changed.* This point is important because many popular books on how to succeed in relationships or in business emphasize appearance. The best-selling *Dress for Success* books in the 1980s epitomized that concern. In the business world, lies, misleading disclosures, expensive suits, intimidating body language, or fancy office furniture may sway the outcome of a negotiation in favor of the deceiver. Those devices are most likely to succeed in a one-time deal.

Family life, however, is a long, repeated set of negotiations that last years, even generations. Deception may be poisonous. If the stakes are high and the bluff is made repeatedly, it may, at last, be called. If that happens, the deceiver has lost face, injured trust, and strained affection, on top of losing whatever point he was protecting by bluffing in the first place. If the bluff is never called, the deceiver may suffer anyway. His ploy may gnaw at his conscience and coarsen his judgment (see Bok, 1978).

To sum up our understanding of bargaining power let's say this: Alma has bargaining power to the extent that she can move the couple eastward along the horizontal axis, in the direction of more value for her. As we saw earlier, when she improves her BATNA, or the appearance of her BATNA, relative to Ben's, she has more leverage to move the couple eastward.

There is also another way that Alma can slide the couple eastward. She can do things (possibly with Ben's conscious cooperation) that push the whole curved line—the possibilities frontier—outward along the horizontal axis. That is, she can do things that increase the *possibilities* for her to enjoy value, but not for him to enjoy value. The new curve would look like this (figure 3.3):

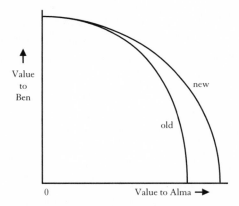

Figure 3.3. Pushing Out the Curve to Benefit Alma

Now, for any given level of happiness for Ben, the best the couple can do is better for Alma than it was before. That makes it likelier, though not certain, that Alma will be better off than before. It doesn't make it likelier that Ben will be better off. (The pleasure that Ben takes in seeing Alma enjoy herself is already taken into account here on Ben's axis.) For example, Alma could talk Ben into moving to the big city, where Alma will have a chance to go to cultural events and foreign restaurants that their small town lacks. Ben is indifferent between the two locations, because he spends all his waking hours watching cable TV.

Of course, any way that Alma finds to push the whole curve northeastward would benefit both her and Ben. For example, suppose fiber-optic info service is available in the big city but not in the small town. After the move, Ben exults in multimedia, interactive, wirehead heaven. If Alma lacks envy, she won't mind changes that push the curve northward, enlarging possible benefits to Ben and leaving her possibilities as good as before. An example would be the long-awaited doubling of the volume of data supplied—at no extra charge—by the fiber-optic info service. Ben is ecstatic. Alma's life is pretty much the same.

Commitment Mechanisms

If you understand bargaining power, you have mastered the hardest part of this whole book. You may begin to notice real-life examples of BATNAs and threat points all around you. Now, we come to one of the most colorful aspects of negotiation: commitment mechanisms. When someone pulls a commitment mechanism on you, you know it. You feel squeezed. In family life, however, it usually doesn't look like the person purposely crafted the commitment mechanism. It's just the way things are. That's what makes it so powerful.

A commitment mechanism is anything that makes it very expensive for you not to do something that you want to do. It lets you say to your negotiating partner, "I want X and I really can't afford to do anything else." Or it lets you say, "Shucks, I'd really love to help you with Y, but I can't." That is, *it traps you into doing what you want to do.* If people are pushing you to do something else, being trapped is convenient for you.

People use commitment mechanisms a lot in business and politics (Dixit and Nalebuff, 1991). They also use them a lot in romantic relationships and in families.

Getting pregnant is a good example. For a woman who wants a baby in a family that does not believe in abortion, pregnancy is a dramatic commitment. Even if her partner doesn't want a baby, or doesn't want one just then, it's a done deed. It has all the elements of a classic commitment mechanism: it is binding (it won't go away); it is credible (she's not likely to fib about it); it's visible (soon it will show); and it is irreversible (if both partners oppose abortion under their circumstances).

Here is another example. Young people who go to a private college or professional school often leave with large debts. Many new graduates feel an obligation to work full-time for years at a high-paying job to pay off the loans. If they don't, and default, they will hurt their credit rating. They may also feel dishonest. School loans can be a commitment mechanism that traps people into devotion to a career. When they discuss with their partner who should ratchet back to care for a new baby, they can point to their loans and say, "Sorry—gotta work." If they had wanted to emphasize career over baby all along anyway, they're in luck. Of course, that argument works only if they earn more than their partner.

Here is another example. When my husband and I started talking seriously about having a baby, I was concerned about what effect a baby might have on our work. He is a professor, with scheduled classes to teach, faculty meetings to go to, and exams to give. I'm a writer. My only schedule is the one I make for myself every day. My husband and I wanted to share the work of raising our baby fifty-fifty. However, I was afraid that I might wind up doing more baby care than we planned, just because my schedule was so much more flexible than his.

What could I do? My friend Raquel said, "You need a book contract. Something that commits you to delivering a manuscript by the baby's first birthday." My husband and I laughed, but then we looked at each other with our eyebrows raised. She was right. I did, in fact, manage to get a book contract. It has helped us, subtly and not so subtly, stick to our plan. You are reading the result.

Commitment mechanisms also give us a new way to understand the notion of credibility. For example, suppose a young man trying to persuade his jittery partner that he will be a devoted father tells all his friends, relatives, teachers, and neighbors that if he backs down, they should revile him. By mobilizing social pressure, he has created a big cost that will fall on him if he reneges on his promise. That makes his promise more credible.

This example makes it easier to understand the destiny of promises. Some promises are hollow from day one. There is no way they are going to be kept. Other promises are self-enforcing. There is no way they are going to be broken. One difference between them is that an intrinsically weak promise costs much more to keep than to break. Or it results in much higher benefits if it's broken than if it's kept. Self-enforcing promises are just the opposite.

For example, if you promise yourself that you won't eat one bite of dessert for the next whole month, you are making an intrinsically weak promise. Your skeptical side—or your friends—will say, "Yeah. Real credible."

On the other hand, think of Neil Simon's *The Odd Couple*. Two divorced men get an apartment together in New York City. Felix is a fastidious opera fan who enjoys gourmet food. Oscar is a messy sportswriter with lowbrow tastes. In many ways, they seem like a poor match. They are a funny match, which is why the play got turned into a movie and two television series.

Because there is a big difference in their tastes for neatness and cleanliness, Felix and Oscar can make binding promises to each other, explicitly or implicitly. Suppose Felix promises to keep the kitchen spotless if Oscar ponies up some sort of promise in return. Oscar can be sure that Felix's promise is self-enforcing. The psychic cost to Felix of a dirty sink far outweighs the cost to Felix of scrubbing it.

The costs and benefits that set up commitment mechanisms and that create credibility can, therefore, be emotional as well as material. After all, a very big percentage of what happens in relationships is emotional.

Here is an example of a weak promise to oneself that bears directly on the sexual division of labor. A young, egalitarian couple is contemplating parenthood. The woman is a little concerned that they might, in spite of their intentions, drift toward giving her more responsibility for the baby. She tells herself, "Well, if that happens, I'll just walk out on him and leave him with the baby for a day. Or even for a weekend. That'll shape him up."

This promise to herself is intrinsically weak. It flies against big costs—all emotional—that she will incur if she keeps it: damage to the relationship, disapproval from friends or relatives, anger from her partner, and—most unanticipated by this nontraditional young woman—her worries about exactly how well her angry partner is taking care of the baby. All these things combined will probably make it hard for her to walk out, even for twenty-four hours. Because she most likely can't make a binding promise like this, her bargaining power is lower than she thinks it is. That is, she overestimates her bargaining power. Because she is overconfident, *she may fail to make other arrangements* that would help her and her partner stick to, and enjoy, their commitment to their baby. The evidence suggests that many young women are wildly overoptimistic about how much child care their partners will do (for example, Cowan and Cowan, 1992). Partly, that is because intrinsically weak promises to ourselves make us feel temporarily like heroes. They cast a seductive spell, and then collapse. All dieters know it, and so do many women on AFDC.

Let's return to the question of commitment mechanisms themselves. Is there a way to counteract them? Yes. The magic counterspell is not to see or perceive them in any way. Remember that one of the essential elements of a commitment mechanism is that it be visible. It can't be visible to someone who is unavailable for communication. In the old days, a young man who enlisted in the army the morning after the senior prom couldn't be pressured into marrying the young woman he might have impregnated the night before. Nowadays, in the United States, those pressures are weaker than in the past. In some places still, though, skipping town is the only way for a man in those circumstances to escape marriage.

Some negotiators skip town, in a sense, by taking a mental holiday. How many women have you heard make this complaint: "You just can't talk to him about housework; it's like talking to a brick wall"? A man who, from the beginning of the relationship, has stopped listening whenever the subject of housework has come up has put himself in an advantageous position. On certain topics, he is simply unavailable for negotiation.

People who stonewall like that are claiming value. They are protecting their slice of the pie. As we saw earlier, they are forgoing the opportunity to jointly invent a new arrangement that might be better for both partners. Stonewallers believe—consciously or unconsciously—that the status quo is acceptable to them. Or, that the status quo as they can modify it without cooperating with their partner is acceptable.

That brings us to a very interesting question. A book about the whys and wherefores of the sexual division of labor might be said to be about, more fundamentally, the whys and wherefores of the status quo. I will approach this question as one approaches a hippopotamus: stealthily and from the side.

Focal Points and Tipping

Consider this problem. Mott and Schaeffer have parachuted separately into a dangerous location. They are in big trouble. To make things worse, neither knows where the other has landed. In order to be rescued, they have to get together quickly. They can't signal, radio, or communicate in any way, but each has a map of the area (Schelling, 1980, pp. 54–55). Take a look at figure 3.4. Where should they go to meet each other?

Mott would like to figure out what Schaeffer is likely to pick as the meeting place. He knows that Schaeffer is thinking, "Where would Mott think I'm likely to go?" Does the map suggest a place that each can expect the other to pick? What place would you pick? Many people who see this map in nonscientific experiments pick the bridge. They think it might stand out for the other person, and that the other person might conclude, therefore, that it will stand out for them.

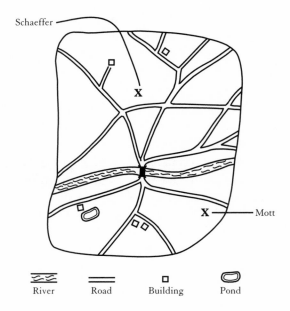

Figure 3.4. The Parachutists' Map

(Reprinted from Thomas C. Schelling, *The Strategy of Conflict,*
Harvard University Press, 1980)

Here is another example. You and your mother are shopping in a big department store. You get separated. You need to find each other quickly because you are both late for a lunch appointment and you came in one car. Where should you go to meet her? Where do you think she will go? Where will she think you will go? Where do you think she will think you will think she will go—and so on? The answer depends entirely on you and your mother. What would work for you?

In both these situations, two people want the same thing, each wins or loses along with the other, and they have some sort of problem communicating. They need to coordinate what they do. All they have to go on is their shared past experience, cues in the environment, and hunches about how the other will read those cues. If a solution stands out so conspicuously that both gravitate toward it with confidence, we call that solution a *focal point.* For Mott and Schaeffer, the focal point might be the bridge. On the other hand, if they have joked for years about starting a fish-farming business together, the focal point might be the pond.

Notice two things about these situations. First, there really isn't any answer that is correct in the abstract. What works will depend entirely on the culture, family history, and personal idiosyncrasies of the people involved. In some families, the answer might "of course" be the door they came in; in others, it might "of course" be the shoe department.

Second, the parties' need to coordinate can overwhelm whatever conflicts of interest exist between them. Mott might be close to the bridge and far from the pond, but if he knows that Schaeffer will go to the pond *and* expect Mott to go to the pond, Mott has to go to the pond. The difficulty they have in communicating subjects both Mott and Schaeffer to the tyranny of expectations in its most naked form. When a focal point stands out, it will advantage one party more than the other, disadvantage one more than the other, or be roughly equally good for both of them.

The economist Thomas Schelling, who was the first to see the importance of focal points and who coined the term, came to realize that many features of our everyday life probably result, in some sense, from coordination. We wear bell-bottoms when they are in style because we know that everyone else will expect us to and because it is easier to go along than to be deviant. For the same reason, we stop wearing them when they go out of style.

The same process explains a large part of the stability of many institutions and traditions. The weight of mutually consistent expectations helps hold them in place. I said earlier that we were about to stalk a hippopotamus. It just came into view: the mutually consistent expectations of women and men. They explain a large part of the stability of the sexual division of labor. That is, the sexual division of labor is a giant focal point. This is true within certain couples and within certain societies.

Which couples? Which societies? Very small families, infant formula, and men and women's nearly equal familiarity with baby care mean that a father and a mother are very good substitutes for each other in the home. They are more substitutable now, in rich countries, than they have ever been before in human history. However, even modern, egalitarian couples rarely flip a coin. Why? In part because tradition creates a focal point.

Focal points are a fruitful concept for us because they operate even without the consent of the parties. Even against their political beliefs. Even against *both* their interests.

Consider the Cough Syrup Conundrum. Ruth and Karl have two young children. Ruth works days and takes care of the kids after 4 P.M. Karl works nights and takes care of them during the day. They don't hire out any child care. One result is that they are both very rushed. Sometimes, one barely talks to the other before handing off the kids, like batons in a relay race, and dashing out the door. One week, both kids get colds. On Tuesday, Ruth and Karl each notice, on their separate shifts, that the supply of cough syrup is getting low. Who will pick up more cough syrup for the kids? It's Karl's job to do the food shopping, which he does on Sunday. However, Ruth realizes that he will expect her to buy the cough syrup, because she buys most of the children's clothes, toothbrushes, toys, and so on. All week though, she is too busy at work to leave early and stop at the drugstore. That evening, when the cough syrup runs out, she has to rush to the drugstore before it closes— with the kids wailing in the car.

This unpleasant incident happened because even though Ruth and Karl have pledged to take equal responsibility for child care and for earning, they share a background set of expectations about the ultimate responsibilities of mothers and fathers. Those expectations are like a strong prevailing wind. When the two have trouble communicating, they get pushed hard in one direction. In other words, the focal point was that Ruth buys cough syrup. The focal point operated even though it made everyone unhappy: Ruth was frazzled, the kids were in an uproar, and Karl was unhappy to learn about Ruth's stressful experience. Every day that week, though, he honestly figured that Ruth would pick up some cough syrup on the way home from work. Because Ruth was able to figure that he figured that, and he was able to figure that she would figure it, and so on, they were all stuck.[3]

Is there any way to counteract focal points? Yes, but it takes advance preparation. People overcome a focal point they dislike by making some other solution very conspicuous. A businesswoman who wants more than 50 percent of her partnership's mining profits will, from the very beginning of their discussions about forming a partnership, stress the importance, for example, of rewarding people according to the amount of personal risk they take—if she foresees that she will be the risk taker. She will emphasize the point every way she can think of. She'll get her partner to read *The Fountainhead,* take her to documentary movies about famous explorers, wear a pith helmet on neighborhood strolls, and crack jokes about armchair slugs who exploit the masses. She will try to make her solution seem like the natural one or, at least, natural for anyone in a partnership with her.

People who want to overcome the focal point of the traditional sexual division of labor use the same sort of pre-bargaining behavior to reshape the expectations of their potential partners. They must create *new,* mutually consistent expectations. They face a big job, because tradition has labeled the most minute features of our social landscape as appropriate for either males or females. Many women try to dislodge the traditional focal point by setting precedents from the very beginning of their relationships, behaving in an egalitarian way, being very education-oriented or career-oriented, and being consistently feminist, for example, by splitting restaurant bills, taking their education seriously, learning how to do routine maintenance on their cars, and playing sports instead of only watching men play sports.

Also, people who are wary of focal points that are disadvantageous to them can make an extra effort to prevent breakdowns in communication. For example, Ruth and Karl could keep a message board on their refrigerator.

Focal points are not only hard to escape, they are easy to fall back into. That gives them uncanny power. Consider, for example, racial segregation in residential neighborhoods. In the United States, most neighborhoods are either predominantly white or predominantly black (or Latino or Asian-American). A neighborhood that is, say, 60 percent white and 40 percent black and stays that way is a rarity, because white residents flee, or are duped into fleeing by greedy real estate operators, when the number of black residents climbs over a modest percentage.

The result is that there are only two stable situations: a neighborhood is mostly white or mostly black. In between, blacks are entering but whites are leaving. Another way of saying this is that there are two focal points: mostly white or mostly black. In between, the composition is tipping very quickly toward the next focal point.

This phenomenon is, in fact, called *tipping* (Grodzins, 1957; Schelling, 1980). It happens in many different settings. For example, at the end of a rock concert, either the whole audience is clapping for an encore or no one is. Rarely do ten people keep on clapping if the rest aren't. After the second encore, the whole audience claps, but each person stops quickly as the rest fade. Everyone tips toward the next focal point, which is silence (and a rush for the parking lot).

Tipping gives tremendous stability to the focal point of the traditional sexual division of labor. Unlike in neighborhoods and rock concerts, in child care there is only one focal point: women do it. Even couples like Ruth and Karl who have achieved a 50-50 split still face a perilous balance. Anything that nudges them away from the 50-50 focal point they have carefully cultivated for their family could send them skittering quickly all the way back to 100-0. Say, for example, Ruth wrenches her back, can't do her paying work for six months, and so stays home full-time for that period. If Karl gets a big raise, all the machinery of social approval, lurking background expectations, and other forces will make their new arrangement surprisingly stable. There is a good chance that Ruth will stay home with the kids and Karl will become the sole breadwinner.

As we will see, couples who think they have escaped the pull of the traditional focal point often get snapped back into it, as into a black hole. The only remedy for tipping is unceasing vigilance and countertipping.

Status

My aunt's favorite story is about the night the Prince of Wales washed her dishes. Imagine that: the future king of England in her very own kitchen in Hingham, Massachusetts, swabbing plates and pots with Ivory liquid. When she starts to tell it, everybody within earshot goes perfectly still to listen.

Unfortunately, I made that up. My aunt tells no such story. Still, it is instructive. Simple acts have different meanings depending on the status of the person who does them. A small favor, such as washing the dinner dishes, seems more generous when a famous or rich person does it.

When relatives give presents, neighbors babysit, or bystanders help an injured jogger, the recipient tries to figure out what kind of gesture would be fair in return. Psychologists call the trading of those sorts of favors *social exchange* (Brown, 1986). They distinguish it from economic exchange.

In social exchange, people need to figure out how large a favor they owe in return. Favors aren't like merchandise in a store. They don't come with price tags. To calibrate how they will reciprocate, recipients take into account many characteristics of the person who extended the favor: the effort it cost that person, the amount of money it cost relative to the person's means, whether the person is extremely busy, whether the person is a local or even national big shot, and other elements of that person's social status. Those elements make the favor they give in return seem either fair or unfair. When it's unfair, recipients feel ashamed or guilty.

This concept of fairness in social exchange is useful for us for two reasons. First, nearly everything romantic partners do for each other could be called social exchange. Alma does some chores, Ben does others. Alma contributes a certain amount of money to the family pool, and Ben contributes something, ranging from zero to millions. Is the arrangement fair? The arrangement that seems fair to both of them will vary, in part, with the characteristics I just listed. If Alma comes from an old aristocratic European family, now fallen on hard times, and is extremely busy fending off newshounds, Alma and Ben might both feel it's fair if Alma does much less than Ben around the house. Those characteristics don't sound like they create bargaining power, but because of the peculiar qualities of social exchange, they do change the arrangement Alma and Ben will probably fall into, to Alma's benefit. (They give Alma bargaining power by making it more likely that Alma can push the arrangement eastward, toward value for her.)

This concept is helpful to us for a second reason. Another thing people take into account when calibrating the fairness of favors is whether the giver is male or female. Compelling evidence suggests that when a man does a favor the recipient feels that he or she should reciprocate with more than when a woman does a favor (Brown, 1986; Jasso and Rossi, 1977). That is, other things equal, maleness confers social status for the purpose of weighing favors.

Clearly, the consequences for housework could be profound. On Monday, Peter washes the dishes. On Tuesday, Lisa washes the dishes. If on Wednesday Lisa feels in her bones—despite what she believes intellectually—that *she still owes Peter,* because her favor didn't quite cancel his out, Peter is going to have an easy time doing less housework than her. That is, in male–female couples in which the woman feels deep down that the man really is the Prince of Wales, the man has an extra dollop of bargaining power. That extra dollop makes the traditional division of labor even more stable than it would be otherwise. In couples so afflicted, the woman can barely keep up with returning favors to the prince who deigns to live with her. Is there any way to expunge the glittery aura of male status? Only by changing one's feelings. Women who can't will scurry like a scullery maid or live with guilt.

Moral Language

When a person is trying to persuade someone to accept her position, she can appeal to a general principle he believes in, argue that her proposal serves a need that he has, improve her BATNA, craft a commitment mechanism, subtly emphasize her status, or suggest that he owes her a favor.

Another thing that she can do is say that her position is the fair one. That is, that her position is morally superior to anything else they have discussed. People use moral language like that for several reasons. First, moral arguments are often persuasive, since most people want to do the moral thing. Most people want to believe that their family lives are moral and fair, too. People also use moral language because it makes them feel good about themselves. When two people begin to grapple with a decision on a moral level, instead of just a practical level, they have in most cases already taken a step toward the possibilities frontier. In other words, it doesn't only help the person get a bigger piece of the pie, it helps make the pie bigger.

(That's true even in unlikely situations, such as bank robbers debating whether to murder the vault guard, who could identify them, or conk him on the head, in hopes that the blow would muddle his memory. When they begin to discuss the issue in moral terms, they awaken a flickering part of themselves that, probably, they like the best. For that reason, honor among thieves is an ancient principle.)

Families use moral language all the time. The first argument a three-year-old is usually able to produce is, "It's not fair!" Most feminist critiques of male power in families and elsewhere advance as their main argument, explicitly or implicitly, that the status quo isn't fair.

Many nontraditional couples in which the man is a very involved father or a househusband use moral language to describe their choice, too. They make statements like, "We are a team. It just seems fair that way." Or "She was making enough to support us and then I threw my back out and I wasn't going to stay home and do nothing. That wouldn't be fair." That is true even of romantic partners who say they don't think of themselves as feminist (Ehrensaft, 1987; Kimball, 1984).

Since many people have a strong need to believe that the world is just and that their situation is fair, it's not surprising that nontraditional couples use moral language to describe their choices. However, I think that many couples with an involved father may also be using moral language as an important tool to protect their arrangement—as a commitment mechanism. If their arrangement were to fall apart, they would run the risk of seeming less moral, or at least hypocritical, to themselves and maybe to others. Moral language can also make the new focal point they have created more conspicuous and help set up new, mutually consistent expectations. ("Ruth would never make a special trip after work to get cough syrup; she'll expect me to do it during the day. It's only fair.") Of course, it gives the partner who initiated the arrangement—in many cases, the woman—more bargaining power. It might be her way of counteracting the glittery aura of male status I just discussed. Also, if she began using moral language to frame her view of equality in the family when she was a teenager and from the very beginning of the relationship with her partner, that behavior has probably created precedents that increase her bargaining power. Even if her husband is egalitarian, moral language might nudge him into doing more household work than he expected to do. That can happen whether or not she intended to nudge him. Mostly, of course, in families as elsewhere, people use moral language simply to express their moral feelings.

Love

Negotiations within a couple are different from many other sorts of negotiations. For one thing, most spouses love each other. That has many implications. One is that love makes us generous. That means that the high-bargaining-power spouse often gives things to the other that she or he could never have bargained out of an unloving spouse. In turn, the low-bargaining-power spouse may show loyalty, tenderness, and effort in all conjugal endeavors far above what an unloving spouse may have received. To have a balanced view of negotiation in families, we need to keep those facts in mind.

Still, we also need to keep in mind that even though it feels good to be generous, there's a limit. Let's say Al has to choose between two potential partners. He thinks he could come to love either one very much. Bea is healthy and psychologically sound. Colombe is sickly and haunted by irrational fears. Al is a high-earning breadwinner and knows that love makes people generous. Colombe is so needy that Al would probably give her lots of money to spend, leisure time to spend it, and lots of attention to try to make her better off. Because he doesn't want his feelings of love to cause him to give away to his partner too high a fraction of the fruits of the marriage, he chooses Bea. With her, he can be generous but still keep a lot of the fruits of the marriage for himself.

This example may sound artificial, but at some level people probably do take such considerations into account. It is one of the reasons for a fact we noted earlier: healthy, attractive people from upper socioeconomic backgrounds tend to marry people who are also healthy, attractive, and from upper socioeconomic backgrounds. That way, they won't have to shore up their spouse in a loving attempt to make them as well off in the marriage as they themselves are. It also helps explain why people don't on a large scale marry down in characteristics other than expected income.[4] (It is also one reason some people with a serious physical or mental disability, who would make devoted and charming spouses, have trouble finding the partner they deserve.)

The negotiated result that Al expected to unfold within a loving marriage influenced his decision about who to marry. In general, the typical deal that husbands get and wives get within marriage in a given society probably does have a big influence on who marries whom. For example, when laws, marriage contracts, or customs dictate that wives get a big fraction of the fruits of marriage, then women have more incentive to marry up. A big fraction of a big pie is nicer than a big fraction of a small pie.

This point is an upside-down version of a point I've made repeatedly: who marries whom can influence the deal the husband and the wife get. Their relative bargaining power influences how they split the pie. This point shows that we are facing a system with feedback loops. The typical deal influences who marries whom *and* who marries whom influences the typical deal. Social scientists are just beginning to figure out how those feedback loops work. We will return to this point in chapter 10, when we discuss what changes in the status of homemakers might be necessary to entice millions of men to marry women who earn lots more money than they do.

The Marriage Market

How does a woman find a romantic partner to share her life with? How does a man find one? It's not totally random. There are places to go (luaus, foxhunts), customs to follow (bathe regularly), and friends and relatives to ask help from. The results are not totally random, either. Some people are very appealing to lots of potential partners. They can be choosy, or have many partners, or both. A few people are unappealing to most potential partners. They can't afford to be choosy. If they are, they'll stay single. Because the world of romance has definite structure, and because people get roughly ranked (have different values, if you will) and sort themselves accordingly, social scientists say that there is a marriage market.

The expression "marriage market" may sound peculiar. But it does help us understand some important things about relationships and the sexual division of labor. For one thing, everything we have to say about negotiation within a couple takes place in a bigger context. That context puts some limits on what will probably happen within the couple. That context is the marriage market.

This is how it works. In *Jane Eyre,* Rochester's chances of success in the marriage market were good. He was handsome, intelligent, and rich. He was attractive to lots of highly desirable women. Jane, on the other hand, had poor prospects. She was not pretty and had no social connections. In nineteenth-century England, those were big handicaps. Imagine that Jane had been able to support herself independently at a decent standard of living. Imagine that Rochester had never married his first wife. What would have happened if Jane and Rochester had met under those circumstances? How would Jane have perceived the potential match?

Undoubtedly, Jane would have understood that if they got married, he would have more bargaining power than her because his chances in the marriage market would be better than hers should they split up. That is, her BATNA—her best alternative to staying with Rochester—didn't only include her ability to support herself economically; it included her ability to find another partner. If she was very unlikely to find someone as appealing to her as Rochester, and Rochester could easily have found another kind, intelligent woman, that would give Rochester some leverage in a marriage with Jane.

Charlotte Brontë saw that clearly. That's why she doesn't have Jane marry Rochester until Jane has an independent fortune *and* Rochester has been blinded and maimed. That way their economic position *and* their position in the marriage market have been roughly equalized.

The marriage market is important for our purposes because it limits the divisions of labor that women are able to create in their families.[5] If 99 percent of men are looking for a housewife, it is hard for 10 percent of women to pursue careers *and* get married. Still, men don't dictate the terms of marriage single-handedly. Even in a world of 99 percent highly traditional men, some men will have to settle for career-oriented wives. The thing is, they may not be the most desirable men. Women don't dictate the terms of marriage, either.

Men's traditionality is not the only thing we need to look at. Sometimes the number of men is the important thing. If there are only a few men out there, they will have their pick of the most appealing women. If those women don't work hard to keep them happy, the men can credibly threaten to leave. They'll shout from their armchairs, "Hurry up with those chips! What's taking so long?"

The ratio of men to women is called the *sex ratio.* It has a big impact on the lives of millions of people. It shows quite nicely how the marriage market works and how it affects the sexual division of labor. For example, among African-Americans between the ages of twenty-five and fifty-five, the sex ratio is 86.5 men for every 100 women (M. Williams, 1990). That contrasts sharply with the sex ratio among whites in the United States, which is 100.5 men for every 100 women. The African-American sex ratio has been falling since 1840, the last time it was even. Nowadays, the causes of the imbalance include the tragically high homicide rate among black men (51.4 per 100,000, as opposed to 11.3 for black women), their higher rates of suicide (9.9 per 100,000, as opposed to 2.0 for black women), and their higher rates of death from disease and accidents.

Many African-American women are keenly aware of this problem. They may be wondering how much they can improve their bargaining power with black men. Their troubles are exacerbated by the fact that black men are more likely to marry nonblacks than black women are. In 1985, so-called interracial marriages included 133,000 between a black man and a nonblack woman (117,000 of whom were white) and 50,000 between a black woman and a nonblack man (47,000 of whom were white) (M. Williams, 1990). The squeeze black women face is painful.

Does the sex ratio ever help women? Historically, yes. For example, Chinese-American men far outnumbered Chinese-American women in the United States between 1890 and 1965. U.S. immigration laws, which Congress passed with explicitly racist rhetoric, helped create that imbalance. The result was that Chinatowns were full of men and had hardly any women or children. By 1950, Chinese men in the United States between the ages of twenty and thirty-four still outnumbered Chinese women by 20,099 to 14,184 (Kung, 1962). Many of those men never married. Twenty-five percent married non-Chinese. On the other hand, nearly all the women married. In the early decades of this century, when parents arranged most marriages, many young Chinese daughters married middle-aged men with well-established incomes and reputations (Kung, 1962). That is, the parents were able to achieve economically safe marriages for their daughters. (Although that might not have been what the daughters themselves preferred.)

Some male college students and graduates may think that Chinatown sounds familiar. For example, at Yale University in the 1970s, men far outnumbered women, since Yale didn't start admitting women until 1969. Older male graduate students poached the undergraduate women away from the undergraduate men. Many of those women, in their happy ignorance of the bargaining dynamics swirling around them, thought it natural that twenty-five-year-old Ph.D. students should find them fascinating.

Skewed local sex ratios also explain why many women scientists, engineers, and doctors are married to men in the same profession. In graduate school, the men fall all over each other trying to court the few women in the class. Those dynamics have, I think, another subtle result. They deceive some of those women into thinking that they will have a lot of bargaining power in the future, too, when it is time to have children. As we will see in the chapters that follow, they usually don't.

Sex and Culture

If you think about it, very few of the basic elements laid out in this chapter depend for their effect on a sexual difference within the couple. Lesbian couples and gay male couples face the same forces as male–female couples. Of course, the traditional focal points—woman as homemaker, man as breadwinner—will not carry much force. The special privilege conferred by male status is irrelevant in female–female couples and washes out in male–male couples. However, other sources of status—such as an upper-middle-class background or a degree from a fancy college—can give the higher-status lesbian or gay man an extra dollop of bargaining power.

For example, in many male couples in the United States, money is the topic that generates the most arguments. Guides for gay men caution readers who have a higher income than their partners, "You may feel that you've earned the right to make all the decisions.... You don't, or at least your partner won't think you do" (Marcus, 1992, p. 211). Also, in gay male couples, slobby Oscars have an easy time getting neatnik Felixes to do the housework (Marcus, 1992).[6]

Consider also lesbian couples. Most lesbian mothers had their children while they were in a relationship with a man. Some have trouble persuading a new female partner to pay half the rent and do half the child care (Lewin, 1993). The new partner is less emotionally attached to the child than the biological mother is and doesn't owe the child any legally or socially enforced support.

The division of labor at home, then, is an issue in all romantic relationships. It is also an issue in all sorts of families, cultural settings, and religious environments. Research in anthropology, the sociology of families, and the history of family life reveals hundreds of examples of bargaining power, its sources and its results, that fall neatly into the framework set out here. To list enough examples to convince a skeptic would take more than one book. Here I'll give just two more examples of bargaining power in families.

First, consider a culture and environment very different from ours. Researchers studying small, nonliterate, tribal societies have found that the more that women outnumber men, the more likely the society is to be polygynous. Some men have many wives, and many women have to share a husband with three or four wives (Becker and Posner, 1993).

Second, consider an example close to home. Among Mexican-American families, men are likely to do housecleaning, shopping, and child care mainly in couples in which the wife is employed and earns at least one-third of the family income (Pesquera, 1985; Ybarra, 1982). As one Mexican-American wife said, "We only have a say if we are not under them economically" (Pesquera, p. 152).

Can our framework explain the details of family life, the rituals that tie families together, the commitment that outlasts searing hardship, the diversity of cultures, the idiosyncrasies within cultures, the sweetness that makes families worth forming, generation after generation? Of course not. What it does explain, and what we cannot ignore, are certain forces that have locked women into raising children and locked men out, for centuries.

In the following chapters, I use this framework to analyze four kinds of marriages: a traditional marriage, two transitional marriages in which women with a weak to medium-strong bargaining position seek a lot of participation in child care from their husbands, and a nontraditional marriage. We will see how BATNAs, babies' effect on threat points, the focal points created by tradition, the power of tipping, and the role of status all combine to make women's primary responsibility for child care much more enduring and harder to change than it would be otherwise. We will also think carefully about what each of these women can do to achieve her goals.

II

Negotiating Women's Lives

4

A Traditional Marriage

Man's love is of man's life a thing apart, 'Tis woman's whole existence.

—Byron, *Don Juan*

W E MAKE DECISIONS EVERY DAY. SOMETIMES WE MAKE THEM after a lot of thought. Sometimes we just plunge in. Other times we make a decision by not taking a particular step because it never entered our heads to consider it. If by not taking that step we close off an option that we'll never have again, that inaction was tantamount to a major decision. Occasionally, we briefly consider doing something (moving to St. Louis, applying for a union apprenticeship) but don't do it because it seems foreign, because we're afraid other people will make fun of us, or because it doesn't fit somehow with the rest of what we are. And so, with each step we take and each step we don't take, our life grows into its distinctive shape. Those decisions, summed up over time, make each person's life unique.

Another reason each person's life is unique is that we face so much unpredictability. Strange things happen. Little events sneak up and suddenly make a big difference. For example, my brother-in-law was trying to decide whether to go to medical school in San Diego or New Haven. One night, he had a dream that he was at a gray, frigid train station in New Haven. He got into a taxi and told the dream-cabbie about his predicament. The cabbie turned around and said, "Are you nuts? Go to San Diego!"

So he did. There he met his wife, they bought a house, and they just had their first child. If it hadn't been for that dream, there's a good chance that my brother-in-law would have gone to New Haven. The rest of his life would have been different.

Sometimes I remember a story by the science fiction writer Ray Bradbury (1983), in which a time-traveling tourist visits the dinosaur era, steps off the carefully marked trail he's been told to follow, and crushes a butterfly underfoot. When he gets back to his own time, things have changed. The frightening militarist who lost the presidential election the day before his trip is now president. Even the English language is slightly different. The life course of that little butterfly would have rippled its effects down into the twentieth century. Its early death changed history.

Decisions, then, have peculiar properties. We make them consciously and unconsciously. Chance events can alter their outcomes. Their outcomes depend on *other* people's decisions. (If the woman who married my brother-in-law had moved to Chicago, he couldn't have met her in San Diego.) Also, chance events alter the outcomes of *other* people's decisions. (She might have had a good dream about Chicago.) Moreover, the outcomes of some of our decisions don't reverberate until many years later, like the death of the butterfly.

Decisions have yet another peculiar quality. Seen from the right angle, certain decisions that people make when they are young are *moves* that set up the negotiations they will have with their romantic partners when they are grown up. In the language of the last chapter, young people's decisions set up their best alternatives to a negotiated agreement (BATNAs), their bargaining power, their commitment mechanisms, their own personal focal points, their social status, their attitudes toward status, and so on. That means that decisions—whether or not they are conscious, intermeshed with other people's decisions, or contingent on chance events—have repercussions through the years.

Because young people's decisions help shape their BATNAs and bargaining power as grown-ups, they help determine the *outcome* of negotiations that romantic partners face. Because girls and boys make different choices, on average, women and men have different BATNAs and different levels of bargaining power, on average. The most important decisions that girls and boys make in this regard are about their education and jobs, their choice of romantic partners, and how they assign responsibility for the care of their babies.

How do those forces work in real people's lives? In the next few chapters, we'll see. We'll look closely at four kinds of marriages. Each marriage is hypothetical, in large part a composite built up from findings in scholarly studies, memoirs, and oral histories.[1] I have also drawn on my own survey of sixty-five nontraditional couples. I surveyed only nontraditional families to fill in a hole I found in the scholarly literature. Studies of traditional families, and families in which the wife worked for pay but also kept most responsibility for managing housework and child care, gave many hints about negotiation in those families. However, studies of families in which the father did half or more of the child raising did not. In this chapter, we'll consider a traditional marriage, in which both the wife and the husband expect the wife to specialize in homemaking and raising the children.

A Traditional Girlhood

A traditional girl prepares to be a wife and mother. Consider, for example, Alice, born in 1948. Her father loaded trucks at a warehouse and her mother was a full-time homemaker. They were a socially conservative family and lived in an area where women's job was to run the house; shop; do the laundry; cook nourishing meals; raise the children; give their children a strong sense of discipline and morality; help them with their homework; make sure their friends weren't leading them astray; stay in touch with the relatives; cook a big dinner every weekend for the grandparents, aunts, and uncles; volunteer at church now and then; and, every day, keep the house clean and neat. It was a big job. It was the job that Alice intended to do when she grew up.

Alice's daydreams, her games, the way she dressed, the skills her parents taught her, the things they praised her for and criticized her for, the stories she read, and the television shows she most enjoyed were all consistent with her ambition to specialize in homemaking. Also, the decisions she made as a young woman made it very hard for her to do anything later *but* specialize in homemaking.

Education

First, there was her schooling. In high school, Alice liked English, gym, and social studies. She took as little math and science as she could get away with. They were hard. Most of all, what was the point? She never even considered technical courses such as drafting. Her main goals in school were not to embarrass herself with low grades, to be a good person, and, with luck, to find a kind, honest, cute young man with lots of energy and discipline who would earn a steady income—higher, she hoped, than her father's. She was looking forward to marrying before she turned twenty-one. The prom was serious business. She did not work for pay, except for occasional babysitting. She did not plan to get any schooling after high school graduation.

What did Alice's education consist of? She was busy acquiring the skills, attitudes, and connections she needed to meet a desirable young man and to be a good wife and mother: paying close attention to her appearance, knowing the calorie content and nutritional value of different foods, learning how to bake delicious desserts, being a good listener and a supportive friend, learning how to do housework, attentively watching mothers take care of babies. She was not picking up any skills, attitudes, or social connections that could lead to a paying job with a wage that met her income goals for her own family. At best, she could do filing in an office, be a waitress, or learn to cut hair at a beauty salon. To her, that sounded reasonable. After graduation, she did in fact get a job at the beauty salon. She got to see lots of her friends that way, and older women, too, when they came into the shop.

From a negotiating standpoint, we can say that Alice created a *commitment mechanism*—she was trapped into what she wanted: to be taken care of by a loving, breadwinning husband and devote herself to her children. To any traditional young man looking for a wife who would put her family first, Alice looked terrific.

Alice not only created a commitment mechanism but she *burned a bridge* behind her. Burning a bridge is a very powerful commitment mechanism. The expression comes from a decision Hannibal made over two thousand years ago. Hannibal led the armies of Carthage against the armies of Rome in a terrible war that lasted decades. Finally, he marched his soldiers and elephants from North Africa right down into the Italian peninsula. To persuade his soldiers that they had no option but to fight with every ounce of determination they could summon, he burned the bridges behind them. They could not retreat.

Alice burned a bridge behind her when she decided not to take any math beyond first-year algebra and no science beyond first-year biology. She closed off certain options. Young women today who make that choice close off even more options. For example, many young women from working-class and lower-middle-class families were able to break into jobs with middle-class pay during the mid-1990s by becoming nurses and technicians. The job market in the United States and other rich countries, and even many developing countries, is evolving in a direction that puts a higher and higher value on technical training (Rivera-Batiz, 1992).

Because Alice passed up her chances in high school to pick up any distinguishing, remunerative skills, we can say that she *trained down*. She was simply not thinking about the job market. She was totally focused on the marriage market. Alice also gave up valuable opportunities by not continuing her education after high school. Alice's parents did not want to spend the money to send her to college, but she could have worked part-time, scrimped, and borrowed to put herself through junior college. She didn't make that extraordinary effort because it didn't fit with her plans for the future.

More schooling would have raised her *social status* a little as well. By itself, that change in status would probably have had only a minute effect on her relationship with her future husband. It might have offset just a little the edge that his special social status—being male—gave him.

Going on to college also tends to change young people's attitudes in crucial ways, especially those who live away from their parents. For example, they develop more flexible views about which chores in the home are appropriate for men and women (Goldscheider and Waite, 1991). Boys have to do their own laundry. Girls have to take out their own trash. In other words, living away from home shakes up the traditional *focal point* of the sexual division of labor in the home for young people.

One reason, then, that Alice's views about her future stayed so fixedly traditional is that she never moved out of her parents' house until she got married. Also, had she gone on in school, she might have qualified for a higher-paying job (for example, as a dental hygienist). The decision not to continue her education reinforced all her earlier decisions.

Marrying Up

Next, consider the man Alice married. Jack began working part-time at his cousin's motorcycle shop when he was fifteen. He became a full-time employee when he graduated from high school. He was a hard worker, proud of his perfect attendance record on the job, and at the time they got engaged, he was looking for ways to increase his income. Maybe he would learn how to drive large trucks or construction machinery. Because he was three years older than Alice, he seemed wiser in dealing with the practical problems of life. Alice liked that.

Notice that the age gap between Alice and Jack did two things. Even if they had both started the same kind of job after high school graduation, Jack's pay would have been higher because he was three years ahead of her on the wage ladder. Therefore, the age gap made it even likelier that Alice would be the one who stayed home when the first baby came. It also reinforced the deference Alice was taught to give to the man of the family, because he was more experienced. That made it a little more likely that Jack would get his way in major family decisions.

Of course, because Alice and Jack approached the idea of paying work with totally different attitudes (and because the crowding of young women into low-skill service work lowered Alice's earnings), Jack earned more fixing motorcycles when he was eighteen than Alice did at age eighteen cutting hair. Even without the age gap, his expected earnings, even if Alice continued to work full-time, would have been significantly higher than hers.

We can say, then, that Alice *married up,* both in age and in expected earnings. From an economic point of view and a negotiation point of view, marrying up is the keystone of a traditional marriage for a woman.

Let's take a close look at Alice's position from a negotiation perspective the week after her wedding.

It was June 1966. Her earnings at the beauty salon were a little above minimum wage. On her own, she couldn't afford a decent apartment. In her mind, one of the most attractive things about getting married was living apart from her parents as an independent adult. Alice was also considering quitting her job soon, to devote herself to homemaking. However, it was Jack's income that made possible both her independence from her parents and her concentration on homemaking.

In chapter 3, we learned that people's best alternative to any given agreement, or BATNA, matters a lot. Alice's BATNA had two parts: what she could earn in the job market and what she could find in the marriage market. Her earnings were low. So her alternative to marriage in general was lousy. When it came to particular husbands, though, her situation looked a little better. Her alternative to marrying her first choice was marrying her second choice. Because Alice was a good person and was outgoing, well organized, clearly skilled at homemaking, and (one is sorry to have to say) good-looking by the arbitrary local standards, her second-choice young man would still have made a decent husband. At age eighteen, she was at the peak of her marriageability. If she and Jack got divorced in a year or two, she could still probably find a dependable, kind, attractive young man to marry.

A Declining BATNA

Now consider what happened after several years of marriage. Alice's BATNA started to fall. If she had been unhappy, her alternative to staying in the marriage would have been to leave Jack. However, her expected earnings were so low that this alternative would have looked unpleasant. Her main hope would have been to remarry quickly. However, as she got older (the beauty problem) and as she had more children (who would probably stay with her), she looked less and less attractive to other men.

In contrast, Jack's earnings increased as the years passed. So did his marriageability, at least until his mid-forties. The sags and wrinkles that aging brought to Jack didn't hurt his chances of remarriage as much as the same sags and wrinkles hurt Alice's. So his BATNA and bargaining power increased relative to hers.

The change in their relative bargaining power had subtle effects on their relationship. Even though both Jack and Alice were loving and generous, they disagreed sometimes. Occasionally, they disagreed about something important. The increase in Jack's bargaining power over time made it easier for him to get his way.

Picture Alice at twenty-seven. She and Jack had four children. When she was a girl, Alice had no clue how much work it would be to take care of that many children. Confronted with the reality, she decided she wanted more help from Jack around the house when he came home from work. However, Jack figured that after a long day at his construction job, he was entitled to a good dinner and some rest. As a favor, Jack sometimes took the kids outside to play so Alice could put dinner on the table in peace. Doing any more, though, seemed beyond the call of duty.

Neither Jack nor Alice was aware of the process, but their BATNAs were reinforcing the traditional sexual division of labor in their family.

Alice made other influential decisions along the way. She was a stickler for neatness and kept the kitchen and bathroom spotless. Those *high standards of housework* were hard for Jack to meet, when he was inspired to try. He would never have put away his socket wrenches or screwdrivers without cleaning them, but he saw nothing wrong with leaving dirty forks in the sink overnight. Alice couldn't stand that. Her criticism of his methods discouraged him from taking regular responsibility for washing the dishes. Her failure to compromise her standards meant that she was stuck with most of the housework nearly all the time.

Alice also liked to *spend money*. She grew up in a family that had very little to spend, so was thrilled that Jack made a steady, decent income. She liked to stroll the shopping center with her friends, buy things on sale, and make the house look cheery. She wasn't greedy; she just wanted her family to enjoy the good things in life. Therefore, she encouraged Jack to find ways to increase his income. Supporting five dependents on a construction salary put a lot of pressure on Jack. He worried about what he would do if business dried up, or if he got sick or injured. With those sorts of worries, and the thousand details he always had to juggle in his mind about his rig, his coworkers, and his boss, Jack was unlikely to volunteer to take on another huge and taxing mental job—helping to manage the housework and the kids. If Alice had a lower target for the family income or if she earned a significant share of it, Jack would have had more mental room for responsibilities at home. But she didn't. So he didn't.

Having Children

Other choices that Alice made influenced her negotiating position. As soon as she got married, she wanted a baby intensely. Why not? Her life's work, as she saw it, was raising children.

Jack also wanted kids. Waiting a few years would have been fine by him, though. Relative to Jack, Alice was impatient. Here, as always, *the impatient person pays*. Because Alice wanted a baby more strongly and sooner than Jack did, he didn't need to make any moves or shows of commitment in order to persuade her to have one. For example, Alice had always dreamed about moving to the mountains and buying a little old house with a stream in back. He did not have to concede that or anything else to her in the early years of their marriage.

Before she turned nineteen, then, Alice got her wish. She got pregnant. Her traditional girlhood and traditional marriage led her briskly and ineluctably to traditional motherhood.

Alice's pregnancy set into motion another force that lowered her bargaining power relative to Jack's. During her pregnancy, Alice's *emotional attachment* to the fetus grew and grew. That extra attachment made her devoted and predictable. It gave Jack the ability to manipulate her, even if only unconsciously or only with her best interests at heart.

Do *all* mothers love their newborn babies more than the fathers do? Probably not. Research suggests, though, that the *average* mother is more emotionally attached to her newborn than the average father is. For example, mothers' grief at the death of their newborn baby or infant is usually more intense than fathers' grief (Zeanah, 1989). Mothers also grieve more intensely than fathers after the loss of a baby to sudden infant death syndrome (SIDS). Those studies do not find that *all* mothers are more emotionally attached than all fathers. In fact, in one study of fifty couples, over 20 percent of the fathers had higher grief scores than their female partners (Benfield et al., 1978, cited in Zeanah, 1989, p. 468).[2]

Why are women's feelings toward their newborns different from men's? No one knows for sure. I suspect, though, that the experience of being pregnant is fundamentally different from the experience of watching one's partner be pregnant.

For example, physicians know that mothers' feelings toward their fetuses undergo a change at about the twenty-week mark (roughly four and a half months), when they can start to feel the fetus moving inside them (see citations in Zeanah, 1989). Mothers show more intense symptoms of grief if they lose a fetus after that point than before (Zeanah et al., 1993). For the average woman, the fetus's movements seem to ratchet up her awareness that she really does carry a developing life inside her. Her partner may enjoy feeling those same movements when touching her stomach, but the emotional impact is probably different.

Second, the pregnant woman probably thinks about the fetus much more often than her husband does. Just picture what went on at Alice and Jack's house. During her pregnancy, she ate food she normally didn't eat, such as cottage cheese and spinach. She wore different clothes, her gait was different, and every glance from passersby reminded her that she was pregnant. She was tired. She had to slow down. By the time the baby arrived, she was used to sacrificing her routine, her time, and her energy to take care of it. Those sacrifices seemed less outlandish to her than they did to Jack.

Third, few things make us love people more than actually taking care of them. Psychologists know that in certain circumstances, if we believe one thing but have to do something that contradicts it, over time we change our belief so that it is consistent with what we are doing. They call the mental state of believing one thing but doing another *cognitive dissonance* (Cooper and Fazio, 1984). A woman who doubts that she has any interest in baby care may have her feelings transformed by the many things she does every day during her pregnancy to take care of the fetus. She looks both ways *twice* before crossing the street, she avoids the freshly painted corridor to stay away from fumes, she turns down a glass of wine at her parents' house. The last five or six months of her pregnancy—when she knows for sure that she is pregnant—give the forces of cognitive dissonance (and other forces—social, neurochemical, and who knows what) time to bend her emotions into a new shape.

Of course, many expectant fathers take on new chores, too. They earn extra money, paint the nursery, and buy lots more milk at the grocery store. Still, they don't have as many opportunities per day to take care of the fetus as the mother does. Their emotions probably don't get bent as far into that new shape as mothers' emotions do.

Does this phenomenon mean that men are doomed to a weaker bond with their children than women have? I doubt it. Instead, I think it means that the typical mother has a head start in developing strong feelings toward her newborn baby. She has been consciously taking care of it for six months. He has just begun to hold it in his own hands. In a sense, she is six months ahead of him.

(Of course, the headstart effect does not influence adoptive parents, since the mother didn't carry and deliver the new child. In most adoptive couples, the mother is the primary parent. All the other elements of negotiation that I set out earlier help lock her into primary responsibility for raising the children. Another important difference between adoptive and biological parents may be that in an adoptive couple, one or both partners have a stronger desire to raise children than do the average couple who become biological parents. No one becomes an adoptive parent by accident. If only the adoptive mother, and not the adoptive father, has that extra-strong desire to be a parent, that affects her negotiation position, much as the headstart effect does for a mother who has just given birth.)

The main consequence of the headstart effect is that when a woman delivers her first baby, her bargaining power takes a big plunge. She probably has less bargaining power now than she has had at any time before in the relationship. For example, no matter how unhappy or angry Alice might have been with Jack, it wouldn't have been credible to Jack or anyone else that Alice might walk away from the baby. That rarely happens. In negotiating lingo, we say that her *threat point* has risen. Jack would have to be much more intolerable to get her to leave now than he would have to have been in the past.

In happy couples, the change in the woman's threat point may not have much influence. Unfortunately, many couples with babies and young children are not happy. Babies create stress. In one study of seventy-two couples with children, for example, 97 percent of them reported more conflict after the baby arrived than before. Over 12 percent of them separated or divorced before the baby was eighteen months old (Cowan and Cowan, 1992). For many young parents, the possibility of serious conflict is not distant or theoretical.

Also, notice how incredible Jack would have found any threat Alice might have made—even if only subtly or implicitly—to refuse to take care of the baby in an effort to get him to contribute more time to taking care of it. Without being in the least bit cruel, he could easily outwait her. He loved his baby, but he hadn't already invested the months of effort and discomfort—the pregnancy—that gave Alice's feelings such urgency. Five minutes of listening to the baby wail and she would rush into its room to check the diaper.

In short, at this dramatic period in her life when the housework had quadrupled overnight and she was temporarily physically disabled, she was completely dependent on her husband's generosity and goodwill. She had practically no leverage at all.

Alice did not make use of the one thing that would have made Jack catch up with her in emotional attachment to the baby: stretches of solo time during which he was completely in charge of the baby. She had no intention of doing that because it was obvious to her that when it came to babies, men were complete knuckleheads. They shouldn't even try. Jack shared that belief. Thus, their childhood training, their attitudes, and their plans all meshed beautifully.

Once, though, when Alice was busy on the telephone, on the spur of the moment Jack changed a wet diaper. He folded the new diaper crookedly but effectively, caked the baby with powder, and put the wet diaper in the hamper. The baby cooed at him.

"Not so tough!" thought Jack.

When Alice got off the phone and went to the changing table, she shrieked. It looked like an explosion in a flour factory. The hamper lid was ajar. The baby was crawling toward it curiously.

Alice told Jack that he was an idiot, a slob, that the baby was about to drown in filthy diapers, that he'd just wasted two dollars' worth of baby powder, and that the next time he got any bright ideas he should do her a favor and go sit in the cellar.

Jack didn't like it. The tender bud of experimentation, the first stirrings of self-confidence, the delicate dawn of realization that hands-on baby care had its own pleasures and rewards—all frozen out and buried as under an avalanche. Jack never again volunteered to change, dress, feed, or bathe any of his babies.

Psychologists call Alice's reaction *gatekeeping*. In later years, she would pay for it. It made her indispensable. If she was ever laid up with lumbago, had to travel to the state capital to take care of legal business for her parents, or wanted to go on a one-week vacation with her church's women's group, Jack would be at a complete loss. He had no clue that Jamie was allergic to wool, who Sally's best friend's babysitter was, or how to scramble an egg in such a way that Paula would consent to eat it. Successful child care equals the mastery of two million details, times the number of children, plus inter-action effects for every possible combination of children. Jack didn't even know there was an equation.

Alice had never planned to become so indispensable at home. How did it happen? The more children there are in the family, the less substitutable the father is likely to be for the mother at home. Alice's third child was unplanned. It turned out to be twins.

An *unplanned pregnancy* may be a happy surprise or an unhappy surprise. If it's an unhappy surprise, the mother may decide to have an abortion. The important point for our purposes is that an unplanned child seldom results in the father increasing his responsibility for raising the children. It may increase the absolute amount of child care work he does, but the mother is still the child specialist and may be forced to become even more of one.

When an unplanned baby arrives, the mother often has to interrupt her education, training, or paying job. The father feels pressure to increase his earnings. A woman who is already a full-time homemaker will have to post-pone any plans to work for pay or volunteer outside the home. Babysitting will now cost more. Several more years just got tacked on to her period of indispensability at home. In short, an unplanned pregnancy usually rein-forces the traditional sexual division of labor.

What about unmarried couples? As late as the 1970s, many working-class young people got married simply because they got "caught": the young woman got pregnant accidentally (Rubin, 1976). Their counterparts today are less likely to get married; people don't pressure young men to behave like responsible fathers anymore, nor do they scorn young women who've obviously had sex outside of marriage. The results may seem liberating to some. But one consequence is that mothers—biological, foster, or adoptive—wind up providing nearly all the care for those children. Thus, unplanned pregnancy has the same implications for the sexual division of labor today as it did twenty years ago.[3]

Gains from Specialization

Can we find any advantages in the way Alice and Jack decided to run their lives? Without a doubt. Because each concentrated on a few tasks, each became very good at them. Jack handled large machinery with confidence, was good at fixing things, and knew how to get along with his co-workers. Alice was very attuned to the needs of her children and the moods of her husband, was a good cook, and was skillful at sewing, removing stains, throwing birthday parties, giving first aid, growing vegetables, inventing ways to make the house run more smoothly, and defusing disagreements among her friends. Economists would say that Alice and Jack reaped the gains that come from specialization.

Gains from specialization are very valuable. For one thing, specialization saves time. Because Alice always did the grocery shopping, she knew exactly which aisle in her supermarket to go to for shoelaces. When Jack ducked into the store once in a while to pick them up, it took him much longer to find them.

Saving time is important after a baby arrives, because time becomes much scarcer. It is nearly impossible for a nonparent (or someone who hasn't had similar caretaking responsibility) to appreciate how breathtakingly scarce time is for new parents. All they seem to do is take care of the baby, work, and sleep. Under that regime—sleepless nights and bleary days—it becomes crucial for each household chore to get done by someone who won't goof up or waste half an hour trying not to goof up. For that reason, babies increase the pressure on a couple to specialize. Typically, whether it is the father or the mother who does the grocery shopping doesn't matter. It does matter that it usually be one or the other.

Unfortunately, in many families the pressure to specialize pushes the woman toward a more traditional sexual division of labor. Alice quit her job at the beauty parlor before her first baby was born, so she couldn't be pushed any further than she had already leapt. Imagine, though, a woman who decides to switch from a full-time job to a part-time job after she has a baby. Some of the household chores her husband used to do will start to look more compatible with her work (half for pay, half unpaid with the baby) than with his work (all for pay). For example, she could take the baby to the grocery store during the day instead of waiting for her husband to go after work. If this couple saves time and effort by having her do the shopping, fine. It makes them better off (as a couple). However, it also starts *tipping* them toward an arrangement in which she does more and more unpaid work, an arrangement in which she might be much worse off. Tipping might lead her to give up her paying work altogether.

Still, gains from specialization are called gains for a reason. In addition to saving time, specialization lets people develop skills that the nonspecialist doesn't have. Alice could decorate a cake; Jack could use a jigsaw to make fanciful wooden toys for the kids. Specialization can also prompt people to raise their standards and achieve things that would never even occur to a nonspecialist. For example, Alice sewed imaginative Halloween costumes for the kids that everyone in the neighborhood marveled at. The whole family treasured the memories of those costumes for years. High levels of performance in unpaid family work can create a special, warm atmosphere at home. Couples in which both parents work for pay full-time at demanding jobs cannot bring off many of those extra domestic touches. They may pay that price willingly. Still, they pay it.

Middle Age

Luckily for Alice, Jack was a gentle, loving husband. They were happy together. After many years, when the last twin got a full-time job, Alice was no longer indispensable at home. She was thrilled. She was forty-one years old and more confident than she had been at eighteen. She knew more about the world and more about what she wanted. What she wanted was to work for her church twenty-five hours a week to launch an outreach and community services program she had been designing in her head for the last ten years.

It is no coincidence that Alice's dream job was *idealistic, low-paying, and flexible.* Her caregiving experience, and freedom from the pressure of supporting her family for the previous twenty years, made that kind of work seem natural to her. Jack, of course, couldn't have imagined switching at this point in *his* life into such a job. He had to continue to earn money. He and Alice still had expenses, and his children might need help in the future. Alice's new job, then, did little to change their relative bargaining power. Even if she had looked for the highest-paying job she could get, her starting pay would have been low anyway.

Alice enjoyed her new job. Five years later, though, Jack's mother, who was sixty-nine years old, fell and broke her hip. She couldn't get around her own house anymore. She had to come live with Alice and Jack. Of course, she couldn't get around their house on her own, either. Someone had to check in on her once or twice a day, get her meals, and help her in other small ways. Not surprisingly, that someone was Alice, since her job was low-paying and flexible. She could telephone from work often and come home once or twice during the day.

Soon, Jack's mother's condition deteriorated. She needed help many times a day: to get dressed, to walk to the bathroom, to avoid falling again, and so on. Plus, Alice's oldest daughter now had two preschool children but wanted to return to work as a physical therapist. She wanted Alice to help with babysitting.

It started to make sense for Alice to leave her job and veer back into care-giving at home. She and Jack would obviously lose less if she stayed home, rather than he, because her wages were much lower. Second, all those years she spent raising the children had created habits of thinking and feeling that made her want to give direct, physical care to Jack's mother more than he did. She knew how to soothe. She knew how to learn the thousand details that would best comfort her.

However, it *was* surprising to Alice that after spending twenty years at home raising children and five years at her dream job, she now faced years of caregiving work at home again for an elderly relative and her grandchildren. She realized, with a clarity she had never known before, that *the mommy track lasts a lifetime.*

Millions of women, like Alice, take on big responsibilities for caregiving in their middle age. In one study by the U.S. Bureau of the Census, 70 percent of the people who gave informal care to elderly people with functional impairments were women. Daughters made up 29 percent of caregivers; sons made up 9 percent.[4]

Another recent study of 13,000 middle-aged people in the United States found that women were two and a half times more likely than men to babysit their grandchildren. Married grandmothers gave on average fifteen hours of care a week; single grandmothers gave twenty hours.[5]

Taking care of your grandchildren and your own parents when you are middle-aged has both good and bad consequences. It strengthens family ties. It helps people come to terms with their own mortality and the miracle that they, one day, will be replaced by other people whose passions are as idiosyncratic and intense as their own.

It is also expensive. Time spent diapering your grandson or buying groceries for your frail mother-in-law is time you could have spent doing something else. In particular, many middle-aged caregivers reduce their hours of paid work or quit their jobs entirely. One study, using the census data just mentioned, found that 29 percent of caregivers to the elderly changed their work hours or quit their jobs to accommodate their new responsibility (Stone and Short, 1990). Women were more likely to make a change in their jobs than men were. Highly educated white women were much less likely than other women to quit their jobs entirely. Presumably, their pay was higher and their jobs were more interesting.

Alice did not lose much money when she returned home to be a full-time caregiver. Just a job she had worked up her courage to aspire to for thirty-nine years. Who can say that loss was small?

One thing to note is that Jack is not the villain of this story. He might even have felt oppressed by his job. Nevertheless, what he did all day long gave him a degree of practical independence, social status, and bargaining power at home that Alice never had. He benefited from the traditional sexual division of labor in another way, too. He got an attentive person to take care of his mother for free. (The only cost to Jack was Alice's lost wages.) Moreover, that person's life experience made her *want* to do the work. That was quite a windfall.

Jack had no inkling when he married Alice that things would turn out this way. He simply didn't think that far ahead. Neither did Alice. Neither do the millions of other young women in the world who train down, marry up, and fail to give their partners solo time with their babies.

Class and Race

How many of the decisions that Alice and Jack made hinged on their class background, their income, or their color? They both grew up in white working-class families. Jack was able to earn a lower-middle-class income. Are the negotiating dynamics in a traditional marriage the same for a poor couple, an upper-middle-class couple, or a black couple? Basically, yes.

Of course, each type of relationship that we could imagine—and each relationship itself—is unique. For example, a young woman from a poor family has unattractive options in both the job market and the marriage market. If she gets married, her husband is likely to be poor, too. She may work to supplement the family's income before and after they have children. Her income gives her little independence, however, because it is so low. It doesn't give her much bargaining power, either, especially after she has children. Because she is probably more emotionally attached than her husband to the babies, his bargaining power increases greatly. As chapter 1 showed, poor mothers endure a disproportionate share of battering from their male partners. In the United States, poor mothers who leave (or get left by) their male partners have the option of receiving welfare payments—Aid to Families with Dependent Children. Instead of depending on the earnings of a male breadwinner, they then depend on the government. However, the sexual division of labor in their household stays firmly traditional; the government does no housework.

Young women from upper-middle-class families enjoy many more options. The traditionally minded ones forgo most of them, however. They don't get training in remunerative fields. Instead, they seek a young man who has. When they have their first baby, their life's work begins. Materially, psychologically, and in every other way, it may be a deeply satisfying life. However, those women are very dependent on their husbands. If they are beautiful or glamorous, their chances of a good second marriage may give them some bargaining power while they are young. The beauty problem soon drains that away, though. At forty, their threat point will be high.

African-American women have always worked outside the home in large numbers. In this century, married black women have worked for pay at about twice the rate white married women have (Wallace, Datcher, and Malveaux, 1980). Earning a high share of the family's income has, by itself, probably helped black women's bargaining power within their marriages. The catch nowadays, of course, is that so few black men get married and live with their wives and children. That may be partly because the earnings of many black men are so low that their picture of a good family life and their ability to deliver it are very far apart.

Also, we need to keep in mind the unusual sex ratio that African-Americans now face: about 87 men for every 100 women. That ratio gives African-American men who are the least bit desirable as romantic partners unusual leverage. For example, a woman whose husband does live with the family and helps support it might hesitate to criticize him if she suspects that he is having an affair. His remarriage options are much, much better than hers. Her threat point is high. Given that her earnings are probably close to his, it is remarkably high.

Thus, traditional women in many different circumstances, enjoying different opportunities and bearing different burdens, all face the same basic forces. They all must negotiate as best they can, whether they know they are doing it or not.

What happens when the traditional ground rules change, when women who get a college education become common, and divorce becomes even commoner? New opportunities, new burdens, and new ways for the forces of negotiation to shape family life.

5

Two Transitional Marriages

OR MOST AMERICANS, THE WORLD OF TRADITION THAT CREATED
Alice's marriage has crumbled away. Families are small, divorce
rates are high, real wages have fallen for many men, and the number
of service jobs that are close to home has grown hugely. Consequently, millions of mothers work for pay.

Women in Canada, Sweden, France, Germany, and England have lived
through similar changes (Bakker, 1988). In those countries, too, since the
1970s, millions of mothers have been working for pay. Economically speaking, women in all the rich countries are behaving more like men than ever
before. Why have men changed so little? In this chapter, we'll see why.

A Traditional Girl Changes Her Mind

Laura's father is an engineer and her mother is a librarian. When Laura was
small, her mother worked part-time. Her grandmother watched Laura and
the other children when her mother was working. Laura was a good student in high school. She took two years of math and one year of chemistry,
but no physics. She enjoyed her history classes most of all. She went to the
state university, majored in psychology, and then got a master's degree in
social work. Her first job was as a caseworker with the state agency that
monitored child abuse. Her starting pay was $18,000.

Laura married her college boyfriend, Rob. Rob's father is an optician and
his mother is a medical secretary. When he was small, his mother stayed
home with Rob and his sisters. When he started primary school, she got a
job as an elementary school teacher so that she could be home when her
children got home from school. Rob's mother did not take a forty-hour-a-
week job until her youngest child started the eleventh grade. In high school,

Rob took four years of math, including probability and statistics. He also studied biology, chemistry, and physics. He did not enjoy the math courses, but his father insisted that he take them. In college, he majored in economics and took lots of computer science courses. His first job after graduation was for a big insurance company downtown, doing computer programming. His starting pay was $33,000.

When they married, Laura was twenty-four and Rob was twenty-six. The choices each had made until then about their education, jobs, and romantic partners were typical of young Americans in the 1970s, 1980s, and 1990s.

Even for people with master's degrees, like Laura, social work pays poorly. Many social workers are idealists for whom a high salary is not the most important thing in life. Because Laura did not get training in high school, college, or graduate school that would lead to a salary at the high end of what she was capable of earning, we can say that she *trained down*. She also *married up*. Rob was two years older and, at the time they got married, he already earned almost twice as much as she did. That earnings gap was likely to widen.

Those choices were sensible for Laura because she had always planned to have children and take primary responsibility for raising them. She never planned to be a breadwinner. She always expected that while her children were small, she would work part-time or stop working for pay altogether. She knew that she would not become obsolete if she dropped out for a while, since the field of social work changes slowly.

Rob's choices made sense for him, too, since he had always assumed that he would be mainly responsible for supporting his wife and children. His wife might help, but the ultimate responsibility would always be his. In the computer field, companies buy new machines, operating systems, and applications software every few years. He chose a job that penalizes breaks and rewards continuity.

So far, the choices that Laura and Rob made mesh together beautifully. They agree implicitly about what mothers and fathers should do at home and outside the home.

Soon they have two sons. Rob never spends more than three hours alone with his infants. That time usually includes a nap. He calls it "babysitting." Laura switches to a part-time job right after the birth of the first baby. When the kids are small, they spend twenty-five hours a week at a day care center a mile from Laura's office. Almost immediately after she reduces her work to part-time, she starts picking up some of Rob's household chores: doing the laundry, washing the dinner dishes, buying the groceries. She continues to do all the other housework that women have traditionally done. She also manages all aspects of child care. Those years are frazzling, but she knows that later she will cherish the memories. She is thankful she doesn't have to work full-time when her children are small. She also knows that Rob is working fifty or sixty hours a week. He has switched companies, been promoted several times, and now earns $45,000.

When Laura's younger child enters the third grade, Laura gets a full-time job at a nonprofit family-services agency. Her salary is $23,000. Suddenly, a series of unexpected events take place at Laura's office. The assistant director leaves and Laura is promoted to replace her. Laura happens to see a notice for a federal grant and takes the initiative to write a proposal. She wins the grant. Now she has to develop a project plan, hire staff, and meet with city officials.

Laura loves the work. She discovers a flair for management she never knew she had. Then something wonderful happens. The local TV station features her project on the nightly news. The mayor offers her a job at city hall. She discusses the opportunity with Rob and he supports her, proudly. She takes the job. It pays $33,000. It is a thrilling challenge and Laura excels at it.

A year later, Laura and Rob's house is in disarray. Laura is exhausted. She does *not* think she will cherish the memories of trying to find a babysitter for her fifth-grader who has the mumps, while prying loose a Power Ranger action figure that took a dive into the toilet, while a week's worth of laundry lies unfolded on top of the dryer and she is worrying about being late for a breakfast meeting. Something has to change.

Laura wants someone else to take on a significant share of the housework and responsibility for the children. She figures that they can afford to hire some help, but not all the help she wants. Her husband, and possibly the boys, will have to do more work at home. How can she get them to do it?

Laura faces formidable obstacles. First, she chose a romantic partner who expected to be a breadwinner, who assumed that women are better equipped to handle children than men are, and who expected to be waited on just a little at the end of a tough day at the office.

All the precedents that she set during their courtship and marriage reinforced Rob's expectations. He always imagined that the sexual division of labor in his home would be similar to the one in his parents' house. Also,

Laura has been specializing in housework and child raising for ten years. She has built up valuable knowledge and skills. She knows which babysitters to call and which not to bother on the particular Thursday morning when her son comes down with the mumps: Carole has her own kids on Thursday mornings, Beth has an art job this week, but Nancy or Paula might be available. There is nothing trivial about the databank of information about babysitters, best friends, and teachers, and *their* babysitters, best friends, and teachers, that a primary parent builds up after ten years on duty. She is also intimately familiar with her children's moods, quirks, strengths, and weaknesses. She "just knows" things about them that are hard for her to put into words. For example, Robbie would never secretly drop a water balloon on the head of a hated gym teacher in an empty alley. His pranks are elaborate, he performs for an audience, and he always takes the credit. Her husband honestly doesn't know those things.

Rob also has an excellent commitment mechanism. He can credibly say that he *has* to work fifty or sixty hours a week to keep his job. It is hard for Laura to assess independently how many hours he really *must* work. He can argue that he doesn't have the time or energy to take on more responsibility at home.

Even though Laura has no thoughts of leaving her marriage, she is probably also dimly aware that her alternatives to the marriage are not as good as Rob's. That is, her BATNA is worse than his. She couldn't bear to lose custody of the boys, but supporting them on her salary plus whatever child support Rob provided would mean accepting a much more abstemious style of life. At thirty-six, with two kids, her remarriage options are not stellar. Rob would bitterly miss the boys, but wouldn't seriously want to deprive her of custody. He is thirty-eight and has a high salary. He could easily support himself. He is an honorable guy and would probably pay child support, but if he stopped, there is little effective enforcement. Finally, since he is kind, appealing, and well paid, there is a good chance he could get remarried quickly, possibly even to a woman who is younger (and therefore, according to convention, more attractive) than Laura.

Because Laura's BATNA is not great and because of her tremendous emotional attachment to the children, her threat point is moderately high. To keep the family together, she would tolerate the level of exhaustion she suffers now for years. Rob knows that. No matter what Laura says or does, that bedrock fact greatly limits her bargaining power.

Other negotiating problems stand in Laura's way, but their impact is secondary. For example, Rob's status as a man subtly influences how Laura behaves toward him. Even when she is justifiably angry at him, she can't help but defer a little to his conception of the family's future. The focal point of tradition also makes it harder for Rob to imagine calling the babysitters himself.

What does Laura have going for her? Most important is that Rob loves her. He will not be happy if she is miserable. He will give up some things in order to make her less miserable. Second, Rob is a moral person. If she explains how she feels and what she needs in *moral* terms, he will sympathize. He will yield on some issues because it is the right thing to do. Third, Rob is by no means a rigid male chauvinist. He is willing to consider new arrangements if they take into account his tastes and abilities. That is, he is willing to make trade-offs.

A Traditional Woman Renegotiates

What should Laura do? The negotiating framework outlined in chapter 3 shows us, in a broad-brush way, which proposals may work for Laura and which ones will fail utterly. Our analysis can't take into account the nuances of personality, culture, and people's history together that make each family unique. It can't give us a detailed script for Laura to follow. It does reveal to us, however, that certain types of compromises are likely to last longer than others. Some promises she might get Rob to make will be self-enforcing. She can gradually create a new focal point for her family. Throughout this process, what she *does* will be more important than what she says. The renegotiation of who does what at home will probably last for the rest of Laura's married life.

Let's take one step back. Remember why we say that Laura is in a negotiation with Rob. The two of them are interdependent; they need each other emotionally and practically. They have some conflict; at the moment they disagree about the assignment of chores in their home. They can use strategic behavior; they can look ahead and decide what to do based on how the other is likely to react. Finally, there is room for agreement between them (figure 5.1).

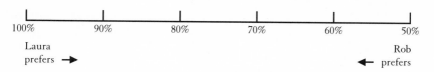

Figure 5.1. Room for Agreement

Laura's ideal is that Rob do half the housework and child care. Rob's ideal—at least before he learned how unhappy Laura was—is that Laura continue to do all the family work she has been doing for years. Their location now on this line is marked "100%." Laura is doing 100 percent of the traditionally womanly work in the home.

Because Laura's BATNA is worse than Rob's and her threat point is higher, the bottom line is that she will almost certainly not get Rob to move all the way to 50 percent. He can say no and make it stick. When he makes a final stand, her options will be either to accept that result or leave the marriage.

There is only one condition under which Laura might get Rob to slide all the way to 50 percent. If Rob is unusually generous, he will simply give it to her.

Beginning

Laura should consider the following approaches.

Let Rob know that she is miserable.

This information alone will make him want to do more housework. The question is, How much misery for Laura can Rob tolerate? The more he can tolerate (the more selfish or hard-hearted he is), the less he will give. The more loving and empathic he is, the more he will give.

Let Rob know how much work she is doing.

This information may startle him and, therefore, make him want to give. The more analytical and open-minded he is, the more it pays for Laura to give him this information in detail, even in writing. For example, she could make a list of all the unpaid family work that gets done in their house by her, by him, by the children, and by any hired helpers they now employ. Then she could highlight the chores that she does. She should remember to list things such as preparing income tax returns, taking the car in for maintenance, buying clothes for the kids, monitoring the kids' clothes to see when they need bigger sizes, sending get-well cards to sick relatives, managing the family's savings and investments, taking responsibility for the kids' religious instruction, and deciding time limits on the kids' consumption of certain types of entertainment, such as video games. If she is very thorough, most of the page will be highlighted.

Making this list may help Laura see that not all chores are alike. Some happen once a year, such as tax preparation. That job takes a long time and has a deadline, but the work can be scheduled for whenever it's convenient. Dinner, on the other hand, has to be on the table every night by 6:30. Some chores are mechanical, such as taking out the trash. Some involve mental work, such as monitoring a situation, deciding when certain things need to happen, and either doing them or getting someone to do them—that is, they consist of management. Some chores require skill; others don't. Some go together naturally (coaching hockey and buying the gear for the kids); others are easily divisible (buying groceries and vacuuming).

The more Laura understands that each chore has many dimensions—each of which makes the chore easy, hard, pleasant, or unpleasant for Rob to do, and easy or hard for him to wiggle out of—the more success she will have in devising a new routine.

Talk about fairness and partnership.

Laura can tell Rob honestly and nonaccusatorily about her goals for her life, the marriage, and the family. She can tell him that it seems very unfair that he should have more leisure time than she does. She may also tell him she thinks that some of the extra hours he spends on the job aren't necessary. They won't lead to higher pay or more job security, so she'd rather have him put in the effort at home. Or she might think that they *will* lead to higher pay or security, but she'd rather he put in the effort at home. She can tell him that she has been happiest in her marriage when she thought each of them was working equally hard to build up the family's resources and to create a loving environment for each other and the kids. Her goal is a fair, equal, loving partnership. As noted in chapter 3, moral language both helps persuade people and helps them feel better about the result, whatever it is.

Nag.

Very few game-theory textbooks cover nagging. However, it's an everyday part of family life. It's also an everyday part of the negotiation that goes on in family life. Nagging may get Rob to give a little more. The question is, How miserable is Laura willing (and able) to make him? The more scathing she is and the more sensitive he is, the further he gives. But it won't be pleasant for either of them.

According to the stereotype, wives nag and husbands gripe about it. If that is sometimes true, it's because traditional wives' threat points are so high that they have few other options. They hope they can make their husbands just miserable enough that doing the chore will be preferable to hearing the nagging. Of course, being forced to nag is at least as unpleasant as hearing it.

STUMPERS

Laura and Rob talk about rearranging their housework and child care many times, in different moods, with different results: Rob withdraws, Laura cries, new routines break down after a month, one of them stonewalls, they make threats that do and don't get carried out, and good-faith promises that do and don't get kept.

Occasionally Rob says something that completely stumps Laura. She keeps doing 100 percent of the chores for a long time because that line silenced her. The better she understands her feelings and her negotiating position, however, the less likely she is to be stumped. Consider the following lines.

"I make much more money than you. You ought to do much more work at home than me."

This comment contains two slightly different arguments: (1) "I'm the primary breadwinner, so you should do most of the homemaking"; (2) "I earn more per hour, so my time is worth more than yours, so I shouldn't spend my time doing unpaid chores."

Laura's best bet is to switch immediately to moral language. Each person's life has dignity and intrinsic value. No matter how much they earn, how famous they are, or how royal their ancestors, people are equal in a fundamental moral sense. Laura's life is worth just as much as Rob's. Her time is worth just as much as his.

If she were working for pay only part-time and had no other important commitments, then it might be fair for her to do more housework and child care than Rob. But she is working full-time. Just because her work is paid less doesn't make it less valuable.

"If you're too stressed out, switch to part-time work."

Rob says this angrily and then leaves the room. The first question is, Is he bluffing? If he really wouldn't want to lose Laura's income, or see her give up the satisfaction she gets from her job at city hall, Laura can easily counter the proposal. What if he isn't bluffing? She must point out that she wants to keep the job. She really enjoys it. Maybe she thinks that his salary alone isn't enough to meet her goals for the family. Maybe she thinks it's important that she earn a full-time salary herself (to increase her economic security, bargaining power, whatever). Of course, if she has mixed feelings about the job, she *should* consider switching back to part-time work.

What if Laura flips this argument? She can say to Rob, "Look, if you don't think you can hold down a demanding job and meet your family obligations at home, maybe *you* should switch to a less demanding job." If Laura is bluffing, because she really doesn't want to see his salary fall, then she is wasting time. If she is serious, she has proposed a radical change in Rob's day-to-day life, self-conception, and economic future. If he is very ambitious, risk-averse, or traditional-minded, or just plain loves his job, he won't switch jobs.

Only two things will make him switch. Either Laura will have to get a job that is high-paying and very secure, or they will have to decide together that they can get by with a lower family income. Some men in their thirties do decide to leave the fast track and focus on other things, but not many. Rob will be more likely to switch when he's fifty-five. However, notice that *even* if Laura persuades Rob to get a less time-consuming job, she still has to negotiate to make sure he spends some of his newly freed hours doing housework and child care. All in all, her odds of succeeding with this approach are low.[1]

"You have no idea how stressful it is to be the breadwinner. I just can't handle any more responsibility."

This argument is sophisticated. It has some merit. However, Laura is earning 40 percent of the family income; Rob is only a 60 percent breadwinner.

He probably *feels* like more than a 60 percent breadwinner because he can't be sure that Laura will continue to work full-time. She has never given any sign that she will try to maximize her income. What if a new mayor gets elected and Laura learns about an interesting job at a nonprofit agency for two-thirds her current salary? She might take it, rather than look for a high-paying but grueling business job.

Laura can counter this argument in several ways. She can become more of an income maximizer. That will probably let Rob ease up at work.

Second, she can suggest chores for Rob to take on that won't add to the stress he feels. That is, she can keep responsibility for managing housework and child care, but farm out mechanical tasks to him.

Third, if she suspects he's only whining, she can say, "My stress level is clearly higher than yours, because I'm going out of my mind and you aren't." She can let him know again how miserable she is.

"I just can't see myself doing the laundry (or the grocery shopping, or going to the PTA meeting). I guess I'm just an old-fashioned kind of guy."
Laura should point out that the last time she checked, Rob did not spend his day stalking saber-toothed tigers, shooting arrows at attacking cannibals, or lugging water from the well. He is *not* an old-fashioned kind of guy. He is a college graduate, pampered by high technology, with only two children, and a wife whose income pays for 40 percent of every bit of food he puts into his mouth.

Basically, Rob is waving a hand at the focal point of tradition. Laura can say, first, that tradition really shouldn't govern what happens in their house. In a hundred ways, they are not a traditional couple, nor do they live in a traditional world. That world is gone.

Second, people's emotions change more slowly than the facts that surround them. Sometimes she feels awkward, too. Sometimes her confidence wavers when she takes her car in to the shop to get the tires rotated, when she has to criticize the performance of an older man who reports to her, or when she has to make a decision at work that involves large sums of money. We are living in a time of transition. It's rattling. But she and Rob are grown-ups. They can handle it. They can also help each other keep their qualms in perspective. People—their own relatives, even—have survived revolution, famine, and civil war. Surely Rob has the grit to take on Safeway.

HOW TO OFF-LOAD THE HOUSEWORK AND CHILD CARE

What chores can Laura really get other people to do? The answer has nothing to do with clever repartee or sensitive persuasion. It has to do with the nature of the chores themselves and the tastes and abilities of Laura, Rob, and their kids. This question brings us deep into the game theory of housework. Laura should raise the following questions.

How much housework can they hire out?
The more services they can buy from housecleaners, repair people, restaurants, convenience food manufacturers, babysitters, drivers, and so on, the less Laura has to persuade Rob and the kids to do. At $70,000, their family income is much higher than that of the average American household, so

they can afford to hire out a lot. They can discuss how much they are willing to spend, and then learn by experience whether hiring out changes the atmosphere at home in ways they don't like. This change is the easiest, most conflict-free, most lasting one Laura can make.

What chores can Laura outwait Rob on?

In what situations is Rob a Felix and Laura an Oscar? If the answer is none, then Laura is in trouble. The best kind of promise to extract from Rob is a self-enforcing one. For example, if he can't stand to wash dishes by hand when they're out of clean ones and it's time to set the table, then his promise to take responsibility for running and emptying the dishwasher is self-enforcing. Or, if he is more nervous than she is about the bills getting paid late, she should put him in charge of paying bills.

If Laura thinks carefully, she is bound to come up with a few chores that meet this description. What does he nag *her* about? Of course, after they've agreed to the new arrangement, she has to back up her implicit threat not to do the chore with firm inaction. She won't ever have to nag him, because he'll always do it before she starts to worry about it. In fact, Laura doesn't even need to *ask* Rob to take on the chore in the first place. If she cuts back on it, then stops doing it entirely, he will drift into taking responsibility for it. My husband drifted into taking responsibility for the dishwasher, paying the bills, and taking out the recyclables in exactly that way. On most housework, he can outwait me. But not on those chores. Once I saw that, I scratched them off my mental list of things to do. If Laura sees a few things like that, she can spend her effort to *explicitly* negotiate change on other matters.

What can Laura trade off?

Laura should think of things Rob might enjoy that are fairly easy for her to deliver to him in exchange for doing more housework. She must be careful to exchange like for like. That is, it would be unwise for her to trade something big up front, such as moving to the neighborhood he prefers, in return for a promise of a future stream of chores from him. Instead, she should offer a stream of small revocable things, such as going with him to basketball games or on weekend fishing trips, letting him and the kids spend extra time at the video arcade together, or visiting his mother more often. The more urgently she wants him to do a chore, or the more he resists, the more she should consider trading off something he really wants that is difficult for her to deliver.

Can she accept Rob's standards?

The answer depends on how low his standards are relative to Laura's for tasks he might take on. If they are much lower, either those are the wrong tasks to give him or Laura will have to compromise and live with it. It also depends on how flexible Laura is in accepting a different *style* of performance.

This point is important. Conflicts about standards lie at the heart of nearly all arguments about housework. For example, when my husband was a bachelor, his kitchen table was covered with three or four alternating layers of crumbs and newspapers. Was I going to be able to persuade him to start cleaning up the newspapers and crumbs every night? No way. He didn't even see them. My standards of neatness are much higher than his. Ergo, I will always be the one to pick up (at least until our kids are old enough to help).

He did agree readily to do my laundry along with his. I just had to accept that he was willing and able to make only slight changes in his routine. He washed the colored clothes together with the whites, one gigantic load at a time. Occasionally, mysteriously, he splashed in bleach "by mistake," creating a unique polka-dot pattern on our clothes. I didn't care that our whites were not dazzlingly white; I had never separated whites and colors when I did my own laundry. But we did need to discuss the bleach issue. Now, he never touches it. Luckily for me, my laundry standards are not high.

Thus, the lower Laura's standards are, the more she can get Rob to do and be happy with the results.

Differences in style can create more puzzling conflicts. My husband, for instance, is slow and haphazard, and he mixes work with play. I get the chore done quickly and then relax. Watching him clear the dinner table over the course of thirty minutes, carrying one glass or one plate at a time into the kitchen while he reads *Sports Illustrated* and spills crumbs on the floor, drives me nuts. But, short of a brain transplant, I can't change his personality. Either he does it his way, or help a little, or I do it all. Often I help a little, then go somewhere else so I won't have to watch him.

Here are more concrete examples. On the nights that my husband is in charge of cooking dinner, take-out food is acceptable. So is a store-cooked barbecue chicken, a baguette and several kinds of cheese, or even grilled cheese sandwiches. Pancakes are not acceptable; they depress me.

One very busy two-career couple I know agreed that the husband would cook dinner on Tuesday nights, when the wife gets home late because she takes a class after work. He makes tuna fish sandwiches. It's not her idea of a beautiful dinner to come home to. It *is* a compromise she can live with.

If Laura can relax her standards and gracefully accept her and her husband's differences in style, she will be much more successful in getting Rob to take on new chores. She should remember that her standards and style aren't intrinsically superior to his. Rob may care more about saving time and mental energy and may care less about appearances than she does.

What if Rob purposefully bungles a task so that Laura will take it over again herself? The comic strip "The Lockhorns" has featured that ploy. Once Mrs. Lockhorn confided to a friend: "I don't mind that Leroy doesn't help around the house. Last time he did, he washed the dishes and laundry together" (August 7, 1994).

That's a tough problem. Laura can call his bluff by outwaiting him. If she can't outwait him—because, say, he really can live with clumps of undissolved soap powder on his clothes, but she can't—then she needs to use moral language to snap him into good-faith behavior. She can remind him what is at stake: their relationship, her respect for him, and his view of himself as a good person. She can also try new trade-offs. Persistent bad-faith behavior by Rob will lead to real conflict. Unfortunately, given the difference in their threat points, that's a conflict Laura is unlikely to win. That unpleasant fact explains why some women lose the effort to get their husbands to take on more housework.

Actually, though, I suspect that many more lose the effort because they fail to lower their standards or to accept differences in style. Laura may find that a little flexibility on her part goes much farther than she ever imagined. The house won't run the way she would run it herself. But she won't be exhausted.

Can Laura delegate management tasks?

Laura's two hardest jobs are managing the housework and managing care for her sons. Can she divide those two jobs into five, six, or seven jobs, and give a few to Rob?

The difficulty is that the last thing Rob wants is more management responsibility. From his point of view, the ideal new chore is one that can be done whenever it's convenient for him, is low skill or easy to learn, is pleasant for him given his idiosyncrasies, and that he can do his own way without getting criticized.

From Laura's point of view, the ideal chore to give Rob is one that is hard for her—that is, it has to be done frequently, at a set time, and is mentally taxing, physically unpleasant, or socially complicated.

Management is mentally taxing. Her only hope of delegating any of it is to carve off small slices. The good news is that this is easier to do than most people realize. The bad news is that the precedents Laura has set in the past, and her own high standards, may create obstacles.

Here is an example. From the time our baby was born, my husband has been in charge of buying all the diapers, wipes, and formula. He is also in charge of deciding when she needs to move into a bigger size. I never remind him to buy diapers; I never even think about them. I just reach into the drawer of her changing table and pull them out. In the beginning, I figured I was running a significant risk of being caught short, because my husband is absentminded. But, I never have. He rose to the challenge, partly, no doubt, because if we run out, he is just as likely to be home alone with her as I am.

The point is, I am willing to pay all the costs of not managing the diaper issue. And there are some costs. One summer my daughter and I left for our vacation three days ahead of my husband. I had to buy the diapers there. In blissful ignorance, I bought size 3 instead of size 4. (My husband said, How could you?) I had to go back to the A&P and exchange them.

Another example. I tell our babysitter what little things I want her to do each day: give our daughter a bath, brush her teeth if she eats raisins, or do an arts project. My husband doesn't think of things like that. However, he is in charge of paying the babysitter every week and doing all the tax forms related to her work. Given the difference in our standards, I can't happily delegate to him many aspects of managing the babysitter. But I can split up the job, and delegate to him the part most closely related to other chores he does willingly and well: paying bills and doing taxes. Also, my delegation is credible and complete; I don't even know exactly what we're paying the babysitter now.

What about Laura? Because of the precedents, high standards, and valuable skills and knowledge that she has built up for ten years, she will not be able to get Rob to take over a large percentage of her management of the housework and kids. (Not unless some electrifying change hits the household, such as an accident or illness that leaves her bedridden for months.) Even if they hire out more housework, she will have to tell the housecleaners what to do and how often.

Laura may find it easiest to delegate things that she can describe as new chores (making it sound as if old precedents don't apply) and as related to traditional male concerns. For example, buying clothes for the boys. She can say, "They are growing up. They are *not* children anymore. You may be better at buying clothes for preadolescent boys than I am. Take a stab at it."

Of course, she will have to live with the results.

What if less housework gets done?

If Laura takes a look at the total set of chores she is doing, can she simply eliminate some before trying to hire them out or to get Rob to do them? If so, she will reduce her workload and find it easier to nudge Rob toward 50 percent (of fewer chores).

I've heard of households in which kids get freshly laundered bath towels every couple of days, because they leave their wet ones wadded up on the floor. Laura can say, "New rule, guys. You wad it, you live with it. You get a new bath towel once a week, period." She does less laundry, and the kids learn the consequences of being messy (and may change their behavior).[2]

Another example. Instead of buying a stylish shower curtain and washing it and drying it in the sun when it gets mildewed, Laura can buy a cheap shower curtain liner. It will be plain but serviceable. When it gets mildewed, her fifth-grader can throw it out and hang up a new one.

Nearly every chore can be done less often, more simply, or just not at all. The only real requirement—legally speaking—is that the house remain nonlethal.

This approach may sound like a strange way of negotiating. However, remember what Laura's goal is. It isn't to make other people do housework. It's to do *less* housework herself and have a fairer partnership with her husband.

What can the kids do?

The answer is: much more than they are doing now. Laura needs a revolution in child labor. The sooner, the better. The older kid can make dinner once a week, with help from the younger, using a cookbook for children. Bagel pizzas and yogurt smoothies make an elegant meal. Rob gets to wash up on those nights. The kids will improve their skills and their attitudes toward housework. Their parents will get a break. The focal point of the family will shift away from the traditional sexual division of labor. The kids may fuss, but Laura has a secret weapon: she can give management responsibility *to Rob* for those few chores that are low-skill enough for the kids to handle. He will have to regularly motivate and discipline his sons. Also, chances are that he and the boys will have their best talks while they are doing physical chores together.

Laura may also intuitively see that anything she does to make herself more independent economically and more attractive (because of the beauty problem) will improve her BATNA. Taking courses in management or computers, or going to law school at night, will help her in the job market. Exercising regularly and eating healthy foods will improve her physical condition and, with a new hairstyle, may help her in the marriage market. Both changes give her a little more leverage with Rob.

It will not be easy for Laura to change who does what at home. But if she understands that she is negotiating each and every one of those changes, it will be possible.

An Egalitarian Poster Couple

Now let's consider a different couple. Gloria's father is an engineer and her mother is a librarian, just like Laura's parents. Gloria took three years of math in high school, majored in business with a minor in Spanish at college, and has wanted to succeed in the business world as long as she can remember. She has strong, nontraditional opinions about many personal and political matters. For example, she refused to wear gold until Nelson Mandela was elected to govern South Africa. Wherever she has lived since her junior year in college, she has donated small amounts of money to the local shelter for battered women.

Phil's father is a salesman at ComputerShak; his mother runs her own interior design company. He always knew he had no interest at all in business. At college he majored in English, and went on to get a Ph.D. He met Gloria through a friend when he was in graduate school. They are the same age. He finds her high level of energy exhilarating. She finds his intellectuality relaxing.

When they got married, they were both twenty-six. Phil had just finished his Ph.D. He got a job at a nearby college as an assistant professor of American literature, at $34,000 a year. Gloria was assistant manager of a fitness center, at an annual salary of $37,000. Roughly speaking, then, they have married across, in age and earnings. Or we could say that Gloria has married slightly down in expected lifetime earnings. If Phil gets tenure, his salary will plateau at a comfortable upper-middle-class level, say, $70,000. It will be a secure and recession-proof salary. If she is successful in business, her salary could be much higher. However, her job will always be less secure than that of a tenured professor.

One thing Gloria and Phil have in common is that they both have strong feminists attitudes. They both read *Ms.* His thesis was a feminist analysis of several early-twentieth-century American novels. He intends to teach courses of that sort. They have often talked about how, when the time is right, they will have a baby and equally share the work of raising it. Both are aware that Phil's job is more flexible than Gloria's. On mornings or afternoons when he isn't teaching, he'll be able to work at home. He'll also be able to work at home all summer. They figure that will make it easy for them to buck tradition.

A week after Gloria's twenty-eighth birthday, she discovers that she is pregnant. They are delighted. Now what will happen? The truth is that Gloria and Phil don't have a clue.

AFTER THE BABY COMES

And the king said, "Cut the live child in two, and give half to one and half to the other."

But the woman whose son was the live one pleaded with the king, for she was overcome with compassion for her son. "Please, my lord," she cried, "give her the live child; only don't kill it!" The other insisted, "It shall be neither yours nor mine; cut it in two!"

Then the king spoke up. "Give the live child to her," he said, "and do not put it to death; she is its mother."

—1 Kings 3:25–27

According to the Bible, King Solomon was the wisest judge of ancient times. His insight into people's character helped him find fair solutions to conflicts. In the famous case of the fought-over baby, he understood two things that Gloria and Phil don't understand, at least not consciously.

Solomon understood that the typical mother feels intensely protective toward her newborn baby. He also understood that this emotion is so reliable that he could take it into account when deciding what to do. In the language of this book, we say that Solomon acted strategically; he looked ahead, imagined how the real mother and the impostor would probably react to things he might do, and chose the path that looked best.

Did Solomon have any intention of hurting the baby? The Bible tells us that he was a righteous man, so we know he would never kill an innocent child. He was only bluffing.

How did the women react? Just as he expected. The real mother couldn't bear to see her son die. Instead, she proposed a lifetime of longing and suffering for herself, so that he might grow up whole and healthy in the care of the impostor.

For our purposes, this Bible passage is very rich. Many forces are at play in it. They are all important to understanding what happens after a baby is born.[3]

THE HEADSTART EFFECT

I discussed the headstart effect earlier. Research done in the United States suggests that mothers, on average, are more emotionally attached to their newborn babies than fathers are. One reason is that the experience of being pregnant shapes many women's emotions in special ways. Of course, cultural and social forces probably influence women's feelings, too. The key point for Gloria, though, is that she believes she never absorbed the cultural and social messages that more traditional women believe. Many nontraditional women may truly not be influenced by traditional cultural and social attitudes. Still, many of them will, I suspect, experience the headstart effect described here. More generally, even if the sexual division of labor in the home disappears in the United States and our cultural beliefs change to reflect that, we will still be stuck with the headstart effect. It will be an enduring difference between mothers and fathers, until the day medical technology makes it possible for men to carry a developing fetus inside their own bodies.

That enduring difference between mothers and nonmothers has important consequences. Solomon was able to exploit it in his search for truth and justice. Phil will be able to exploit it, too, in his search for convenience, more free time for himself, or his own notion of what is fair. He will be able to exploit it even though he is a loving husband and father and is committed to fifty-fifty parenting.

Why? Because different people have different approaches to baby care. Even devoted mothers have different standards from one another. For example, some people believe that a baby should be picked up whenever it cries even if it seems to want only cuddling. (Many pediatricians in the United States now take this position, in direct contrast to the practice of the 1930s.) Others believe that once food, a clean diaper, the proper temperature, and the chance to sleep have been provided, the baby's needs have been met. Some parents take a high-effort approach. They don't use commercially prepared baby food; they purée their own. Other parents take a middling-effort or low-effort approach. They think Gerber's is fine.

Other things equal, the more emotionally attached parent is likely to aim for a higher standard of care and to favor a higher-effort approach than her partner. Not necessarily in every couple, but on average. Why? Simply because that parent is more enmeshed in the baby's sensations, expressions, and apparent emotions (Ehrensaft, 1987).

How does the headstart effect affect Gloria and Phil? Gloria finds it harder to tolerate Molly's cries without intervening. Even though she is tired after the delivery, she reacts more quickly than Phil does. Phil can immerse himself in the newspaper or a novel until the baby's crying breaks his concentration. Gloria notices that she doesn't need to be yanked out of her activity by Molly's cries. She has been monitoring her, by glancing often at the baby carrier in the middle of the living room floor, as she reads, eats, or talks on the phone. Phil glances at the baby much less often. That means Gloria sees the baby stir, open her eyes, wrinkle her nose, take a breath, and start to cry. She is already in motion before Phil's eyes have left the page.

Soon, Phil notices a pattern. It seems to him that he is doing half the housework, since he does the grocery shopping, some cooking, and lots of neatening up. He is doing his best to do half the baby care. He thinks he is attentive and effective. However, when both he and Gloria are home, Gloria always seems to be fussing with Molly. She criticizes Phil for not checking the diaper every twenty minutes; she tells him to tiptoe, not thud; and she generally bustles and clucks like a mother hen. Phil is mystified.

Gloria also notices a pattern. How can Phil be so distracted, so offhand, and so callous in little ways toward their tiny precious treasure? He forgets to adjust the curtain to keep the sun out of Molly's eyes every single afternoon. Imagine! Somehow, when they are both home, she winds up putting in considerably more than half the effort that is being expended on the baby. What does this bode for the future? Could they be slipping toward tradition?

Gloria and Phil haven't heard of the headstart effect, and they don't understand its implications for their bargaining power. Let's say Gloria's standard of care is just slightly higher than Phil's. *The result is that Gloria will wind up providing most of that extra increment of care* she wants the baby to get, not Phil. For example, she cannot credibly say, "It's your turn to check the diaper. I'm just going to sit here until you do it." Phil can outwait her, just as Oscar could outwait Felix. Even if Phil says in good faith, "I'll get to it," the fact that her standard of care is higher will prompt her to jump in and check the diaper if twenty or twenty-five minutes go by.

Also, if she is monitoring the baby more closely than Phil is, she will see reasons for intervention more often than he does. Either she asks him to intervene (wipe the baby's chin), and so faces a chance of being outwaited, or she does it herself from the start.

THREAT POINTS

I've already discussed how a woman's threat point rises after having a baby. Gloria is not immune. She is economically independent from Phil because she earns a good salary. In fact, she earns more than he does. However, because she is more emotionally attached to the baby, she cares slightly more than he does about the baby's welfare. Her desire to stay close to the baby is also slightly stronger than his. That means any threat Gloria might make to leave Phil and the baby is not very credible. She is likely to put up with more unpleasantness from Phil now than she would have before the baby was born.

Notice that Phil's threat point is higher now, too. If he leaves Gloria and the baby, he will be worse off than he would have been if he had walked out before Molly was born. He will miss the baby. As he would have before, he will also miss Gloria's earnings, even though he can support himself comfortably on his own salary.

Before the baby was born, Gloria and Phil had roughly equal threat points. What about now?

In spite of his heartfelt egalitarian attitudes, Phil was brought up to feel confident as a sole breadwinner. He also knows, at some remote level of awareness, that his remarriage chances are good. Gloria, on the other hand, quite rationally recoils from the idea of being a single parent. She knows how hard that would be. Moreover, she never really imagined herself as a sole breadwinner. With a baby in her arms (and her youthful looks beginning to fade), her remarriage chances are significantly worse than Phil's. Thus, the headstart effect, lingering shreds of traditional manly and womanly self-conceptions, and the difference in their chances of a satisfactory second marriage all combine to boost Gloria's threat point over Phil's.

Phil and Gloria are happily married, so why does this matter? Even if Phil never threatens to walk out, or never comes close to imagining making such a threat, his implicit ability to make it lurks in the background. Gloria is not only more dependent on Phil than she used to be; she is a little more dependent on him than he is on her. If he flat-out refuses to bathe the baby or insists on buying a big-screen TV they had earlier agreed was too extravagant, what can she do? She can try moral language, make trade-offs, do everything Laura tried with Rob, and more. But the distasteful fact of the matter is that Phil has a little more bargaining power than he had before. If he presses, he will get his way a little more often than he did before.

TIPPING

Gloria's maternity leave lasts six weeks. During that time, Phil has to go to work most days, but he comes home early when he can to help. At night, he does most of the baby care. Gloria gets to relax.

Gloria and Phil are really sharing. She is happy. There is only one problem. When Phil is on duty at night, he doesn't seem to be as skillful at comforting Molly as she is. Could it be because the baby spends more time with her? Could it be because she is breastfeeding? When Molly wails for more than three or four minutes, Phil hands her over to Gloria. It becomes their joke. Gloria is the "crying expert." Gloria holds Molly high on her shoulder, just so. Sometimes, she nurses her. She quiets down quickly.

By the time their daughter is four weeks old, Gloria is much better at comforting her than Phil is. Phil hands her over to her once or twice a night. She isn't getting as much time to relax.

Gloria also has a better grasp of many of the baby's idiosyncrasies, because she spends more time with her. For example, she likes her bath water surprisingly warm, she is fascinated by the pink plaid bunny that Grandma sent, and her eyes are very sensitive to sun and wind. At night, Phil finds himself deferring more and more often to Gloria for advice. Phil doesn't mind, but Gloria is concerned.

By the end of Gloria's maternity leave, she is much better at comforting, amusing, and caring for the baby. Phil feels like a lowly, superfluous assistant. That irks him a little. It irks Gloria a lot. On the day the baby was born, they were equally ignorant and equally in charge. Now the baby care is slipping into *her* lap. What is happening?

Gloria and Phil are watching a tipping scenario roll through their living room. Recall that tipping happens because focal points suck people into them. The tradition that women take care of babies is a very strong focal point. When Gloria and Phil stray just a little from their newfangled, home-brewed focal point, they find themselves slipping back toward tradition with breathtaking speed.

Some degree of tipping affects nearly all couples. The simple reason is that women who give birth need rest to recover. During those weeks, in most couples, the woman's partner needs to work to earn money. Thus, even in a lesbian couple committed to shared parenting, the woman who has given birth usually spends more time with the baby in the early weeks than the other woman does. Also, many expectant fathers and fathers of new-borns work even longer hours than they did before the pregnancy. They are trying to earn extra money to cover their new expenses (Betcher and Pollack, 1993). The result is that they spend less time at home than before.

An even greater danger of tipping faces couples in which the mother breastfeeds. This problem arises because breastfeeding is so wonderful. The mother enjoys special pride, and the baby's obvious bliss. A newborn who is purely breastfed will spend between four and six hours a day nursing (thirty minutes times eight sessions). During the nursing sessions, Dad (or the mother's female partner) might as well be on Pluto. It will be hard for him to make himself as salient or desirable in the baby's eyes as the mother is.

Does that mean Gloria and Phil should have planned not to breastfeed? Absolutely not. They just face an ironic difficulty. In the United States and other rich countries right now, couples who hope to give the father lots of hands-on child care duties are exactly the couples who are most likely to breastfeed. They are college-educated and very devoted to children. Most don't see that two parts of their program—breastfeeding and major caretak-ing responsibility for father—are in conflict. If they foresaw the conflict, they could manage it. Because they don't, they tip relentlessly toward tradition.

What could Gloria and Phil do to protect their plans for Phil to be an equally competent, accepted parent? Gloria and Phil need *countertipping*. They need to put into effect *affirmative action for fathers*. That is, when Phil has trouble comforting the baby, he gets extra time to do it, until the baby is comforted. Babies do in fact learn to take comfort from whoever gives it to them. They learn to find the rhythms, smells, and sounds of that person deeply soothing. It just takes time.

Unfortunately, Gloria and Phil never think of countertipping. They don't understand what is at stake; the crying is too jangling; they are too exhausted to think clearly or creatively; and it is so easy—so very familiar—to pass the baby to Gloria.

DAY CARE

Gloria's maternity leave is over. Before she had Molly, she figured she'd go back to work full-time after her leave, roughly fifty hours a week. Her goal at work is to become manager of one of the fitness centers in the chain she works for. She would like to do that for three to four years, then find an even more challenging, higher-paying job.

Gloria and Phil sit down to seriously discuss hiring out care for the baby. They have learned about three day care centers nearby. One takes infants for thirty hours a week, one takes them for forty hours a week, and one takes them for fifty hours a week.

Phil says, "Great. Let's go for fifty hours a week."

Gloria says, "Are you nuts? Molly's only six weeks old. She's tiny. We can't warehouse her like that."

Phil says, "This is a terrific center. It's a loving, stimulating environment. You want to become manager; I want to get tenure. This is good for us."

Gloria is shocked. She feels terribly torn. She is devoted to her work, but she wants her daughter to be loved and stimulated by her parents, not some six-dollar-an-hour hireling who will abandon her in three months to sell nose rings at the mall. She never expected that she would feel so strongly about the baby. Nor did she expect to have this conflict with Phil. What is going on?

Gloria and Phil have smacked into yet another implication of the head-start effect. *The more emotionally attached parent is likely to prefer more parental time and less hired care for the baby than the other parent.* That means Gloria is facing a bargaining scenario like the one Laura faced with Rob (figure 5.2).

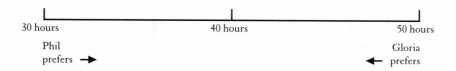

Figure 5.2. Negotiating About Day Care

If Gloria honestly can't stand the idea of her baby staying in the care of nonrelatives for more than thirty hours a week, she faces three options. She could take care of the baby for the twenty additional hours, or Phil could, or some other family member could. As it happens, all their relatives live 500 miles away. It's her or Phil.

Gloria suggests that they choose the thirty-hour-a-week center and that she and Phil split the extra twenty hours a week. He'll do only ten more hours a week of baby care than he would have under the fifty-hour-a-week plan.

Phil says no.

Gloria says, How about we put her in for thirty-five hours a week, and we split the remaining fifteen hours—that's only seven and a half hours extra for you.

Phil says no.

He explains, "Look, I'm not a graduate student writing a thesis anymore. I teach class in the morning, I go to seminars in the afternoon, and in between I'm trying to write research papers to get tenure. In seven years, I either have seven excellent articles or I get fired. These are make-or-break years for me."

Gloria wails, "What about sharing? You said fifty-fifty!"

Phil says, "Calm down. We'll share. We need the day care. We'll share what's left. If you want to stay home with her a little extra, say, in these early months, that's okay. I meant fifty-fifty sharing of a reasonable amount of parental time."

Gloria looks into her heart. The idea of her baby spending more than thirty-five hours a week with strangers makes her feel terrible. She suddenly realizes that she will not go back to work full-time. She'll go back for thirty-five hours a week.

Six weeks after the baby is born, Gloria and Phil have already taken a big step away from their plan. Phil behaved in good faith. He just honestly had ideas about what was good for the family that were different from Gloria's. He got his way because he used his extra dollop of bargaining power. Consciously or not, he has taken advantage of her headstart in emotional attachment to the baby.[4]

GATEKEEPING

Phil's style of taking care of the baby has always been a little different from Gloria's. That's inevitable; Phil and Gloria are different people. Gloria hovers. Phil is able to take his time in responding to the baby.

There are other differences. For example, Phil is willing to tolerate more physical risk. He puts the baby carrier in the middle of the kitchen table, he lets Molly play with a Ping-Pong ball, he swings her by her feet. Occasionally Molly spits up when she's upside-down—who cares?

Gloria cares. Little things about Phil's style irritate her. One day when

Molly is eleven months old, Gloria comes home from the store and finds Phil feeding her ginger ale and potato chips for lunch.

"What is this?" says Gloria.

"What's what?" says Phil. "Oh. This is, uh, good carbohydrates with some bubbles for tactile variety, plus more carbos, with, uh, good vegetable oil to grow on."

"It's junk food, you buffoon!" Gloria shouts.

She forbids him to feed the baby soda pop, potato chips, corn chips, or chips of any kind. Phil shrugs.

Gloria also corrects Phil often: how he fastens the diaper, how he burps the baby, how he instigates the baby, how he ignores the baby.

Phil reacts to this barrage of scolding by gradually feeling less and less competent, and less and less in charge. By the time of the potato chip debacle, the unspoken understanding is that Gloria is the boss of all things related to Molly. Phil carries out instructions.

One result of Phil's withdrawal is that all the mental work of baby care falls to Gloria. And there is a lot of mental work: arranging doctor's appointments and babysitters; worrying about whether she's teething, has an ear infection, or is simply fussy; reading the baby book to see what developmental stage comes next; asking around about preschools and waiting lists.

Just like Alice, Gloria is gatekeeping. Psychologists at Boston University who followed 100 new parents for five years found that many new mothers did it (Betcher and Pollack, 1993). They speculated that the women were assertive in insisting that their style was best, and that the men retreated quickly, because of young people's unconscious expectations and feelings about what women naturally know and what men naturally know.

However, gatekeeping may spring more from the psychology of mothers than from psychological differences between men and women. Sometimes in lesbian couples, the birth mother feels strongly that she is able to parent the baby better than her partner and expects to be deferred to (Alpert, 1988, p. 202).

We don't know for sure why mothers do it, or how many do it. We do know that if a mother wants her partner to do lots of baby care but starts gatekeeping, she is sabotaging her plan.

FAILURE TO RENEGOTIATE

The main forces that knocked Gloria and Phil off their course toward fifty-fifty parenting are the headstart effect, tipping, and gatekeeping. However, other forces are working against them, too.

Before the baby was born, Gloria and Phil shared the housework equally. Gloria was proud that Phil did more household chores than any other husband she knew. He bought groceries, he did a lot of the vacuuming and neatening up, he did some cooking, and he did lots of paperwork. He also took care of the yard work. She did the laundry, some of the cooking, and the bathroom cleaning.

When Gloria came home from the hospital after giving birth, her mother flew in and stayed for a week. When the week was up, Gloria and Phil fell back into their old routine. That meant, for example, that during her maternity leave, on top of nursing the baby for four hours a day, Gloria was doing unprecedented amounts of laundry. Molly spit up a lot, so she went through five outfits on a typical day, plus cloth diapers for burping and the blankets they wrapped her in. That meant one load of laundry every day. Sometimes, the drudgery drove her nearly to tears.

When Gloria returns to her job at the fitness center, the housework routine stays the same. However, because she has cut back on her hours at her job, Gloria feels a little pressure to pick up some of Phil's chores. Phil doesn't ask her to, but as a favor, she quietly takes charge of cooking—or ordering in—all their dinners. One night when Phil comes home late and she has had dinner waiting on the table, she experiences a peculiar sensation. She watched her parents do this, twenty years ago. She is a busy person. Why is she doing more housework than Phil is?

After the baby was born, the *amount* of housework and the *composition* of housework changed completely. But Phil and Gloria never talked about who should do what. They knew their goal was for Phil to share the baby care. So they concentrated on having him change diapers, bathe the baby, and take her on walks. They never took a step back to renegotiate their mundane old chores.

An outsider looking at their work would say, "Wow, if Gloria spends four hours a day breastfeeding, that means Phil has to do four hours of chores a day just to stay even. Let's see. If Phil keeps all his old chores, plus does the laundry, cooks dinner three nights a week, washes all the dishes, and takes the baby in for half the medical appointments, that should just about bring him up to fifty-fifty."

Why does Gloria fail to renegotiate? After all, she is the one who bears the brunt of the new workload. Lots of reasons. Even though she is a good manager at work, she dislikes provoking conflict at home. Also, she is so grateful that Phil is really doing baby care that she doesn't notice for a while that she is buried under the laundry. She also has a niggling feeling that she can ask only so much nontraditional effort of him, and no more. Maybe she also realizes, or feels unconsciously, that she has less bargaining power now than before.

There is one other aspect of housework that Gloria and Phil could renegotiate explicitly, but don't: their standards. If they lower their standards of meal preparation, housecleaning, personal grooming, and so on, they will free up time and energy. Like all new parents, they have already cut back their standards some. One problem is that Phil is willing to simplify the domestic routine more radically than Gloria is. He is by no means a slob, but he would be willing to eat, say, canned soup for supper. In a pinch, he might even be willing to eat it cold. The very thought depresses Gloria. She's no housekeeping wizard. But watching her mother keep her house neat and cheery for eighteen years did leave Gloria with the feeling that housekeeping is important.

The result is that Phil and Gloria cut back, but she does most of that extra increment of chores that she wants to have done but that he could take or leave. Without even trying, Phil Oscars her into it. If they had explicitly renegotiated the housework, she might have found ways to get him to do more, or to take on other tasks to compensate for those extra chores.

SPECIALIZATION

One more force blows like a strong headwind, pushing Gloria and Phil toward a traditional division of labor: the pressure to specialize. Time is scarce. Energy is scarce. Both are unspeakably scarcer now that both Gloria and Phil are back at their jobs.

Now that Gloria leaves work every day at 4 P.M., it makes sense for her to be responsible for dinner. After all, Phil doesn't get home until 5:30 or 6:00. He is responsible for grocery shopping, but sometimes Gloria discovers she needs an ingredient for a recipe. In the old days, when they got home at the same time and Phil cooked almost half the dinners, she would have said, "Oh, I guess I can't make lasagna. Why don't you do your tuna thing?" Now, she zips out with the baby in the late afternoon to buy the missing ingredient. While she is at the store, she picks up a few other things. Phil finds that he needs to go grocery shopping less often than before.

Gloria is now spending roughly ten hours a week at home with the baby while Phil is at work. When the baby spills Cheerios on the rug at 4:30 P.M., crawls over them, and crushes them, Gloria immediately vacuums the mess up. Then she proceeds to vacuum the rest of the room. Phil finds that he needs to vacuum less often than he used to.

There is nothing wrong with Gloria buying groceries or vacuuming. But they are supposed to be Phil's chores. Gloria is discovering that some chores are just a little bit more compatible with baby care than with a paying job. After all, she's home.

The most important chore of all, taking care of the baby, requires mastering many details. Babies change so fast that 20 percent of those details change every month. This week, she loves Gerber's green peas, insists on being read Winnie the Pooh before her naps, and is frightened of the neighbor's cat. Next week, she hates the peas and loves the cat. Keeping up with a baby is hard work.

Parents who are sharing child care have even more work. They have to tell their partner what happened while they were on duty. For example, when my daughter has an ear infection, my husband and I have to talk at length about it at least once a day. We discuss the minutiae of her symptoms, her sleeping schedule, her food and fluid intake, her other activities during our watch, and what instructions we should give the babysitter. All this talk takes time. We are forgoing some of the gains of specialization. In return, we enjoy the pleasures of collaboration.

Gloria, in contrast, doesn't like to talk. She likes to get things done. Phil is different. He enjoys putting his feet up and discussing the ins and outs of things. That's what he loves about being a professor. However, he has a hard time remembering the odd, picayune detail that Gloria occasionally mentions to him as she rushes out the door. For Gloria and Phil, then, the constant, detailed communication necessary to share child care fifty-fifty comes hard. That means the pressure for just one of them to specialize in child care leans on them heavily.

As the months pass, the pressure to specialize, combined with the fact that some bundles of chores are more efficient if done together than other bundles of chores, pushes Gloria toward doing a higher and higher share of the household chores. Gloria and Phil are slipping closer and closer to the black hole of tradition.

THE CATCH-UP EFFECT

What should Gloria and Phil have done? Could they, realistically speaking, have pulled off fifty-fifty sharing? If so, could they have made it last?

Let's remember that Gloria's troubles began with the headstart effect.

Without it, the baby wouldn't have raised her threat point much over Phil's. Without it, tipping wouldn't have started. Nor would she and Phil have had the disagreement about day care that led to her working part-time, but not him. Was there anything Gloria could have done to neutralize the headstart effect?

She tried to involve Phil emotionally in every part of the pregnancy. He came to all the sessions of her childbirth class. He also stayed with her in the delivery room during her labor and the birth of their daughter. For Phil, it was the most thrilling and profound event of his life. Most men feel the same way. Unfortunately, researchers have not found that being present at the delivery has any effect on men's caretaking behavior or emotional reactions to the baby in the following weeks (Entwisle, 1985).

Could Gloria have reduced her headstart in emotional attachment *after* the baby was born? Imagine this extreme case: Gloria comes home from the hospital and immediately goes into a stasis field, a suspended animation energy field that's a staple of science-fiction stories. For the next six months, Phil has sole responsibility for the baby. He bottle-feeds her, he holds her, he takes her for walks, he gives her antibiotics three times a day for two weeks during her first ear infection, he takes mental notes on all her changes and tiny achievements. He is extraordinarily immersed in the day-to-day life of his daughter. When Gloria emerges from the stasis field—not a nanosecond older—odds are that Phil will be at least as passionately attached to the baby as Gloria is. His style may be different, because he is a different person. But he has progressed far along his own curve of emotional attachment. He may even have passed Gloria.

Phil's unusual stint will also have made him more attentive, more skillful, and more confident with the baby than he ever imagined he could be. Even though he is exhausted, he actually finds being with the baby addictive. The more time he spends with Molly the more time he wants to spend with her. Gloria's decision to go in the stasis field has had a peculiar effect. *It has changed Phil's underlying tastes in a way that advantages her greatly.* He craves to do what she wants him to do. Very few negotiators, in any field of endeavor, get a chance to transform their negotiating counterpart in that way.

So much for science fiction. Short of purloining futuristic technology, how could Gloria have helped Phil have an experience like that?

The key to the success of our hypothetical stasis field is that Phil was alone with the baby. The more solo time with the baby Phil gets, the faster he will move along his curve of emotional attachment, and the higher the chance that he will catch up to Gloria (who is moving along her curve every day, too).[5]

However, Gloria and Phil missed this opportunity. Phil has always spent several hours a week alone with Molly as Gloria does errands. That is simply part of their attempt to share equally. It never occurred to Gloria, though, to ask Phil to take Molly for an entire day or an entire week. She didn't know that he needed *extra* time with the baby to catch up. If she had understood, she might have used a lot of her negotiating power in the early weeks to give solo time to Phil. She might even have breastfed less and let Phil give Molly one or two bottles a day.

Gloria and Phil had no idea what the headstart effect would do to them. Nor did they ever grasp the possibility of the catch-up effect. Nor did they ever see that solo time for Dad was the best way for him to catch up. Because the emotional dynamics of baby care are so opaque, and because when Gloria and Phil were tangled up in them they were short on sleep and mental sharpness, Gloria retains every bit of her headstart. It grows into a big lead. Phil never, ever catches up.

When they have a second baby, Gloria takes a leave from her part-time job and stays home for four months. She still hasn't been promoted to manager. At Phil's next review, his department chairman tells him that he probably won't get tenure; he should look for jobs at other colleges. His best offers come from Ohio and Louisiana.

Gloria says, "Good grief, have they heard of fitness there?"

Phil says, "Puh-lease!"

What he means is, he feels like the main breadwinner so she shouldn't complain. They move.

In Ohio, they have heard of fitness, but they haven't heard of Gloria. Phil gets tenure and his career develops nicely. Gloria has to settle for a job at the YMCA. She never, ever catches up.

Gloria wouldn't trade away her children for anything, but what she has isn't what she hoped for. Nor is she likely to learn how close she came to making those hopes come true.

6

A Nontraditional Marriage

By NOW IT SHOULD BE CLEAR THAT MANY ELEMENTS OF NEGOTIA-tion reinforce the traditional sexual division of labor in the home. One problem is that some of those elements are self-reinforcing. For example, tipping can snowball once it starts. So can gatekeeping. So can differences in income. For instance, the partner who earns significantly less is the one who pulls back from paying work when more hands are needed at home, but that interruption makes her future salary even lower relative to her partner's. She is getting more and more stuck in the glue of tradition. Another problem, of course, is that each of those forces strengthens the others.

In short, we are looking at a system of powerful feedback loops. The question is, If the feedback loops run so vigorously the wrong way, can they be made to run vigorously the right way? Can bargaining power, commitment mechanisms, focal points, and attachment to the baby all work *in favor* of a mother who wants mainly to succeed in science or politics and a father who wants mainly to raise happy children?

The answer is yes. However, many forces will continue pushing hard the wrong way for decades to come: society's focal point of motherly care for babies, men's special social status, and the beauty problem. So the helpful forces must be hauled around and pointed determinedly the right way. Very few girls who go with the flow will find themselves marrying house-husbands. At least during the lifetime of my children, it will mostly be girls who are hungry for achievement and who really couldn't care less what other people think of them who will wind up married to men who do oodles of child care.

A Nontraditional Girl

Amy grew up in a beach town. Her mother owns an art gallery in the shopping center. Her father used to be head cook at a local seafood restaurant. When she and her brothers were small, her father watched them during the day, and her mother watched them in the evening. When Amy was nine, her parents divorced. Her father moved away. He rarely visited. After the divorce, there was much less money. There were also many more chores for the children to do. Her brothers did the laundry and vacuumed. Amy learned how to weed and water the garden, overhaul bicycles, and do rudimentary cooking.

Amy missed her father. Her childhood years were difficult. She spent her time reading and building with plastic construction sets that her father had bought for her older brother long before. When she was in the sixth grade, she got to work with a computer at school for the first time. She loved it. In high school, she joined the computer club. Most of the kids in it were older, and most were boys. Amy didn't care. She knew she was good at computers and at building things.

One thing she did care about a little was her weight. According to the standards that the other girls discussed constantly, she was plump. Her mother said, "Don't worry about it. Your weight is normal. And looks are not important; what you do is." Amy wavered at times, but chose to believe it.

Amy took four years of math in high school: algebra, geometry, trigonometry, and precalculus with an introduction to probability and statistics. She also took three years of science: biology, chemistry, and physics. Chemistry was great, she thought. It was a lot like building things: atoms had properties, molecules had shapes. It all fit together elegantly.

Amy went to the state university and majored in chemistry. It was much, much tougher than high school. She got discouraged and switched to biochemistry, which was a little easier. She became a research assistant for a middle-aged professor who respected her. He always said, "Edison was right. Science is ninety-nine percent perspiration."

Amy was not afraid of hard work. One day during her senior year, she realized where her drive came from: she had no intention of suffering the reversals, anxiety, and pinched economies that her mother had endured.

That year, she met Dave, a sophomore who was majoring in art. Actually, he couldn't decide between art and music.

He asked her what her major was. When she told him he said, "Oh, a techie."

She said, "No, I'm just going to cure AIDS."

Dave was impressed. They became friends, but only friends.

Amy stayed at school for two extra years to get a master's degree, so she and Dave wound up graduating the same year. By that time, he had decided to major in music. He encouraged her to join the choral group he sang in.

After graduation, Amy and Dave started seeing each other. She got a job at a pharmaceutical company, with a team doing research on retroviruses. Dave waited tables at an expensive restaurant. Mostly, he worked on his music. He created aural collages by feeding into an old Macintosh computer samples of different sounds: the *Beverly Hills 90210* theme music, George Clinton, hoots from an aviary. The result was not in the least bit commercial.

Dave was the third of four children. His parents, like Amy's, were divorced. In spite of his bohemian pose, he was very close to his family. He particularly enjoyed his young nephews and nieces. He took Amy to several family gatherings, where she watched him wrestle with the kids, read them stories, squish Play-Doh, and bathe the dolly. His face shone.

They got married when Amy was twenty-six and Dave was twenty-four. She made $45,000; he made $12,000. He wanted to cut back his hours at the restaurant, and maybe fool around with sculpture.

Amy said, "Sure. If it's not too weird, maybe Mom can even show it in her gallery."

Dave said, "Right. As long as it's got a dory in it."

Amy laughed. One reason they got along was that Amy did in fact respect his art.

Two years after their marriage, Dave started mentioning kids. His nephews and nieces were already growing up. Toddlers were cool, he thought. Three kids would be perfect. Amy had not started to think seriously about children, but more than two didn't sound realistic to her. She told Dave that if her lab won the big grant they had applied for, which would last them four years, she would start to think about getting pregnant. Her company granted an eight-week maternity leave.

As Amy and Dave stand on the threshold of parenthood, let's quickly analyze the choices Amy has made so far. Most strikingly, she *trained up.* Four years of math and three years of science in high school put her near the top of technical readiness for American teenagers. That background made it possible for her to skip the remedial courses and finish the requirements for a B.S. in four years.

Amy also set important *precedents* throughout her preadolescent and adolescent years. She found many interests to sink her energy into. Boys were only one, and not the most important to her. She never thought her appearance was, or should be, her main asset. She stuck it out in the computer club, where she learned not only that computers were only machines but also that boys were only human. Because her father and brothers had done so much child care and housework, it never occurred to her that males should be exempt from such chores. Her friends all knew she would tolerate only a boyfriend who treated her respectfully. Finally, Amy was not materialistic. Her goal was a middle-class standard of living, with health insurance and a house in a quiet, safe neighborhood. Plenty of kids in her high school had not had that much.

Next, she *married down*. Dave was younger than she was and his expected earnings, at least when they got married, were much lower than hers. Note, though, that she married someone who was bright, able, attractive, and responsible. He was just unconventional.

Dave also enjoyed young children. Amy liked that side of him. She never consciously thought, "Oh, great, I'll be able to bargain him into a lot of child care." Instead, because she intended to earn her target family income by herself, she found it easy to tolerate traits that some women might have found disturbing. She saw the good sides of those traits: warmth, affection, playfulness.

Finally, Amy's job was a good *commitment mechanism*. Lab research is very demanding work. If your experiment bubbles to an end at 1 A.M., you have to be there. Her field was also highly competitive. She had to go to training sessions and read lots of papers to keep up with new developments.

Timing Is Everything

Amy's lab did not get the big grant. She told Dave that this was not the time to have a baby. Instead, she decided to look for a job at another company.

Dave protested, "You're twenty-eight. We don't have much time."

Amy held firm. She wanted her job to be secure before she started having children. She found a job at another pharmaceutical company, a small, hard-driving start-up that was a thirty-minute commute from home. Her hours would be longer, but her chances for promotion would be higher.

Amy worked very hard for three years. Her team identified several new compounds that slowed the reproduction of retroviruses. She got a promotion. Finally, she worked up her courage to ask for a raise. She checked with acquaintances at several other companies and learned that she could get hired elsewhere for at least $8,000 more than her employer was paying her. She took this information to her manager, making it plain that she was willing to jump to another company if necessary. She got the raise. The company also got funding from venture capitalists for a three-year extension of the retroviral research.

During those years, Dave worked on sculptures, on aural collages, and on fixing up the ramshackle house they had bought. He was making about $4,000 a year selling his sculptures, mainly at art fairs. He had also found an audience for his music, in a discussion group on the Internet devoted to digitized music. It didn't pay, but it was rewarding.

One day Amy said, "Listen, if we have a baby, it will be a lot harder for you to travel around to those art fairs."

"Why?" Dave asked. "I'll just bring the baby stuff. The Indians used to carry their papooses all over, right?"

"Uh-huh," said Amy. "But that doesn't mean it was easy."

"You can take some time off, or go part-time, right?" said Dave.

"I get eight weeks of leave. I can't take more; I'm the main technical support person on this project. Nobody can replace me. I could maybe cut back my hours at the end of the project, but that's in two and a half years."

"You're already thirty-one. Then you'll be practically thirty-four."

"So we have to decide."

That conversation left Dave with a funny feeling. He had always known that Amy would have to work for pay, but he had never imagined himself as the only parent at home with a baby for a stretch of months, never mind years.

He asked one of his artist friends, a thirty-year-old woman with two children, about day care for infants. She said that there were centers, or you could work out an arrangement with another mother who watched her own plus yours, or you could hire a babysitter to come to your house. She also told Dave roughly what the options cost. None was cheap.

"And don't think you're going to get any work done while the baby is tiny," she added. "I took a year off for each of mine. You're just too exhausted. No time. You won't believe it."

Then she grinned. "But don't get me wrong—I think it's great!"

Dave thought her grin looked just a little fierce.

A Nontraditional Baby

Amy knew that she was ready; Dave decided that he was ready. After seven months of trying, they conceived.

During Amy's pregnancy, the housework routine continued as before. Early in the marriage, they had split the chores evenly. After all, Dave was working full-time, too. When Amy switched to the start-up company, she spent less time at home. The house got messier. They lived with it.

When the obstetrician laid the newborn baby on Amy's chest, Amy laughed.

"Can you believe how beautiful she is? Look at those eyes. She doesn't look at all like those other babies."

Dave stood beside her. He thought little Clara was precious—but she was red, covered with dark fuzz, and skinny as a gag rubber chicken. He couldn't believe Amy was so delighted. She had never been the maternal type.

Amy decided to breastfeed, at least during her eight weeks of maternity leave. Her mother spent a week with them. Neither Amy nor Dave knew a thing about baby care.

Dave was much more nervous than he had expected. He refused to wash the baby's umbilicus; he was afraid he'd hurt her. He was also more exhilarated than he had expected to be.

Amy felt logy and fat. Breastfeeding was a pleasure, but it seemed to take up half her waking hours.

Since Dave's schedule was elastic, he spent every afternoon doing work around the house. He took on more chores, since Amy was tied up with breastfeeding. They also worked out a procedure to include him in most nursing sessions. He changed the baby beforehand and he burped her afterward—which meant carrying her around on his shoulder for twenty or twenty-five minutes. To get Clara to pay attention to him, he made goofy faces, held up a red racing car, and otherwise made himself dementedly conspicuous. Amy said nothing, because she understood. She would be going back to work soon. He wanted to make sure that the baby loved him before he was left alone with her.

After two weeks, the pediatrician said it was fine to begin introducing bottles of formula. Dave took the middle-of-the-night feeding. Each week, they replaced one more nursing session with a bottle. By the seventh week, the baby was half breastfed, half formula-fed. Dave bustled around the kitchen, boiling, shaking, cooling, and sprinkling. He looked self-important, and he loved it. He knew it was all prelude to holding and nourishing his child, the one and only.

Dave deferred to Amy on many of the details of Clara's care. Should they use cornstarch in her diapers? When should they drop a feeding?

He always said, "You're the scientist."

Amy thought what he really meant was, "You're the woman."

What did she know about cornstarch? She gave her best guesses, and Dave accepted them.

Dave was rougher with the baby than Amy would have liked. He plopped stuffed animals on her head and swung her by her feet. Amy told him to be careful.

He said, "She loves it!"

What could Amy do?

Amy decided to ease Dave gradually into taking sole responsibility for the baby. When Clara was seven weeks old, she nursed twice in the morning and twice at night. That meant Amy could go where she liked between 10 A.M. and 6 P.M. She took Saturday and Sunday off, and went out with friends.

When she got home, the kitchen was dirty, no progress had been made toward dinner, and the baby was grimy. When Amy complained, Dave said, "We went to the park. I'll get to it."

Amy did the same thing the following weekend.

Dave said, "We went to the zoo. I'll get to it."

When Amy's maternity leave was over, she felt sad, relieved, guilty, and excited, all at the same time. It was confusing. She felt much more desire to stay home with Clara than she had expected. Work seemed sterile in comparison. But she was also desperate to escape the blockhead drudgery of taking care of the baby. Work seemed exalted in comparison.

Dave also had mixed feelings: pride, apprehension, and a little resentment that Amy was returning to the wide world while he was staying penned up with the baby. However, by that point, he was as skillful as Amy, knew much more than she did about the fine points of formula, and felt deeply protective toward his daughter.

He and Amy had talked a lot about day care. They had different views. Amy's first choice was that Dave take care of the baby at home. Her second choice was that a babysitter come to the house. Dave worked in the shed out back and on the computer upstairs. He could check in frequently. If the baby were out of the house, how could they be sure she was getting good care?

Dave was absolutely sure he did not want to be a full-time parent for an entire year, until Amy's big project at work was done. He was also afraid that having the baby at home might interfere with his work. Plus a babysitter at home would be expensive. He wanted to put Clara in family day care for, say, twenty-five hours a week. That would leave him time alone to work and be less expensive than a babysitter.

Amy and Dave were facing their first serious conflict. They were both too tired to think clearly, so it took them a long time to tack down what each cared about most. Finally they reached a compromise. They had a babysitter come to the house twenty hours a week, in the mornings, freeing Dave up for his most productive work time. Amy agreed to try to get home from work by 6:30 every night at the latest, and take over caring for Clara until bedtime. That would give Dave some time to fiddle with his computer. This arrangement cost a little more than Dave's family day care plan.

Dave felt that Amy got slightly more out of the compromise than he did. They wound up with less hired-out time than he had wanted, in return for a promise that Amy would change her work patterns in the future. That would be hard for him to enforce.

Amy said, "Look, if it doesn't work out, we can change what we're doing. Let's just try it. I need my peace of mind."

Dave felt he didn't have too much leverage, since Amy had to go back to work full-time. Amy, on the other hand, knew that she couldn't push Dave too far. He simply didn't have the same feelings for the baby that she did. He also felt strong commitment to his work, even if it contributed very little to the household income.

As it happened, the compromise worked out well. The babysitter stayed until noon and she did the laundry, by far the most onerous chore. Then Clara napped for two to two and a half hours. So Dave actually had a lot of time to work.

Amy made a tremendous effort to get home early every night. She felt irritated from time to time because Dave had no idea how much self-discipline and cajoling that schedule took. He really didn't understand the pressures she was under at work. How could he? He had only held short jobs doing light office work and waiting tables. Still, she was eager to bask in her island of time every evening with Clara, so she made the effort.

Only one part of their agreement was not working well. Dave was supposed to make dinner every night. (Amy went grocery shopping on Sunday mornings.) On many nights, though, he hadn't started anything by the time Amy got home. She cared more about a hot meal, nicely served, on a decently set table than he did. He always said he was too tired to cook. They would eat take-out, microwave leftovers, or together make something fast and sorry, in Amy's eyes, such as canned soup and a salad of limp greens. It seemed, though, that she would have to lump it.

As Clara got older, Amy began to regret that she was missing many of her milestones. Dave saw her roll over for the first time. Dave felt her first tooth. The babysitter saw her sit up for the first time.

Amy also noticed that when the baby bumped her head or got scared by a dog, she turned to Dave. It made sense, because Dave spent much more time with her. Still, it gave Amy a twinge.

Her mother said, "Well, if he's going to get the hard parts, he's going to get the good parts, too."

"You always said, 'Be careful what you wish for,'" Amy said, a little ruefully.[1]

Let's review the negotiating steps Amy and Dave have danced through together during Clara's first year.

Amy refused to start trying to get pregnant until she had her promotion, raise, and new job in hand. This delay grew out of, and helped to underscore, her commitment to her career. It not only set a precedent, it created a commitment mechanism. Amy's participation was indispensable for the new project at work, which had funding for three years. Dave was forced to choose between: (1) baby now and care by Dad or (2) baby later and some help from Mom. Dave wanted a baby soon because he wanted to have three children in all, before Amy's biological clock struck midnight. He was more impatient than Amy. In the end, he paid for that impatience. He got bargained into having the baby soon and doing most of the care himself.

After the birth, Amy had a definite *headstart* over Dave in attachment to the baby. She countered it by giving him lots of responsibility for feeding the baby, even though she was breastfeeding, and by giving him big blocks of solo time very early on. Feeding the baby four times a day and being in charge for eight hours at a stretch helped Dave catch up.

Dave suspected, on an unspoken emotional level, that Amy's instincts about newborn care were better than his. However, Amy's modesty and desire to make room for Dave prevented her from gatekeeping. Her firm commitment to return to work in eight weeks, since she was the breadwinner in the family, greatly influenced her behavior and his behavior. They simply couldn't afford for Dave to feel second-rate at baby care. The breastfeeding undoubtedly caused tipping in the baby's affections. But Dave's bottle-feeding and early solo time helped Clara learn to look to Dave for comfort, too.

The headstart effect was most conspicuous in Amy and Dave's disagreement about day care. Amy wanted Clara to get lots of parental time during the day. Amy's status as breadwinner, though, helped counteract it. Dave was economically dependent on her. That meant Amy couldn't supply that parental time herself. In turn, Dave's status as a man probably helped him get a better deal than many women would have gotten in his place. It made outsiders take his artwork seriously. It also made Amy take his work just a tiny bit more seriously than she would have if she had seen the wife of one of her colleagues futzing around with red clay and Plexiglas. That edge was an important part of Dave's bargaining power. Note that they were spending much more on child care than Dave earned selling his sculptures.

Of course, both Amy and Dave talked about his work in moral terms. It wasn't about making money, it was about making the world more awake, more beautiful, more meaningful. That sort of talk was another important part of Dave's bargaining power.

What can we say about Amy's and Dave's BATNAs? Both have the uncomfortable feeling that if they remarried, they wouldn't do as well. Amy is thirty-two years old. Given the beauty problem, she is not in her prime. Plus she is a dedicated lab scientist who doesn't want to devote herself to baby care. Not many potential husbands are hunting for a woman like her. Dave is thirty. Peter Pan is delightful at twenty-one, but suspect at thirty. Dave's greatest, most unusual asset is that he is terrific with babies. But not many potential wives are hunting for a man like him, either.

Their mediocre chances in the remarriage market, then, roughly cancel out. That leaves Dave's obvious economic dependence on Amy. His disadvantage is partly canceled out by Amy's headstart in attachment to Clara. She is much more devoted to her baby than the typical breadwinning father is to his. It is not really credible that she would walk out on both Dave and Clara. Her threat point is moderately high.

Or is it? What if she took Clara with her and walked out on Dave? Dave has heard stories of far less deserving women being awarded custody. He suspects that the typical judge would not understand at all what Clara means to him and what he means to Clara. He sees that likelihood as a despicable injustice. It significantly weakens his bargaining power. If he lost Amy and Clara, he'd have to go back to waiting tables. He'd be poor and lonely. Or he'd have to give up his artwork and find a steady job. That makes his threat point high.

All in all, Amy's BATNA is better than Dave's. If the marriage broke down, she would have nearly all the income and an excellent chance of getting custody of Clara. Her bargaining power, though, is tempered by her love for Dave. His weakness is palatable because he trusts Amy.

They are both looking far into the future for ways to swap favors, make concessions, and give what the other really needs. For example, Dave expects Amy to contribute much more time to baby care after Clara's first birthday. Their ability to make long-term trades is one of the greatest strengths of their marriage.

Cracks in the Fresco

As Clara's first birthday approached, Dave got cranky. He was always tired. It was hurting his work. The main compensation was that Clara adored him. She crawled all over the house to be near him. She watched him wide-eyed, with a big, eager, drooly smile. In the house, it was great, but he felt self-conscious when he took her outside in the afternoon. In the park, all the other parents and babysitters were women. They looked at him funny.

Amy said, "You sure it's not the purple granny glasses?"

Dave said, "Absitively. I don't wear them half the time."

He thought he would get over it, but he didn't. Instead he found a little park where hardly anybody went. Going clandestine made him feel stupid, though. Besides, Clara didn't have other babies to play with there.[2]

Having dinner with Amy's colleagues had also become excruciating. He was afraid the subject of babysitters would come up, and then the fact that they hired one for only twenty hours a week.

He would say, "Well, she sleeps most of the afternoon. And I get a lot of work done even when she's up."

He was fibbing.

Amy would say, "He's great with her. You wouldn't believe how self-confident she is. When we go to the zoo, she growls at the leopards."

When Amy said those things in public, Dave felt proud, but also squirmy.

He didn't know a single other father who worked half-time and raised a baby half-time. He didn't know a single other man who was the main, hands-on parent. His feelings surprised him a little, since he had always been unconventional. Being sure that artists were heroes was different from being sure that hands-on parents were heroes, it seemed.[3]

An artist friend bought him a videotape of the 1984 movie *Mr. Mom.* He and Amy watched it together. They both noticed how, by the end, Michael Keaton's character not only did an excellent job of raising the children but gave his approach a masculine spin. They also noticed how he stayed home for only about one year.

Amy told him that she had often felt like an oddball, too, "since about seventh grade." She knew very few women biochemists. On the other hand, women in the sciences did have groups, newsletters, meetings.

Dave went to the library and found a few books and newsletters about stay-at-home fathers.[4] He considered starting an on-line discussion group for men like him on the Internet or putting an ad in the newspaper.

Amy was concerned about Dave. He was lonely. Also, how could he get over his doubts about the manliness of taking care of Clara? Should he start lifting weights or studying karate? Or carry around a chainsaw, like Michael Keaton's character?

Amy had her own problems, too. She was always tired. It was hurting her work a little and her enjoyment of life a lot. She and Dave got almost no time to relax together. Her main problem, though, was that her manager was hinting that she was being considered for a promotion out of the lab entirely, to a job marketing their new anti-viral product. She knew the scientific details better than any of the MBAs in the company.

Amy thought it sounded great. However, she wouldn't be able to go part-time, as she was hoping to, during her first year in such a job. It would also require lots of travel. Dave would have to continue being the number-one parent for much longer than he had expected.

The day she got the job offer, she told Dave all about it. He was very upset.

"We don't need more money! We need time. I need time. You have no idea what it's like. It isn't fair!"

Amy stayed calm. She described the options. First, she could stay in the lab, go half-time for a year, and thereafter work at home one day a week. She wouldn't be very productive at home, given the nature of her research, so she would probably have to take a pay cut, maybe as much as 15 percent.

The disadvantage of that option was that she was getting sick of test tubes. She had only just realized it, while this offer was percolating.

Second, she could take the promotion, work full-time very hard for one year, and then go half-time for a year. After that, she could work one day a week at home. The vice president of marketing telecommuted from his home computer on Fridays, and he got full pay. The disadvantage of that option was that she would have to travel. It would mean spending three or four nights away from home each month. The advantage was that she was interested in the job. Plus it paid a lot.

"You would really go half-time for a whole year at that new job?" Dave said.

Amy said her idea was to try for another pregnancy so that she could spend lots of time at home with the second baby for a year, the way Dave had with Clara.

Dave stared at her. He couldn't believe she was so rational about this. His emotions were so mixed up.

His first reaction was, "That would be great!"

They talked late into the night. Amy told Dave about some ideas she had to make his life easier. They could increase their babysitter's hours from twenty to twenty-five or thirty hours a week. During one of her vacation weeks, Amy could take Clara to her parents' house. Dave would have that whole week at home to himself. Also, he could contact his old computer-music buddies and propose going out with them regularly, maybe even one night a week.

They could hire the babysitter for extra hours once in a while, too. For example, a local college was holding a computer-music contest, leading up to a concert of winning pieces. With some extra time to work, Dave could enter.

They could even think of moving closer to Amy's office to cut down her commute. She would spend the time she saved taking care of Clara in the morning and evening.

Just having this conversation made Dave feel better. He had felt so worn down, unappreciated, and tormented by self-doubt. He was surprised that Amy had put so much thought into his problems.

By the end of the week, they had sorted out a new arrangement. Amy would take the new job, if management accepted her proposal about a half-time stint in the future and working one day at home thereafter. Dave would try twenty-five hours of babysitting a week. After thinking about it hard, he didn't want Clara in the hands of a non–family member for longer than that. It meant getting a new babysitter. He would see how he liked her and the new hours. He relished the idea of Amy taking the baby away for a week. He also decided to enter the music contest. A high school student in the neighborhood could babysit several afternoons a week for a month to give him time to polish some recent pieces. Dave had no interest in moving. He did work up the nerve to call his old buddies and some of them planned to get together with him. He also decided to learn how to start an on-line discussion group. It was intimidating, but soon he ventured forth into cyberspace with a discussion group he called: SuperDads.

Amy and Dave did not talk about one important aspect of their new arrangement. After Amy's half-time year was over, Dave would once again be on duty. If things went as planned, he'd be taking care of two children by then. He and Amy might ratchet up the babysitter's hours further, but he would be the parent who had primary responsibility for the kids. When Amy traveled for work, or if she were promoted again, he would have to fill in for her at home. Amy and Dave didn't need to talk about that. It was understood.

The negotiating dynamics that Dave and Amy faced during this period of stress are clear. Dave discovered that being the primary parent had unexpected costs for him. Most of those costs were emotional. Learning how to take care of Clara was much easier—and more rewarding—than he had expected. But it cut far more deeply into his time and energy than he had ever imagined possible. He also felt more uncomfortable in public, and more emotional conflict about feeling uncomfortable, than he had expected.

Because Amy loved Dave, she wanted to help him. She thought creatively about trade-offs she might make. The main resources she had to work with were her earnings, her time, and her emotional support. They could spend more money on babysitters or a new house. She could contribute a little more time to child care in the future. She could encourage Dave to spend more of his leisure time with other adult friends. She could encourage him in his artwork. She could also encourage him to reach out to other men who were raising children. The proposal that she made to him about her new job contained a long-term trade: less child care time by her now in return for more time and more money later.

Dave accepted the proposal. He was able to, first, because he trusted Amy to keep her promise. Second, she made the proposal affectionately and respectfully. She obviously cared about him.

Amy and Dave had a second child. Amy stayed home half-time for the baby's first year. Afterward, for months at a time, she was able to spend one day a week working at home. But for long stretches, that was impossible.

Her earnings grew; Dave's did not. While the children were small, he made slow progress in his work.

Dave found himself talking to his sisters on the phone more and more frequently. How had they toilet-trained his nephews and nieces? How much milk did a three-year-old really need? His sisters encouraged him to join a play group they knew about that consisted of eight mothers and thirteen kids.[5] Dave was shy at first. However, the moms did not look at him funny. They were awed by his artwork. They thought that Clara and Annie were absolutely wonderful. Dave's face shone.

Nine men logged in regularly to his on-line discussion group for stay-at-home fathers. They shared "hairy eyeball" stories; one-line retorts to give to meddlesome strangers; tips on discipline, children's books, movies, and activities; and, of course, sports trivia. Slowly, Dave felt himself being drawn into a whole new social circle—the real and virtual world of hands-on parents.

One night Dave lay on the couch.

Amy sat beside him and said, "So, you want to work on that third kid?"

Dave opened his eyes and looked at her.

He said, "Hardee-har-har."

Then they both laughed.

Amy and Dave continued, often, to run smack into unexpected costs, conflicts, and complications. Both were shocked to discover that teenagers needed just as much time from their parents as toddlers did, and much more patience. They compromised, invented, swapped favors, and made concessions with all the energy, creativity, and love they could muster—all four of them.

III

Setting New Precedents

7

A World in Transition

THE THREE SORTS OF MARRIAGES WE'VE JUST LOOKED AT—TRADI-
tional, transitional, and nontraditional—are each typical in three
quite different worlds. In the world of tradition, women specialize in
raising children and in tasks they can do close to home for most of their adult
lives. In a transitional world—the world most people in the rich countries live
in now—confusing changes are taking place. Women triumph in jobs that
their mothers never dreamed of, such as flying jets or mapping rain forests,
yet they struggle unsuccessfully to persuade their male partners to do more
unpaid work at home. In the possible future world that this book is conjur-
ing, the sexual division of labor will have melted away. Many homemakers
will be men. Many primary parents who interrupt their careers or work part-
time in order to raise children will be fathers. Things will be different.

It's no surprise that the old division of labor hinged on sex. How could it
have been otherwise? So many things worked together to enforce a traditional sexual division of labor: law, religion, custom, high birth rates, the
social training of girls and boys, and an economy in which many paying jobs
required muscle power rather than brain power.

What is curious is that in places where all those things have changed, the
sexual division of labor has not. Why not? Because we are stuck in a peculiar transition. In this chapter, we will look closely at its topography. Which
features are holding us back? Which don't matter as much as we think?
This chapter, like the preceding ones, will mainly use ideas from economics.
Not because law and psychology don't matter, but because when we look
at the terrain before us through our economics spectacles, the mudholes
and rocky patches look different. We may even see a path that leads beyond them.

In the marriages described in part II, certain patterns appeared again and again. The education of the young woman and young man, their relative earnings, and their expectations about parenthood all mattered a lot. To understand why so many women are like Laura and Gloria, we need to take a closer look at particular key decisions that women make. For millions of girls, the old certainties of the world of tradition are out of reach, because divorce rates are high, or undesirable, because they look forward to the challenge of working outside the home. Still, many of them can't quite see themselves acting like Amy, happily earning nearly all the money their family will spend.

Instead, their feelings are caught betwixt and between. Taking a close look at what girls are doing as a group, compared with what boys are doing as a group, will show us clearly what needs to change if we are ever, finally, to spurt into a world in which women enjoy real equality with men.

Education: Training Up or Training Down

When I think back to high school, I remember long corridors of scuffed linoleum, rooms full of desks with creaky wooden tops, a couple of teachers who scared me, and three or four I would have gladly followed on a hike into the Atlantic Ocean. Everyone remembers it differently. Some recent research suggests that how people remember high school depends in part on whether they are male or female (AAUW, 1992). That is, girls' experience there is different from boys' experience.

For one thing, girls take fewer science courses in high school, especially in advanced courses. One national study of 58,000 students in the 1980s found that 11.6 percent of high school boys could be called science concentrators but only 7.1 percent of girls could. Concentrators had one or more credit each in biology, chemistry, and physics (West, Miller, and Deodato, 1985).

The survey also found that young people's decisions about math and science in high school correlated strongly with their aspirations for the future (West, Miller, and Deodato, 1985). Students who expected to go to a four-year college or to become professionals were much more likely to study algebra, geometry, and trigonometry and at least one advanced life science or physical science.

Researchers have also found that girls, on average, think that math is less important than boys think it is for courses they will take in the future. In surveys, many say that math-related occupations are "for men" (Fausto-Sterling, 1985).

Anyone who has read a newspaper regularly for the last four or five years has seen reports like those before. We can't heap all the blame on schools. I would be very interested in reading the results of a survey of *parents* that asked whether math was more for boys than for girls.

What the news stories have not made clear, though, are the ramifications of that difference in attitudes and behavior between boys and girls. For working-class girls, who may begin full-time work immediately after high school, having skipped certain courses limits the sorts of jobs they can get. For example, in 1986 a group of banks in New York City promised to hire 250 graduates of South Brooklyn high schools for entry-level jobs but, a year later, had hired only 100. Most of the applicants flunked the entrance exam, which was equivalent to an eighth-grade math test (Rivera-Batiz, 1992). The unfortunate truth is that a person who can't tell when her calculator is off by a factor of 100 will have trouble getting a job as a teller.

Middle-class girls who take only one or two years of math in high school also limit their options. Many college majors will be inaccessible to them. For example, there is no way they can study engineering. Engineering majors begin the program their freshman year. There is no time for remedial trigonometry. To lose that opportunity is a shame, since for decades an engineering degree has been a ticket out of the lower middle class and into a stable, good-paying job for thousands of young people, many of whom were the first in their families to go to college. Few engineers get advanced degrees. Four years of college is enough to get a challenging professional job.

Girls who don't take chemistry or physics in high school also miss the opportunity to learn that they are good at it and that it is fun for them. How many of them might have invented new vaccines, or spaceships, or computers that eat pollution? The choice dismissed out of hand and the choice never considered shape our lives just as surely as the choice we ponder for weeks.

The difference between what boys study and what girls study widens in college. In 1990, women made up only 15 percent of graduating engineering majors, 31 percent of graduating physics majors, and 30 percent of graduating computer science majors. They made up 78 percent of education majors and 72 percent of psychology majors (*Digest of Education Statistics,* 1992, table 250).

As it happens, I agree with proponents of the liberal arts philosophy who say that college studies should expand the mind and soul rather than mainly inculcate vocational skills. However, when young women study liberal arts and young men study science, something very predictable happens. The men earn more money.

In 1987, college graduates who had been working full-time for one year since finishing college made the following average annual salaries (in 1987 dollars): engineers: $26,600; physics, math, and computer science majors: $22,500; psychology majors: $17,300; education majors: $15,800 (*Digest of Education Statistics,* 1992, table 375). Only one year out of college, then, an engineering major is already earning almost 70 percent more than an education major. As those graduates get older, the gap may widen.

We do not have a good, simple story that explains why girls and boys, and college women and men, study different subjects. However, two pieces of evidence suggest that it may have a great deal to do with how young people envision their own future.

First, researchers have found that girls and boys have different attitudes toward money and toward children. In one large, nationally representative survey of high school students in 1982, 41 percent of senior boys said that "having lots of money" was "very important" to them. Only 24 percent of senior girls did. Only 37 percent of senior boys thought that having children was very important to them, as opposed to 47 percent of senior girls (*Digest of Education Statistics,* 1992, table 362).

Another study analyzed data from a nationally representative sample of more than 12,000 young people to find out what things made a girl likely to pick a traditionally male job (Waite and Berryman, 1985). It found that fourteen-year-old girls who believed they would be working for pay when they were in their thirties were much more likely to pick a traditionally male occupation than girls who imagined themselves as future homemakers. Girls who thought they would be working full-time in their thirties were even more likely to choose and stay in a nontraditional field.

Even so, girls' vision of their future can't be the only thing determining whether they study calculus or lunar stratigraphy. At many colleges, women drop out of science majors at twice the rate of men (Muller, 1992). Women may come to college with weaker science backgrounds or unrealistic expectations, or they may find the atmosphere in math and science classrooms chilly or offensive. Some college administrators are concerned about the atmosphere problem and are working on it (for example, see Dartmouth College, 1992).

Keeping that qualification in mind, the bulk of the evidence suggests to me that the typical seventeen-year-old girl already has a picture of her future in her head. The picture may be fuzzy and it may flicker, but it shows her working full-time for pay until her first child is born. After that, she's not sure, but she might very well stay home. Her brother has a completely different picture in his head. The main point—which we saw as we watched Alice, Jack, Laura, Rob, Gloria, and Phil negotiate their way through their thirties and forties—is that those two pictures are different, but complement each other. Boys are investing in arduous apprenticeships to become breadwinners. Girls are still investing a bit less.

Will young women in the future be able to catch up with men's earnings, yet avoid working very hard at paying jobs as men do? Unlikely. Women's full-time, year-round earnings pulled closer to men's in the 1980s than they had ever been before. Two things accounted for that advance. First, women went into traditionally male jobs, such as accounting, law, and business management (Sorenson, 1991). Second, more women stayed at their jobs continuously, year after year, rather than dropping out to become home-makers or stay-at-home mothers (Blau and Kahn, 1994).

As best we can tell, girls' decisions not to study math and science, and what-ever barriers stand between them and those courses (and I have no doubt that such barriers do loom, inexcusably), will matter more in the future, not less. Labor economists predict that the high-paying, fast-growing occupations in the next decade will be managerial, professional, and technical. They'll include engineering, medicine, nursing, law, computer science, and manage-ment. Researchers know that the most important factors in women's deci-sions to enter those jobs are strong educational goals early in life, three or more years of math in high school, and a science major in college (Sorenson, 1991). What tenth-grade girls are studying this week will determine, in part, whether they can get high-paying jobs when they are thirty.

Parents who hope their daughters will have some measure of indepen-dence and power over their lives when they are grown up face many per-plexing decisions. Those many decisions may collapse to a few if they insist on one simple discipline: that their daughters take at least three years of math in high school. They don't have to like it and they don't have to get A's. They just have to take it and try their best.

It should be clear that I am devoting this attention to education not merely because it is vital as end in itself and as a bridge to better lives but because of the effect education has on women's bargaining power. Women who train down—and so earn low wages—are likely after marriage to get bargained into lots of unpaid work at home, whether they enjoy it or not. Women who train up are not. That is, this enduring difference between what young women and men study in school helps perpetuate the traditional sexual division of labor in the home. We are looking at a big fat feedback loop. Most girls want to have children and to be close to them, so they enjoy the freedom to major in French. Once they have children, the labyrinthine processes of negotiation we have explored in this book guarantee that they'll get what they want, and then some.

As a practical matter, what evidence do we have that high income alone helps a woman lever her husband into housework? Meticulous studies using data from 1974 and 1975 showed that husbands of relatively high-earning wives did more laundry, dish washing, and cleaning than other husbands (Hill and Juster, 1985). However, the sex of each partner, other things equal, also had an impact on who did what housework. Since attitudes toward housework have loosened since the mid-1970s (that is, the focal point has been greased just a little), we need more careful research of this sort using recent data. (Interviews of nonrandom samples of couples, such as those gathered together by Arlie Hochschild in *The Second Shift* [1989], are valuable, but can't substitute for time-diary studies of nationally representative samples of households.)

Of course, predicting the future earnings of a French major or a geologist is an imperfect art. The fruits of any given education can be surprising. That point came home to me vividly as I was interviewing couples about their housework and child care arrangements for this book. Several couples consisted of a female nurse married to a male plumber or carpenter. During the late 1980s and early 1990s, the pay of nurses rose dramatically, but pay in the trades and the construction industry shriveled because of the recession. Both of those changes were unexpected. The nurses I interviewed had gone to nursing school expecting to be supported by their future husbands. Later they discovered that they were outearning their husbands.

Some of those husbands were at home full-time. One told me, "What with the price of child care, it doesn't make sense for me to work. So I'm taking care of the kids."

But experience, anecdotal evidence, and such books as *The Second Shift* make it glaringly obvious that even a woman who gets an advanced degree in jet-engine design can't be sure that her husband will cheerfully contribute lots of time to housework and child care. That is, training up is *necessary* to increase a woman's bargaining power, but it may not be *sufficient* to create a nontraditional allocation of housework. All the other elements of negotiating that we have learned about clank into action. Overlooking those other elements was what made a mess of Gloria's newfangled plans.

Our hypothetical, egalitarian Gloria is not the only one who made that mistake. In a survey of 902 women who graduated from Harvard University's medical, law, and business schools from 1971 to 1981, nearly all of whom had had at least one child, 70 percent said they had reduced their hours of paying work because of their children. Over half said they had changed jobs or specialties to accommodate their child care responsibilities. Almost 40 percent said that parenting had slowed their career advancement. Only one was married to a househusband (Swiss and Walker, 1993).

The researchers found it scandalous that those highly educated women had had to make such sacrifices in their careers. To me the most fascinating aspect of the study was that the authors didn't ask any questions about husbands or other romantic partners. What sort of work did *they* do? What were *their* incomes? When the authors asked the women what would have made it easier for them to combine career and parenting responsibilities, most wrote "a more supportive husband" (p. 180).

One California lawyer who left the partnership track for a shorter work-week said that her husband "just knew that he would never help much with child care" (p. 65).

What the researchers overlooked, and what the 902 women surveyed overlooked, is the same thing that Gloria overlooked. What you study isn't the only thing that determines who does what work in your home. Whom you marry does, too.

Marrying Up and Marrying Down

If you were to read the following passage from *Émile* to a roomful of teenagers or college students, you'd get a roomful of giggles:

> It also makes a great difference for the good order of the marriage whether the man makes an alliance above or below himself. The former one is entirely contrary to reason; the latter is more conformable to it. . . . [W]hen the man allies himself with a woman above him . . . then the woman pretends to authority, acts as a tyrant toward the head of the house, and the master becomes a slave and finds himself the most ridiculous and most miserable of creatures.

Most young people don't think they believe that sort of thing anymore. However, if Rousseau had a chance to inspect the spouses most of them wind up picking, he'd approve. Today's young people are caught between believing and disbelieving, between the old way and a new way.

THE RULE OF AVERAGES

I noted earlier that most women marry men who are like them in certain ways. Most wives and husbands have similar cognitive test scores, levels of schooling, race, wealth, religion, ethnic origin, and so on (Becker, 1991). There is one important way in which wives and husbands are usually different, however. Husbands make more money. There are several reasons for that difference.

One is that, in general, men make more money than women. The same process explains why most husbands are taller than their wives. We might call it the rule of averages. When the average twenty-five-year-old woman earns less than the average twenty-five-year-old man, we expect to see the average *married* twenty-five-year-old woman earning less than the average married twenty-five-year-old man.

There is more to it than that, though. Women looking for a husband make decisions that exacerbate the underlying difference in average earnings between women and men. Those decisions widen the gap in earnings between themselves and their husbands and make their bargaining power in their marriages that much weaker.

THE AGE GAP

One of those exacerbating factors is the age gap. In most first marriages, the grooms are older than the brides. This pattern is especially strong in traditional societies. For example, the parents of Ning Lao T'ai-t'ai, a girl born in China in about 1867, sent her into an arranged marriage when she was thirteen years old to a man who was twenty-seven years old. Lao T'ai-t'ai got to visit her mother once a month. Both she and her mother struggled not to cry when their visit ended (Pruitt, 1945).

Fourteen years is a very big age gap. Nowadays, in modern countries, that big a gap is rare. Grooms are usually only two or three years older than brides (Cherlin, 1993).

Even a two- or three-year age difference can have a big effect, though. Other things equal, a spouse who is two or three years older will earn more than the other, just because he is two or three years ahead of her on the salary ladder. The spaces between the rungs are even larger for many people during their twenties than, say, their forties, because the earnings of young workers grow much faster from year to year than those of older, more experienced workers (Mortensen, 1988). That means that during the years when the typical couple is having their first child, the husband may earn *significantly* more than the wife just because he is two or three years older. The age gap, then, is an important part of husbands' advantage in earnings over their wives. That means the age gap is also an important part of their advantage in bargaining power.

Why do women marry older men? Or, put the other way, why do men marry younger women? Psychologists, biologists, historians, and economists all give partial explanations. Here is one story. (See if you can guess which sort of person came up with it.)

In the olden days, most young women wanted to get married. Same with young men. Since young men and young women did different things after marriage, they competed for desirable partners in different ways. The young women worked to perfect their homemaking skills: cooking, sewing, running a house and vegetable garden, tending chickens. The young men worked to get the training and credentials they needed to earn cash in the money economy. They took apprenticeships (in colonial America) or took exams (in imperial China). Young women finished learning nearly all they could about homemaking without actually having a house of their own at an early age, say, seventeen or eighteen. Young men, however, might not finish mastering a skill or might not pass an exam, and so distinguish themselves from their rivals, until they were twenty or twenty-one. Ergo, young men who were ready to marry were older than young women who were ready to marry (Becker, 1991; if you guessed "economist," you were right).

Another way of putting this is that women looking for a husband were balancing men's earnings potential against their other attractions. Earnings grow with age. Most of men's other attractions stay the same or dim with age. A man looking for a wife was assessing women's skills, physical attractiveness, fertility, personalities, and so forth. None of the assets women brought to a traditional marriage grew with age. Instead, their fertility and physical attractiveness diminished. I noted these facts in the discussion of the beauty problem earlier. Here, they illuminate something closely related. In a traditional world, because earnings power and actual earnings rose with time (because, or where, men did nearly all the earning), when desirable grooms and desirable brides married, the grooms were several years older than the brides.

It is also true that a man who is three years older than his wife seems wiser than she is. He should, because three years is a big percentage of 18. He has, in fact, 16 percent more experience in the world than she has. Therefore, when men marry down in age and women marry up, everyone is behaving consistently with the belief that men should lead their families.

This sort of thing can make you scratch your head. Which came first, older grooms or male headship of families? Cultural anthropologists generally shy away from puzzling out causality. Instead, they look for congruences and contradictions (Geertz, 1973). This congruence is certainly neat. Some research suggests, as you might expect, that age gaps between brides and grooms vary quite a bit across cultures. The gaps are smaller where women's status is closer to men's.

For example, in the United States during the twentieth century, the age gap has shrunk a lot. In 1900, in first marriages for both, the average groom was 4 years older than his bride. Now, the difference is 2.2 years. What's more, many more women are marrying younger men. In 1970, in first marriages for both, only 12 percent of brides were older than grooms. By 1988, 20 percent were (Cherlin, 1993).

Is Americans' behavior changing because women are getting more schooling to prepare for work outside the home? Is it changing mainly because fewer women feel they need a man who is "older and wiser"?[1] So far, there is no way to tell. However, we do know that the reduction in the age gap probably improves the bargaining power of the average married woman. When roughly 50 percent of brides are older than their grooms, and when the average age gap is zero, then we'll know that young men and young women have really made it out of this confusing transition and into a new conception of marriage.[2]

HIGH-EARNING WOMEN

We now understand two components of the earnings gap between husbands and wives. First, on average, men earn more than women. Second, women marry up in age.

There is a third component, which we see in the marriages of highly educated young people. Among people with two or three years of graduate school, the men tend to marry women who earn less than they do, but the women manage somehow to marry men who earn even more than they do. Consider, for example, people who graduated from Stanford University's MBA program between 1973 and 1985. In 1987, the average married male

MBA earned $144,461 and the average married female MBA earned $101,204. That difference in earnings is striking, but much more striking is the difference in the earnings of the MBAs' spouses. The average *husband* of a female MBA earned $120,124, while the average employed *wife* of a male MBA earned only $30,323 (Harrell, 1993b).

What does that mean? It is a little hard to tell for sure, unfortunately, because that study did not distinguish between people who were employed full-time and those who were employed part-time. The male MBAs' spouses, then, could have had low earnings because they trained for low-paying fields, because they trained for high-paying fields but then entered low-paying jobs, such as public-interest law, or because they were working part-time.

I suspect that, in fact, the male MBAs married women with much lower earnings potential than theirs. I suspect that because we have a good idea of how married women with the exact same earnings potential as the male MBAs behave: the married women MBAs make over $100,000.

So, high-earning men marry low-earning women. High-earning women marry men who earn as much or even more than they do. Why? Is there an Iron Law of Marrying Up that women can't escape, no matter how sparkling their diplomas and paychecks might be?

I don't think so. I think we can account for this oddity and that no iron law of anything is at work. First, the rule of averages helps high-earning men marry down in earnings, but it makes it hard for high-earning women to. Remember that most men try to earn as much money as they possibly can. A lot of women, on the other hand, do *not* earn as much as they possibly can. That means that when a high-earning man looks out at the pool of women who are like him, socioeconomically and otherwise, and whom, therefore, he is likely to marry, he sees a lot of appealing women who earn less than he does. The high-earning woman, on the other hand, sees all those high-earning men staring back at her. We could call this a pool problem. Most of the guys in the pool are big fish. The women come in all sizes—from blue whales to minnows.

For high-earning women to marry down in earnings, then, they face two options. They can keep their heart open to the possibility of finding an unconventional man (or woman), such as a public-interest lawyer, musician, or artist. That's what Amy did, when she fell in love with Dave. Or they can consider marrying someone from a less privileged background. Because women are more likely to meet men who are like them, socioeconomically and otherwise, than people who are different, most high-earning women wind up marrying men like them who have maximized their incomes.

What if most men don't want to marry up in earnings? Unfortunately, I don't know of any reliable studies or surveys that have pinned down information on this tricky subject. We have all heard anecdotes, of course, suggesting that some men would rather not marry a woman who earns more than they do. I heard once about an attractive, kind, and lively woman who grew up in Kansas and got a nursing degree. Several years later she went to Yale Law School and went back to Kansas to practice law. She says now that she can't find any men who will consider her seriously as a romantic partner. She had much better luck as a nurse than she has as a Yale law graduate. (Let's note, however, in qualifying this story as objectively as we can, that she went back to Kansas three years older. Age still hurts women.)

The *Wall Street Journal* has also gathered up anecdotes of this sort. For an article entitled "A Wife's Higher Pay Can Test a Marriage" (Rigdon, 1993), the reporter interviewed a psychologist who said that many men "can't tolerate the ego diminution of a wife who's more powerful than he is." It's possible, though, that the article, and the assignment in the first place, may reflect the anxieties of the *Journal*'s older male editors more accurately than the attitudes of today's young men.

Are most women reluctant to marry down in earnings? Maybe even high-earning women would rather not marry a man who earns less than they do. Those women earn enough to support a family of four single-handedly in upper-middle-class comfort, but maybe they'd rather not.

For one thing, part of a man's attractiveness, conventionally, is his social status. Part of his social status, conventionally, is how much money he has or earns. Thinking along those lines, or *feeling* along those lines, might lead some high-earning women to pass up men with medium or low incomes.

For another thing, marrying a man with a high salary is like buying insurance. Many young professional women are not sure, in their mid-twenties, exactly what they will do when they have their first baby. They are very devoted to their work, but acknowledge the possibility that they may want to reduce their hours for a while to enjoy and take care of their babies. If they marry high-earning men, they keep open the option of reducing their work hours without running the risk of having to cut back to a merely middle-class style of living. They're covered. In contrast, few young professional men admit to mixed feelings, or uncertainty, of that sort. They benefit, of course, when they marry a high-earning woman. But the main benefit they expect is extra disposable income. They aren't thinking about insurance against wanting to stay home with their babies.

We do have good evidence that high-powered women handle parenthood very differently from high-powered men. One study of Stanford's MBA class of 1982, done in 1992, found that most of the graduates had children. Thirty-four percent of the women MBAs were self-employed or working part-time and 19 percent were not employed at all. Among the men, only 16 percent were self-employed, roughly 1 percent worked part-time, and only 1 percent were not employed. Sixty-four percent of the women said they had made a career change for "lifestyle reasons," but only 26 percent of the men said that they had (Kaufman Associates, 1992).

If those women suspected in the early 1980s that there was even only a 20 percent chance that they would want to reduce their work effort that much in 1992, it would have made sense for them to marry across or up (if they wanted a very high and secure family income). Unfortunately, we can't be sure that insurance-seeking explains their behavior. Maybe they found their jobs much less tolerable than the men did. (For one thing, 48 percent of them said they had been sexually harassed—as they defined it—at work, as opposed to only 5 percent of the men.) Or maybe they were like Gloria and expected to share child raising with their husbands, but just got bushwhacked by their husbands' bargaining power, tipping, and so on.

The bottom line is that those MBA women were primary parents and that their careers suffered for it. Their travel duties at work make that plain. Among graduates who worked at least forty hours a week, 42 percent of the men were away from home five or more nights a month, but only 24 percent of the women were. Thirty-three percent of the women were never away from home overnight for work, compared with 8 percent of the men. That's a big difference.

One female Stanford MBA who has two children said, "Travel is a women's issue. I just won't take a job with a lot of travel" (Zich, 1993, p. 21). What she meant was that travel is a primary parent's issue.

The Stanford data show that *if* MBAs and other high-flying women marry across or up because, on an emotional level, they'd like insurance, they are buying a policy that is loaded against them in ways they probably overlook. Most of them are buying a guarantee that they will be the parent who gives extra time to the child and who manages child care. They are buying a guarantee that their career will slow down, and slow down a lot if they eschew long hours and travel. Those hidden clauses explain, in part, why the Stanford MBA men in 1987 made almost 50 percent more than the women.

Something else might make high-earning women reluctant to marry men who earn less than they do. I suspect that many hard-driving women believe so strongly in the value of hard work in a challenging field that a man who takes a more relaxed approach may seem second-rate. A man who earns very little, because he is a community organizer or struggling writer, may even seem lazy or suspect. For example, in one study of how sixty-three women made decisions about their careers and their marriages, most women said they were not interested in marrying a househusband. The women who were very devoted to their paying work wanted a man who was, too (Gerson, 1985). This sample was by no means nationally representative. We don't know how many ambitious women feel that way. We do know that women who feel that way are unlikely to marry down.

I suspect that part of the reason many women may want a man with a turbo-charged work ethic is that American women are growing up in such a strange time of transition. Young professional women see very little variety in how young parents are handling the work of parenting. If they had female aunts, cousins, and professors whose husbands were primary parents, they might realize, emotionally, that that arrangement could work for them, too. They wouldn't look for insurance. Also, the very ambitious young women who wind up in professional schools or in graduate schools in technical fields today must still spend years breaking stereotypes and fending off discrimination. They've mobilized so much psychological energy to defend this choice to themselves and to others that it may be hard for them to cherish as a lover a man who has made a very different choice. In the future, when their younger sisters and daughters don't have to grit their teeth, many more may fall in love with men like Dave, or with men who aspire to be househusbands and stay-at-home fathers.

One more hitch could, I think, make high-earning women reluctant to marry men with lower earnings. A woman who marries far down in earnings is, all of a sudden, the main breadwinner in her family. Having sole responsibility for clothing, feeding, schooling, and otherwise provisioning—*come what may*—one or two or three children and another adult can be a scary and foreign proposition to most women.

David Gilmore, in his brilliant and sensitive book *Manhood in the Making* (1990), sketches out how adults train boys to equate their self-worth with their willingness to provide for their families. In many traditional societies, boys learn that their very right to call themselves "men" will hinge on the zeal with which they throw themselves into the harsh and frightening battle for subsistence. The typical man endures the combat of breadwinning, "standing between his family and destruction, absorbing the blows of fate with equanimity" (p. 48), not because he is naturally brave or noble but because everyone he knows despises shirkers. The alternative is gruesome social and psychological punishment, such as being "robbed of [his] identity" (p. 221).

That system of training and punishment is breaking down in the United States. Millions of men seem to have fled their traditional duty to provide for their children and the mothers of their children. However, new training is not being given to women. Parents, ministers, teachers, and video games do not teach girls that their very right to call themselves "women" or "human beings" hinges on the zeal with which they throw themselves into breadwinning.

The result is that we're stuck betwixt and between. Even high-earning women don't happily contemplate the possibility of marrying a man who has low earnings. Because they don't, the negotiating dynamics in their families make it hard for men to discover a new way of building up their families: tenderly, bravely, and imaginatively raising their children.

None of the things I've discussed here amounts to an Iron Law of Marrying Up. As noted in chapter 1, the earnings gap between young men and women is narrowing. It has disappeared entirely among young people who are college-educated and white. The age gap is also narrowing. The remaining interesting question is this: Will the average ambitious, hard-driving young woman begin to look for the same things in her romantic partner that the average ambitious, hard-driving young man does?

When I ponder that one, I sometimes think back to law school in the early 1980s. My class was graced with many young men from Texas, who banded together for Lone Star beers, barbecued ribs, and, I'm sure, philosophical talks in a group they called the Armadillo Club. At that time, a woman's college stood a few doors down the street from the law school. It was a good school, but the average SAT scores of the students there were lower than the average scores of students at the law school. The Armadillos threw parties to which they invited only women from that college. The women wore long gowns, special hairdos, makeup, and high heels. The Armadillos wore business suits.

One night, a woman on the steps of the student union caught my attention. She stood in a long gown with her hair piled high. She was feigning composure, but she kept tightly clasping and unclasping her hands. For her, something was at stake.

Why did the Armadillos throw those parties? Partly, they may have been looking for, shall we say, very short-term relationships. Partly, though, I'd say the Armadillos were looking for women whose notion of marriage was compatible with theirs. They were looking for a wife who would be a mother, homemaker, and helpmeet first, and a paid employee outside the home second. They knew that that wasn't the destination of their female law classmates.

Did women students at the law school throw parties for male students from good but not stellar local colleges? Not that I ever heard.

What if they had? What if they had leaped a leap of imagination, collected excellent stereo gear, lots of great music, and worked hard to advertise an outstanding party? A few women might have started lasting relationships with kind, funny, companionable young men. Years later, the women's high salary and bargaining power might have convinced their husbands to stay home for a few or many years to raise their children.

I suspect that there is more play and looseness in the world of dating—if you'll forgive that anachronistic usage—than many women are taking advantage of. But it's up to women to take the first step. When they do, we'll know that they have made their way through the transition and into the future.

Other Decisions Women Make Before Having a Baby

In the hypothetical marriages examined in part II, the women did many things that affected their future bargaining power. Here we will very briefly review some of those other opportunities.

Some women try to maximize their incomes, but some do not. Gloria and Amy both tried to maximize their incomes, but Alice and Laura did not. Even though more women are going into high-paying business and scientific fields now, they still outnumber men in the low-wage helping professions. For example, I went to law school but then took a job in legal services. I worked for poor people, and a combination of federal and charitable funds paid my salary. In 1984, I started at $19,000. My classmates who went to Wall Street started at $70,000 and above. I did the right thing for me; I was idealistic. However, it's no coincidence that women are overrepresented among legal services lawyers. Partly it's because many of us feel less pressure to be breadwinners than our male classmates do.[3] Our marriageability doesn't depend on it.

I'm all for idealism. One of my hopes for the future is that men will feel freer to be moral on the job. The main way to make that happen, of course, is to make it easier, practically and psychologically, for men to marry up in earnings. I'll concede, though, that being a do-gooder is expensive. One study at Cornell, for example, found that even after controlling for gender, grade point average, and courses taken, recent graduates working at for-profit firms earned roughly 59 percent more than graduates working at nonprofit firms (Frank, n.d.).

High pay doesn't only require training up, taking a job in a for-profit company, and working long hours. It may also require, every once in a while, asking for a raise. Anecdotes make me wonder if men might, on average, be more likely to ask for raises than women.

One female friend, for example, started work as a law professor in 1991. The other women who started as assistant professors at her school that year got the same salary she did, but the one man in their cohort got $5,000 more. Why? My friend learned that during his hiring interview, he asked pointedly whether there was any stipend, bonus, or other emolument they could offer him to boost his starting salary. There was. He got it.

It had never occurred to my friend to make such an aggressive request. She felt grateful to be considered for a teaching job and didn't feel entitled to ask for extra pay. Even now that she's heard of the ploy, she doubts whether she has the gall to use it next time around.[4]

If women on average feel less entitled to ask for extra pay (and we don't know that they do), it may be an example of the social exchange theory mentioned in the discussion in chapter 3 of the effects of male status. Men's experience can give them a feeling that their contribution is at least as valuable as and maybe more valuable than what other people are contributing.

We also need to keep in mind that for purposes of negotiating within the family, pay is not the only thing that matters about a job. A job that is very inflexible can create a commitment mechanism. We saw that process at work when Rob told Laura he had to work long hours in order to keep his job and when Amy told Dave she was an essential part of the team at her lab.

Some jobs are extremely inflexible. One of the stay-at-home fathers I interviewed, for example, had been a Navy SEAL. He had to exercise five hours a day, practice sneak attacks at night, and be ready to ship out to the

Arctic Ocean with no more warning than a phone call. Putting any time at all into baby care would have been very impractical. He left the navy after a twenty-year hitch and began taking college courses. His wife was a physical therapist in the navy when they had their first baby. At that point, her schedule was the relatively inflexible one. It made sense for him to be the primary parent.

Many jobs traditionally dominated by women offer part-time arrangements, a variety of shifts, a short week, or the ability to drop in and out easily. Think of substitute teachers, sales clerks, nurses, waitresses, or even self-employed consultants who work out of a home office. Flexibility is nice, but it makes it easier for your partner to bargain you into doing lots of unpaid work at home. Many women *switch into* a flexible job in anticipation of having a baby, to make life easier for themselves. They may not realize that the move *reduces* the amount of time their partner will probably contribute to child care and housework over the decades ahead, which makes life harder for them.

I mentioned earlier that women are overrepresented in helping and do-gooder jobs. The opposite of being idealistic is being materialistic. Materialism is good for a woman's bargaining power if it leads her to make lots of money, develop uncrackable commitment mechanisms, set impressive precedents, and so on. However, being nonmaterialistic can also create opportunities. If a woman earns an average or above-average income, doesn't want a posh style of living, *and* finds a partner who feels the same way, she is in luck. They will be able to pull time out of their paying work, devote it to their children, and still make the modest amount of money they aim to spend. Obviously, the higher their hourly wage, the more comfortable they can be.

One husband and wife I interviewed, for example, share a job entering data into a computer at a music library. Each works for pay twenty-four hours a week and spends the off-hours with their two children. They don't need to hire any child care. Poor and working-class people don't have the option of cutting back on their hours of pay work. They are struggling just to get by. However, many middle-class people and most upper-income people do have that option.[5]

Women who set their spending targets low and find a partner who agrees that family life is a high priority will find, then, that they are rich in *time*. They have time to invent all sorts of arrangements, trade-offs, and new ideas to make themselves, their partners, and their children happier.

Of course, the lower a woman's spending target, the more willing she is to marry down in earnings. That flexibility made it possible for Amy to follow her heart when she fell in love with Dave.

Amy had a lot of other things going in her favor as she negotiated with Dave. One was that she did not passionately crave a baby. Her lukewarm feelings toward motherhood helped protect her devotion to her career. Dave did passionately crave children; he had to give in on some issues to get Amy to go along.

We learned at the beginning of this chapter that many more girls are like Dave than are like Amy. By the end of high school, more girls than boys say that having children is very important to them. The difference between boys and girls in intensity of desire for children may narrow in the years ahead. Even if it does, however, we'll still be left with another important difference. Men can conceive a baby much later in life than women can. In the future, scientists may tinker their way around that difference. Until then, a woman who wants a baby faces a much higher cost of waiting than her male partner does. Relative to him, she is impatient. That impatience may hurt her bargaining power. Concretely, she may have to give up something to persuade him to have the baby when it is best, medically speaking, for her to conceive. Moreover, that time may interfere with her paying work more than his paying work.[6]

There is no way for women to make that disadvantage disappear in the short run. It does help reinforce the traditional sexual division of labor. Women can make it matter less, though, if they boost their bargaining power in the other ways described in this book.

One particular choice that women make when they marry has fascinated me for a long time: what they do about their last name. Traditionally, in Europe and the United States, a wife dropped her last name and became "Mrs. John Q. Husband." Nowadays, some women decline to change their names. That refusal can come as a blow—small but perceptible—to the average guy.

That point was made vivid in the 1988 movie *Die Hard,* in which Bruce Willis plays John McClane, a New York City cop visiting his estranged wife in Los Angeles. We learn early in the movie that when they got married, she didn't change her name, and that he didn't like it. He happens to be inside the building where his wife works when brutal thieves take it over. Single-handedly—enduring gunfire, fistfights, lacerated feet, and exhaustion—he defeats the bad guys. His wife falls in love with him again. At the end, she introduces herself to an L.A. cop as "Holly McClane." She changes her name.

That scene tells us a lot about the symbolism of last names right now. The cop's wife is acknowledging that he excelled in the traditional manly virtues: cunning, strength, persistence, and risk-taking in battle. The least she can do is give him the traditional recognition. Nor does he seem to want more; he'll treat her as an equal as long as she gives him the respect that he deserves as a *man*.

Because some people are challenging that definition of manhood, and men's exclusive claims to those character traits, they are also changing their views about last names. A woman who keeps her last name, in spite of pressure from her fiancé and relatives, is setting a valuable precedent. It may help her bargaining power.

So much is obvious. What really fascinates me, though, is the question of *babies'* last names. In the vast majority of cases in which the wife keeps her last name, the children still get the husband's last name. Some women make that choice because they think it will increase their husband's feeling of attachment to the children. They see the name as a way to counteract the headstart effect. Mainly, though, most women never think of proposing a different last name. The focal point of this tradition is very strong.

What if Amy had proposed that Clara get a last name other than Dave's? There are two possibilities: Dave might have gone along or not. If he had resisted, because he really wanted the baby to have his last name, he might have had to give up something to Amy to persuade her to follow tradition. He might have given up something surprisingly juicy. Laboratory studies and surveys consistently find that people pay a much higher price to keep something they already have—such as a traditional prerogative—than to acquire the identical thing when they don't already have it—such as a privilege that tradition does not award to them (Kahneman and Tversky, 1979).

A couple who makes a nontraditional choice has also set a distinctive precedent. Every time they say their baby's last name, a bell rings. Every time they explain the baby's name to someone else, they implicitly defend their choice. Over time, the decision seems righter and righter, and less and less radical. The precedent bends their feelings, expectations, and shared experience into a new shape. That new shape may help them defend a nontraditional focal point, such as a nontraditional division of labor in their home.

Children and Housework

The family is a school of despotism, in which the virtues of despotism, but also its vices, are largely nourished.

—John Stuart Mill, *On the Subjection of Women*

In most discussions of work, children get left out. But what children do and don't do at home when they are young influences what they'll know and not know, and like and dislike, when they are adults and live on their own. Their early experience shapes the focal point that will seem most conspicuous to them later.

Like educational and marital patterns, the work that children do at home is in a state of transition. Modern gadgets and new attitudes have freed most kids in the United States from the early risings and daylong toil that nineteenth-century farm children endured. However, parents don't seem to be teaching both their girls and boys how to handle all the modern gadgets or teaching them new attitudes toward housework. Girls and boys do fewer hours, and a lower share, of housework than ever before. Most parents still teach their daughters only the skills traditionally needed by women and their sons only the skills traditionally needed by men. The result is that nowadays most young people in the United States leave home with only stereotypical training, and with only a very low level of it, at that.

For example, one study that looked at the chores a nationally representative sample of 5,000 people did at home found that how much housework children did depended heavily on their age and sex. Housework was defined as including cooking, cleaning, laundry, washing dishes, buying groceries, yard work, and paperwork. Mothers reported that their children did a lot of dishes and cleaning; a little laundry, cooking, and yard work; and very little of the other chores. Teenage girls did more housework than other children. In fact, parents with a teenage girl shared *five times* more of the traditionally female tasks with children than parents with a teenage boy did. Teenage girls did roughly three-quarters of the dish washing and laundry, and substantial amounts of cooking and cleaning. Teenage boys did more housework than younger children, but only because they did more yard work (Goldscheider and Waite, 1991).[7]

As children got older, their housework contributions diverged even more. Daughters over age eighteen who were still living at home began to buy groceries, do more laundry, and take more responsibility for the care of younger children. Sons over eighteen who were still living at home *reduced* the amount of housework they did. They did less than children ages six to twelve. They even stopped doing yard work and home repair. They were in some cases working outside the home for pay. However, most of the evidence from other sources shows that such sons rarely contribute any of their earnings to the family pool of income (see Goldscheider and Waite, 1991, p. 148). It seems that in the 1980s, parents subsidized their young adult sons, but relied heavily on the household labor of their young adult daughters.

Research studies don't tell us directly what sort of historical changes have taken place in children's housework responsibilities, but they do give us some good clues. In the national surveys that covered 5,000 people, rural children did more household work than urban ones. Children living in the smallest towns did 18 percent more than children in the biggest cities (Goldscheider and Waite, p. 162). Children of less educated mothers did more than children of highly educated mothers. A mother's employment status did not have any impact at all on the amount of housework that her children did.

Those patterns suggest that over time, as mothers have gotten more schooling and more families have moved to big cities and their suburbs, children's share of housework has fallen.[8] What has caused this change? Nobody knows for sure. It's possible that more parents may want their kids to get good grades than to learn how to bake a pie. Pies won't get them into college.

I suspect that one reason parents are asking less housework from their children is that the status of homemaking has fallen over the past four decades. The fact that more mothers in general are working for pay outside the home has changed everybody's (or lots of people's) attitudes toward housework.

In another compartment of our minds, though, we *know* that homemaking is valuable. All those small good deeds—fresh-smelling clothes, silk flowers in a bud vase on the table, a good dinner—make an apartment someplace deeply soul-cheering to come home to.

The good news is that not everyone is being brought up to be a housework ignoramus. This fact is one of the most intriguing, and least appreciated, features of the transition we are now living through. According to the national survey just mentioned, in one large set of American families children do *twice* as much housework as average children. Their girls do lots of yard work and home repair. Their boys do significant amounts of cooking, cleaning, and grocery shopping. The boys even do plenty of child care.

Who are those young people? They are growing up in one-parent families headed by women.

Single mothers are strikingly nontraditional in how they assign housework. Their teenage sons actually do more chores than teenage *girls* do in two-parent families. The differences between mother-only families and two-parent families do not seem to be correlated with the mother's hours of work or her income. Nor do they hinge on race; black and nonblack single mothers make similar demands on their children (Goldscheider and Waite, p. 161).

No one knows for sure why single-mother families are different. Some researchers speculate that single parents may form a different kind of relationship with their children than couples do. Their relationship is like a partnership (Weiss, 1979). Another way of saying this is that single women may find it more urgent, or easier, or both, to negotiate for a partnership in homemaking with their children than with a male partner. After all, a young son has much less bargaining power relative to his mother than a typical male adult has relative to his girlfriend or wife.

The experience of single-mother families suggests several things. First, one result of higher rates of divorce and of childbearing outside marriage—combined with custody by women—may be that more children, especially boys, learn how to run a house. That is an unexpected social benefit of a privately difficult situation.

Second, their experience shows that it can't be all that hard—psychologically, practically, or otherwise—to get boys and girls to do nontraditional household tasks and lots of them. Millions of single American mothers are doing it every day. That means the sexual division of labor *among children* is much more malleable than we might have thought. Politicians, professors, and newspaper editors make a lot of critical comments about single mothers. Yet, on their own and almost unnoticed, single mothers and their children have achieved a breakthrough.

Finally, single-mother families give us a periscope to peer into the future. After years of doing traditionally male chores (and watching their mothers scrimp), their daughters are much more likely than other young women to enter traditionally male jobs, with higher pay and more chance for advancement (Waite and Berryman, 1985).

What if a young woman from a single-mother family, such as Amy, fell in love with a young man from a single-mother family, such as Dave? Neither would have grown up with traditional notions about housework. In their houses, girls used screwdrivers and boys sorted laundry. In other words, neither would have grown up under the befogging spell of the traditional focal point. They might find it easier than other young people to talk about housework in terms of their real needs: their budget, their time, and what was best for their family.

This reasoning suggests that in the short run, career-oriented women who are willing to be breadwinners should consider men like Dave: graduates of the Single-Mother, No Baloney, Egalitarian Housework Academy. It also suggests that the long run—a future without a sexual division of labor in the home—might be closer than we think.

Religion

Wives, submit yourselves unto your own husbands, as unto the Lord.

—Paul, in a letter to Christians in the city of Ephesus, Asia Minor, where Turkey is today; Ephesians 5:22

Nevertheless let every one of you in particular so love his wife even as himself.

—Ephesians 5:33

In 1991, I went to the wedding of two friends of mine, a woman from a French Catholic family and a man from a Greek Orthodox family. Both were professors at colleges in the northeast. The presiding priest was an old friend of the groom's family. The wedding itself was a traditional Greek Orthodox ceremony, with lots of marching around the altar, modified by the groom and bride to include vows they had written themselves. Partway through the ceremony, the priest addressed the congregation. He concluded by describing the essence of marriage. "The wife is the handservant of her husband, just as the Church is the handservant of Christ."

I couldn't believe it. Had John imported this fossil just to say those words? Had Anne had any clue that this lesson would be the centerpiece of her wedding? If I had been Anne, I would already have shot six degrees past apoplexy. Yet, up there on the altar, she looked unruffled.

In the receiving line, I said, "Whoa! Anne! Did you know that was coming?"

She laughed in a relaxed way. "No, no. We'll have to have a talk about it." She tilted her head toward John.

I marveled. Clearly, Anne was very secure. She understood that the point of the day was for people to enjoy themselves. Minor questions of Biblical interpretation could wait until later.

Secular people are used to thinking of religion as a conservative force. But it's also true that throughout history and all over the world, social reformers have used religious language. Think of the activists in the anti-slavery movement, the labor and civil rights movements, and human rights organizations.

The impact of the faithful on the political and economic status of women is much too sprawling a topic to cover here. I will note briefly only two things. First, religious training helps shape people's view of the world in fundamental ways, including their feelings about the proper place of men and women in the world. Second, teachers and believers of traditional religions are now living through an extraordinary period of debate and flux. Moreover, new sects, doctrines, and cults are springing up in rich and poor countries alike. Some traditional attitudes, strengthened by religious teachings, reinforce the sexual division of labor. Certain new religious ideas, however, are propelling us into an entirely different future. To see this, we are going to look at three snapshots. Each snapshot catches a different, traditional American religious group teetering on the brink of something bold and new.

We'll start with evangelical Protestants. Evangelicals' political views are only slightly more conservative than Americans' views in general. They believe in the authority of the Bible as a guide to everyday life. They also believe in the overarching importance of a personal relationship with Jesus. Most begin that relationship with a remarkable, intense experience: they get born again (Stacey and Gerard, 1990).

What many nonevangelicals don't know is that evangelical women have started feminist periodicals, churches, and study groups. They have worked hard to reinterpret Paul's infamous dictum on wifely submission. They have come up with a doctrine of mutual submission: "The Christlike husband takes upon himself the form of a servant, humbles himself, and dies to himself by living for the best interests of his family. He loves his wife as he loves his own body, because he and his wife are one flesh" (Stacey and Gerard, 1990, p. 102).

Even more remarkable is the wide diffusion of feminist ideas among evangelicals who don't consider themselves feminists. Surveys done at evangelical colleges and seminaries in the 1980s found that most students thought sensitive, gentle men and strong, assertive women were as attractive as stereotypical men and women. They cherished family life so highly that they valued men's participation in the care of young children *even more highly* than did young people who weren't religious. In fact, in one study, 98 percent of evangelical students said that both fathers and mothers should take care of their small children (Stacey and Gerard, 1990).

Of course, most evangelicals are conservative on sexual issues, such as abortion, premarital sex, and homosexuality. That also makes them different from most self-identified American feminists. Still, the changes taking place inside this intensely religious crowd are remarkable: a head-on challenge to male domination in the family, openness to new ways of being a man and being a woman, and advocacy of men's ability and responsibility to care for babies and toddlers.

Here is our second snapshot. Many people who hear "conservative" and "religious" in the same sentence hop instantly in their minds to "Roman Catholic." Catholic doctrine takes an absolutist stance against abortion, modern methods of contraception, and marriages between people of the same sex.

However, what church officials teach and what American lay Catholics feel are two different things. This news comes in part from Andrew Greeley (1990), a priest and sociologist. He has analyzed data from the General Social Survey (GSS), which regularly interviews tens of thousands of Americans in nationally representative samples. Greeley has written that American Catholics tend to believe that God is close by and mingled in the people, events, and social institutions all around us. Protestants, in contrast, are more likely to feel that the world is contaminated and sinful, because God is far away. That difference in religious imagery has peculiar ramifications.

In the GSS, for example, Catholic men express opinions that are much more feminist than those of the average American man. Moreover, Catholic men who say they feel "very close" to God have even stronger feminist opinions than other Catholic men. They are the only men for whom feeling very close to God is correlated with increased feminism (Greeley, 1990, p. 239).

Catholics were also more likely than other people to feel a connection between "a passionate relationship with their spouse and a passionate relationship with God" (p. 183). Ninety-two percent of self-reportedly strong Catholics who say that intense sex has strengthened their religious faith also say that their marriage is very happy. As we all know, the official church does not preach that sexual pleasure, sacred experience, and happiness in marriage are all tied together. Yet many lay Catholics in the United States feel that it is so. Protestants in the GSS, in contrast, don't show any link between sex, faith, and happy marriages.

Finally, in a study done in the early 1980s of a large, nationally representative sample of young Catholics, Greeley and his colleagues asked questions about Mary, the mother of Jesus (Fee et al., 1981, cited in Greeley, 1990). Young people who thought that Mary was very warm, patient, comforting, and gentle were more likely to report a very good relationship with their mother as a child, a very good relationship with their spouse, and an excellent sexual life (confirmed by their spouses).

Veneration of Mary may seem musty, or even idolatrous, to non-Catholics. For many Catholics, however, her story seems to connect their memories of tender care from their mothers to their experience as married, sexual, giving adults *and* to their aspirations as parents. It connects parenting and sexuality and holiness. At some level, it suggests that God feels toward us the tender, passionate love that a mother feels for her baby.

Those ideas and feelings have little to do with official church teachings. Instead, they are the legacy—lively and still evolving—of centuries of Catholic familial and imaginative life. If Catholic men are more feminist than most and see hands-on parenting as holy, their religious values in and of themselves will not stand in the way of their becoming more intimately responsible for the care of their children.

American bishops are just beginning to catch up with their parishioners. In a recent pastoral message about family life, they said:

> For, unlike other relationships, marriage is a vowed covenant with unique dimensions. . . . True equality, understood as mutuality, is not measuring out tasks. . . . Mutuality is really about sharing power and exercising responsibility for something larger than ourselves. How household duties are distributed should follow from understanding what it takes to build a life together, as well as the individual skills and interests you bring to your common life. . . . Especially when both spouses are employed, household duties need to be shared. [National Conference of Catholic Bishops, 1993]

In our third snapshot, we will look at American Jews. In the late 1980s, the people who ranked highest on the GSS feminism scale were Jewish women (Greeley, 1990, p. 80). A disproportionate number of feminist leaders in the United States and in Europe grew up in Jewish families, including such luminaries as Emma Goldman and Betty Friedan.

Several recent books suggest that a disproportionate share of househus-bands and of men sharing child care with their wives are also Jewish.[9] That observation may be misleading, though, because women and men who are highly educated are overrepresented among the couples considered in pub-lished studies. Jews are more highly educated than the average American. That means their schooling, not their Jewishness, may explain why they turn up so frequently in studies of nontraditional families.[10]

How can we tell whether distinctively Jewish ideas and feelings—as opposed to merely modern ones—are impelling Jews toward feminism and toward hands-on fatherhood? One good place to look is among traditional Jews, also called Orthodox Jews, who follow religious law in all its details. In fact, Orthodox women and men across the country are questioning many traditional aspects of the religious courts, synagogue practice and prayers, halakhic education (education in religious law), the rabbinate, Jewish orga-nizations, and marriage and child rearing. They are scrutinizing those aspects of tradition that hurt women's dignity or inflict real injustice on them.

One example of this probing is Blu Greenberg's *On Women and Judaism* (1981). Greenberg loves tradition. She keeps kosher, tithes to charity, strictly observes the Sabbath (no working, writing, driving, or turning lights on or off), and is immersed in the study of classic Jewish texts. However, she pushes hard at nearly every point of tradition that non-Orthodox feminists have criticized. She finds halakhic reasons, which she carefully lays out, for traditional Jews to accept women rabbis, divorce from a nonconsenting hus-band, and women's participation in all aspects of prayer, study, ritual obser-vance, and synagogue practice.

She writes, "We once had imagined that women as executives and priests and men as househusbands and kindergarten teachers inevitably would become either masculinized, feminized, or neutered in the process. Not so" (p. 52). Also, "[t]hose few women who will choose the rabbinate, with its open-ended demands, it is hoped, will choose and be chosen by husbands willing to take up the family slack (as countless rebbetzins have done all these years)" (p. 54).

I suspect that what many observers describe as a traditional Jewish ideal of masculinity—gentle, emotionally open, learned, and family-oriented—may help many Jewish men feel that being a househusband is consistent with their own deepest goals for themselves. After all, in the European shtetls there was no heavy pressure on men to be breadwinners. It was more prestigious to be a religious scholar while your wife earned the family's income.[11] How many Jewish men carry in their marrow today memories of that permission to be economically dependent? It is hard to say. Certainly, strictly observant Jewish men who are househusbands are making that permission even more vivid.

Even Muslims—I should say, especially Muslims—are living through a period of confusing transition. Mainstream Muslims (that is, excluding members of the Nation of Islam) number 2 or 3 million in the United States. Many times that number live in Europe. As their incomes and confidence grow, they will become more influential in the rich countries. Their ideas and feelings about what constitutes a good life, and a good family life, will help shape the ideas and feelings of all of us. Of course, they will also shape the destiny of much of Asia and Africa.

Contrary to the atrocious stereotypes that are now commonplace in American movies and TV shows, traditional Sunni teachings emphasize the equality of women and men, including within the family.[12] Mohammed Arkoun, an Algerian-born scholar and professor emeritus at the Sorbonne, is critical of the closed minds and repressive regimes he sees throughout the Islamic world. He writes that ancient customs of kinship are what oppress women in many Muslim countries, and that those customs are not rooted in, or justified by, the revelation of the Koran (1993, p. 119). Young Muslim women in activist groups all over the world agree. As millions of Muslim girls begin the painful process of training up, thousands, then possibly millions, will have the opportunity to marry down. In Islam, too, a devout believer can be a househusband.[13]

It's clear, then, that believers of many traditional religions are lurching toward a new understanding of women's place in the world. Still, some Americans continue to cling to very conservative forms of religion and very old-fashioned forms of family life. They have not even crept close to the transition. Conspicuous among them are Amish people, Hasidic Jews, and Pueblo Indians. They live apart from other Americans. Hasids often work in all-Hasidic or all-Jewish firms and live in Hasidic neighborhoods. The Amish live in separate farming communities, but sell their crops to outsiders. Some Pueblo communities never let outsiders in at all, except to stand at a distance to watch certain celebrations. Members of all three groups have large families, don't pursue higher education, have low monetary incomes, watch very little television, eat and dress and talk distinctively, and couldn't care less what the rest of us do, so long as we let them be themselves. Their lives are intensely religious. Women do all the child care, and little else but.

Just the same, the integrity and durability of their way of life don't reveal any *intrinsic* bias in religion toward traditional sexual divisions of labor. Instead, they show that in the United States there is still room for people who choose to live in the eighteenth century. Three hundred years from now, they may still be with us (that is, with our descendants). More power to them. I hope that organic change from within, called forth by their own principles, leads to the liberation of their girls and women, and others who suffer in their communities. They, of course, may have different priorities.

I'd like to end this chapter with a reminder of how religion enters into negotiations within families. Religious teachings and images help build up people's focal points, the expectations they share with everyone around them about what arrangements make sense. Religion also affects how people talk. Family life is full of talk about what's right and what's fair. For most people, though, it is hard to separate moral language from religious language. They have the same roots.

Religious feelings expressed in moral language (or vice versa) bear directly on the sexual division of labor in the home. That's because the question "What do we do about child care?" brings us very quickly to the question "What is a good life?"

I hope not to sound overly instrumental, but I think that some women who try to persuade men to do more child care by talking *only* about time, fatigue, or paychecks, or make only inchoate statements about fairness, may be overlooking a valuable resource. Protestant men who put a very high value on family life, Catholic men who associate parenting and holiness, and Jewish men who had scholarly fathers who were economically dependent on their mothers may all be open to a style of persuasion that occurs to too few of their partners. A quotation or an allusion now and then may make all the difference. It would be idiotic—and untrue to ourselves—to abdicate religion to the right-wingers. Instead, it's time to see religion as a well of ethical teachings, poetry, and resonant feelings that can sustain our journey toward more fair and loving families. It is the oasis we carry with us.

8

Myths That Hold Us Back

In feminist circles it is often forgotten that masses of women in the United States still believe that men cannot parent effectively and should not even make the attempt.

—bell hooks, *Yearning*

OLD BELIEFS ABOUT WHAT MEN ARE NATURALLY GOOD AT AND about how their early training handicaps them influence many Americans, people in other rich countries, and millions of people in the developing world. Parents act on those beliefs when they make their daughters fold laundry while their sons watch TV. Teenagers act on those beliefs when boys take precalculus and girls take typing. Because of those beliefs, girls in many families grow up with skills that are different from boys. Girls know more about housework, but less about making money. Directly and indirectly, those beliefs help keep us mired in the sexual division of labor that we inherited from the Pleistocene.

This chapter will take a short detour from the economic and negotiating concepts I have concentrated on so far. We need to, to find a way across a chasm that has made many people conclude that the future I am envisioning—a future in which men do half the child care—is unattainable. After all, if men are natural knuckleheads when it comes to babies, as traditional Alice believed, then there is no point in marching down that path and into the chasm.

Luckily for us, the detour leads to a sturdy rope bridge that soars across the chasm, straight to the other side. Scientists call beliefs about what men are naturally good at and naturally clumsy at beliefs about *sex differences*. Psychologists, anthropologists, sociologists, biologists, physicians, and economists have done lots of research on sex differences. We are going to look at the best research that addresses our question: Do men have what it takes to take care of babies and children?

Cavemen Didn't Change Diapers

If men do have what it takes to raise children, why haven't they been doing it for hundreds of thousands of years? Why, instead, since the distant past, have women specialized in babies and men specialized in other things? Doesn't that pattern reveal a difference in our inner natures?

Some people do believe that ancient difference in responsibilities reveals a difference in the inner natures of men and women. However, it may not. It may tell us, instead, about the hardships our ancestors had to struggle against.

Consider, for example, how hunter-gatherer people lived before anyone invented farming.[1] From the start, we have to be cautious. We know very little about what our ancestors' social life was like 10,000 to 15,000 years ago. Our understanding of the social life of hunter-gatherers and simple agriculturalists is based on observations of people who live like that now ("now" being the eighteenth, nineteenth, and twentieth centuries). They may not be good representatives of life in the past.

With that caveat, researchers believe that our hunter-gatherer ancestors had high fertility rates (seven or eight pregnancies per woman), lived in small extended-family groups, and were nomadic or semi-nomadic. They had no domestic animals, except dogs. They walked a lot (see Diamond, 1991). That way of life imposes practical constraints.

If mothers weaned their babies early to reduce the amount of time they spent breastfeeding, it might have raised the infant mortality rate. The hunter-gatherers we know about today want lots of surviving children. Children support their elderly parents, protect them from enemies, perform ceremonies on their behalf, and give them love and comfort. In a regime where death rates are high, you need a high birth rate just to stay even. Moreover, if you're nervous about population increase by rivalrous neighbors, you may want to do *more* than stay even. (See Diamond, 1991, on the fear and frequency of warfare among traditional peoples of New Guinea.)

I repeat those well-known facts in order to answer one question about sexual divisions of labor that has troubled me for years: Why don't hunter-gatherers set up breastfeeding cooperatives? If they did, then pregnancy would be the only irreducibly female chore. For example, the co-op could consist of one nursing mother and one man. The nursing mother feeds her baby and another newborn, and helps the man take care of three weaned infants. That could free up four other mothers. Those women could return to hunting big, fierce animals, sprinting, camping overnight far away, and other tasks that aren't compatible with caring for a newborn. Such a system could make a sexual division of labor unnecessary. Each person in the group could freely choose what chores to do.

There doesn't seem to be any record of this kind of arrangement among very-low-technology people. Why not? A very small number of kinks, any one of which is enough to derail the co-op, accounts, I think, for its absence from the anthropological and historical records. Those kinks will help us understand sexual divisions of labor in general.

The biggest kink is that the typical hunter-gatherer social group is small. A sprinting-hunting-camping mother who has just given birth cannot count on the availability of another woman to nurse her newborn. If there are only one to four other adult women in the group, it *is* possible for all of them to be either unmarried, pregnant, nursing to capacity, or post-menopausal at any given time. If so, the newly delivered mother has to nurse her own baby. That means that for a while, she has to do chores that are compatible with nursing and baby care. If that risk is real, then it didn't make sense to invest time training her to do highly skilled, noncompatible tasks (hunting panthers) and leave her ignorant of skills compatible with baby care (weaving hammocks, trapping rabbits). That problem pushes the group toward adopting a sexual division of labor.

The other big kink is warfare. In times and places in which the group has to fight enemies, and the fighting is at all likely to be lethal or to have high stakes for the group, it makes sense to exclude from the ranks of warriors people who are pregnant. Low-tech military methods put a premium on using clubs and axes and being able to jump obstacles in the dark (see Diamond, 1991, on traditional technology of warfare in New Guinea). When the average woman spends over five years being pregnant, even rigorous training leaves her less attractive as a warrior than the average young man. Right there, we have the nucleus of a sexual division of labor.

Moreover, if certain personality traits make people more effective as warriors, the group may want to begin instilling those traits in boys early. For example, shame at being branded a coward could help reduce the number of young men who slack off and let other men take the risks in battle (reduce the number of free riders). Teaching boys, and not girls, to be good warriors could easily snowball into a cultural view in which the male and the female seemed fundamentally different. That could discourage most boys and men from doing baby care.

The third kink is mothers' preference for nursing their own babies or parents' preference for very closely monitoring the care of their own children. If either exists, it is enough to derail the co-op. In fact, the history of wet-nursing (hired-out breastfeeding) is full of horror stories. (See Badinter, 1981. The mortality of wet-nursed infants was twice that of mother-nursed infants in France during the heyday of hired-out breastfeeding in the 1700s and 1800s.)

The fourth kink is an overarching point, much emphasized by economists who have written on this topic (Becker, 1991): a small difference can make a big difference. If something is a little easier for Robert than it is for Jo, they may find a way to arrange their work to take advantage of that fact. For example, my husband always changes the light bulbs in our kitchen ceiling lamps. He is eight inches taller than I am, so it is easier for him. It is only a little easier, but he's always available, so why should I put myself out? On the other hand, I take our car into the shop for repairs. I know only a tiny bit more about cars than he does. He knows nothing. Since it's better to have a glimmer (and to be seen to have a glimmer) than to draw a blank, we specialize.

Here is another example. Clearing a patch of forest using fire and stone axes in order to plant manioc may be only slightly easier, on average, for men than for women. A group of fifteen people who must clear a plot once every several months might sensibly decide to train only boys to chop. The group might develop proverbs, myths, and attitudes that justified that pattern. That is what anthropologists see among some indigenous peoples in the Amazon today.

So in the Pleistocene, high fertility, the lack of alternatives to breastfeeding, living in small groups, and, for some peoples, labor-intensive, low-tech warfare probably made some chores visibly (even if only slightly) easier for men than for women, on average. From that nucleus, thousands of different sexual divisions of labor could easily have snowballed.

Even if this explanation is right, it is probably incomplete. The main thing is to recognize that just because hunter-gatherer men today don't do as much child care as the women, and probably didn't in the distant past, that does not mean men are naturally inferior at it. It's possible that harsh circumstances, and nothing else, was what stood between them and their children. It's by far the simplest explanation.

In other words, cavemen don't prove anything.

Men Can't Talk

In 1992, I visited an economics professor and his wife, a psychotherapist, who had a little girl and an even littler boy. Both children were under three years old. As the children careened around the living room, the parents noted that the boy wasn't picking up new words as fast as their daughter had at his age. Then the mother put her feet on the coffee table, leaned back in her armchair, and said, "Of course, girls have a verbal advantage until at least age five."

Where did she get that surprising nugget? Out of the ether of popular culture and, possibly, a monograph she had read in graduate school.

Many people share the view of my psychotherapist friend. They are sure that girls are better with words than boys are, and that women are better with words than men are. When asked how they know this, they say they read it somewhere, plus their personal experience confirms it.

This state of things represents a historical flip-flop. A hundred years ago in Britain, everybody who was anybody knew that the opposite was true. The most prestigious course of study elite young men could pursue was classical Latin and Greek literature. Honors in those studies led to highly coveted jobs. Back then, if you had told government ministers or university professors that women were more gifted at studying classics on average than they were, they would have answered "Preposterous!" (I hope that someday a sociologist of science looks into exactly how and why researchers decided to look into the question of sex differences in verbal skills. Now that verbal tasks such as fluency in foreign languages count for little in the job market, we hear that women have an edge. I suspect researchers will claim to have found that women have an advantage at computer science only after self-replicating artificial intelligences make the field obsolete.)

Why does it matter if many people today believe that women are more verbally gifted than men? What is at stake? People find it easy to believe that women are naturally better with words than men are because, in their minds, that talent stands in for other talents. Talking stands in for being good at creating and maintaining familial relationships. Since we assign women the job of rearing children, it makes sense that we imagine that they are better at talking.

We need to remember, however, that only recently, and only in the middle class, has lots of intimate talk been considered the key to good familial relationships. Not long ago, women's skill at handling bulky objects—wagons, cows, cast-iron kettles—counted for much more than chitchat. Part of what is at issue here, then, is what we think about men's ability to rear children and be homemakers, as middle-class people now define those tasks.

What does the research on girls' and boys' verbal abilities show? In some studies, the girls scored higher than the boys. Before we delve more deeply, though, we need to understand one piece of lingo. When scientists announce that sort of finding, they are saying they have found a difference between the *average* male's performance and the *average* female's performance. The spread *among* boys (or among girls) is always much bigger than the difference they claim to see in average scores *between* boys and girls. The purely fictional picture in figure 8.1 shows what they mean.

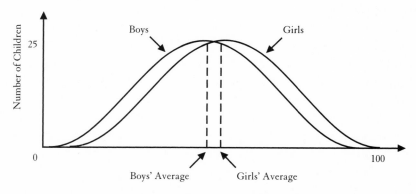

Figure 8.1. Overlapping Bell Curves

Score on test of how much child likes artichokes

Here we see that girls like artichokes more than boys do. However, this difference is only a difference in *average* scores, and a rather small difference at that. The most dramatic results that individual experiments on sex differences have ever found look like this graph. That includes research on verbal abilities.

A 1974 review of the scientific literature in this field found that many studies done on young children turned up no differences. Some studies detected a difference in average scores, but the difference was statistically insignificant. Studies that found a difference found only a small one (Maccoby and Jacklin, 1974).

Another review, in 1978, looked at forty studies of verbal abilities in young people over the age of sixteen. In twenty-three studies, no difference between the performance of the girls and the boys was found. In fifteen studies, girls did better; in two studies, boys did better (Sherman, 1978).

A recent study applying a new statistical technique called meta-analysis to this body of data found that sex accounted for only about 1 percent of all the variance in verbal ability recorded in past studies (Hyde, 1981, cited in Fausto-Sterling, 1985). That is, if you know only a person's sex, you know very little about that person's verbal ability.

In short, the best and most recent work does not find any strong evidence of a significant difference in verbal ability between girls and boys. To the extent that the popular view that women are better with words is wrong, it's a slur on men. It doesn't do women any favors, either.

Scientists and popular culture have awarded to men a consolation prize for being branded inept with words. Boys and men are supposed to be better at math and spatial visualization than girls and women are. Recent reviews of that body of research, however, find that there is, in fact, no good evidence of a sizeable difference between males and females in those skills.

For example, boys score higher on average than girls do on the math portion of the Scholastic Aptitude Test (SAT). However, on average, high school boys have taken more math courses than girls have by the time they take the test. Boys are also more likely than girls to believe that math will be important for courses they will take in the future and for their jobs when they are grown up. Boys may have that attitude because they really are innately better at math, or because adults encourage their math skills more than they encourage girls'. We just don't know. We do know that young people who hold that view, other things equal, score higher on average on the SAT math test than other young people do. When researchers control for the number of math and math-related courses taken and attitudes toward math, the small difference in average math scores between boys and girls shrinks to a tiny margin (see Fausto-Sterling, 1985).

Spatial visualization is the ability to accurately imagine the relationships in space of objects that you cannot see. A review of decades of experiments on spatial visualization abilities found that in more than half the tests, researchers found no sex differences (Maccoby and Jacklin, 1974). On some tests that boys scored higher on than girls, the girls' average score improved when they were given extra time. The boys' average score did not improve with extra time. That may mean that boys are faster learners in this area. Or it may mean that the boys had already had more practice before they took the test, because of the sorts of toys, models, and games they had been given to play with at home. In the few tests that found a sex difference, it explained only 5 percent of the variance in scores (see Fausto-Sterling, 1985).

People who believe the widespread, and apparently incorrect, notion that boys are significantly better than girls at math and spatial visualization may find it easier than others to believe that the traditional sexual division of labor in the home makes sense. After all, even if men are as good at babies as women are, if men are much better at accounting, building, computers, engineering, science, and so on, it makes sense for men to specialize in those high-paying activities. Women can specialize in what is left over.

The Animal Kingdom

We are just beginning to scratch the surface of the rich interactions that exist between infants and adult males, which seem to have such critical repercussions for infant survival.

—Sarah Blaffer Hrdy, primatologist

When I attended elementary school, in the 1960s, we learned about animals. We learned that snakes aren't slimy and that owls can turn their heads all the way around backwards. We also read a little about family life among animals. Our lessons were consistent with what I saw in all my playmates' houses. The daddy wolves, robins, and alligators loped, flew, and slithered off to hunt each morning, while the mommies washed their babies, fed them breakfast, dusted, made lunch, went for a stroll, and waited for Daddy to bring home the bacon (mice, worms, gazelle).

Many people still hold in their minds that picture of life among animals. It helps to reinforce the feeling that women are naturally better with babies than men are. In truth, though, most animals don't carry on like the white suburbanites of 1963. Biologists have recently learned that in many species, males give care to their young that is essential to their survival. This new research has overturned old assumptions and posed new questions. Taken as a whole, it suggests something that the science textbooks of the 1960s never dreamed of. As best we can tell, human males are members of a distinctive group of male animals who have been rigorously shaped and generously endowed by evolutionary forces to care for their young.

What do male animals really do? Biologists draw a distinction between direct and indirect care. Direct care means things done directly to the offspring, such as feeding or cleaning them, or sleeping next to them to keep them warm. Indirect care can be done away from the offspring, but also increases their odds of survival, such as chasing away competitors or building a shelter (Kleiman and Malcolm, 1981). Indirect care is important, but for our purposes, the amount of *direct* care male animals give is more important.

It turns out that in fully 10 percent of mammalian genera, males give a significant amount of direct care to infants and young animals. (*Genera* is the plural of *genus*. Dogs and coyotes, for example, both belong to the genus *Canis;* dogs are members of the species *Canis familiaris,* coyotes of *Canis latrans.*) Male wolves feed their young cubs, watch them when the female is off hunting, teach them, and play with them. Male field mice clean and groom young mice, retrieve them from unsafe places, huddle with them while they rest or sleep to keep them warm, watch them while the female is away, and defend them from predators, such as wolves (Kleiman and Malcolm, 1981).

The most outstanding fathers among mammals are primates—the apes and monkeys that are our closest animal relatives. Among primates, males in 40 percent of all genera give substantial amounts of direct care to their young. In 37 out of the roughly 200 primate species, males invest a large amount of time and effort in their offspring (Hrdy, 1981). In some, males share baby care equally with females. In others, males do more than half the baby care.

Among marmosets (small monkeys that live in Central and South America), for example, the male helps the female while she gives birth, chews food into a fine mush to feed the newborn during its first week of life, and carries the infant at all times, except when the mother is nursing it (Yogman, 1990). Among South American night monkeys, the male carries the infant close to 50 percent of the time during its first week, the mother 33 percent, and juveniles 15 percent. Among nest-building ruffled lemurs, the male stays at the nest caring for the young while the female forages to feed the family (Hrdy, 1988). Researchers have also seen Japanese macaque males become the primary parent of orphaned infants (Yogman, 1990). In general among primates, adoption of an orphaned infant by a related male is more likely than adoption by an unrelated female.

Why do so many male animals spend time and energy on their young? Where did my grade school teachers goof up? To answer those questions, we need to think about evolution. Evolutionary theory tells us that heredity, variation between individuals, and competition to survive and reproduce sculpt all the living things on earth—not only their bodies but also some of their behaviors. That's because some behaviors are inheritable, too. For example, no one has to teach salmon to swim upstream to dig nests in gravel.

Let's say a particular inheritable behavior in a male animal increases the odds that his offspring will survive to reproductive age. Some of his male offspring may inherit the behavioral trait, and some of his female offspring may carry genes to pass it on to their sons, if they have any. Male offspring who show the trait will outreproduce their brothers who lack the trait. Eventually, generations later, a significant percentage of males in that population could show the behavior.

So far, this story sounds familiar. My teachers in the 1960s used it over and over to show one thing: the advantages to male animals of mating with many females, in order to have oodles of offspring. We could call that a quantity strategy.

However, males face another option: a quality strategy. Lavishing attention on a small number of offspring could be as successful as, or more successful than, siring oodles of offspring in producing a target number of grandchildren. The success of the quality strategy depends on several things: the scarcity of food and water, the level of danger posed by predators, how widely dispersed the females are, how crucial care from a second adult is to the survival of the offspring, and so on.

This means that male animals face a trade-off between quantity and quality—between the number of offspring they try to have and the efforts they make to raise the odds of survival of each one. In the wild, it is a trade-off with high stakes. Food is scarce and life is dangerous. Females, of course, face the same trade-off. (That's why women don't routinely bear octuplets. Very few children would survive to pass on the propensity to octuple.)

What biologists have recently figured out is that for many male animals in hundreds of species emphasizing quality is a successful strategy. They lavish care on their babies, outreproduce their brothers, and pass on their propensity to be closely attentive fathers.

Under what conditions is the quality option a good reproductive strategy for males? One setting in which males give lots of direct care to infants is when pregnancy and lactation impose a big burden on the mother. Without help from a second adult, the babies may face poor odds of surviving. For example, female marmosets give birth to infants weighing up to 25 percent of their own body weight (Hrdy, 1981). That is like a 120-pound woman having a 30-pound baby. Imagine! Just gathering the extra food necessary to support the pregnancy and to suckle the young is a tremendous job. It takes two parents to do it.

However, male animals provide lots of direct care in so many different species, in so many different environments, that biologists haven't yet figured out a simple story that explains all the examples. Apparently, the behavior evolved independently, many times, in many parts of the world (Kleiman and Malcolm, 1981).

This diversity does suggest one thing: there is no fixed, universal set of roles for mothers and fathers. Evolution has shaped many male animals to be perceptive and devoted fathers.

Male primates, then, are the champions of the quality strategy. Why should that be? Some biologists speculate that it may be related to a strong trend they see in the evolutionary history of the primate order. On average, the more recently a primate species has evolved, the longer the infants and juveniles are dependent on grown-ups. Where those dependent young animals have needed care from a second adult in order to have decent odds of survival, there has probably been powerful natural selection in favor of more competent and attentive fathers (Hrdy, 1981).

Scientists need to log many more months in the wild watching apes and monkeys to confirm, disprove, or qualify that theory. Still, it is suggestive. As everyone knows, human children are dependent on grown-ups for much longer than the young of any other primates.

Maternal Instinct

Maternal love is a human feeling. And, like any feeling, it is uncertain, fragile, and imperfect.

—Elisabeth Badinter, *Mother Love: Myth and Reality*

Even if natural selection made prehistoric men better fathers with each generation, surely it put still *more* pressure on prehistoric women to become excellent mothers? Surely, evolution has made women better than men at taking care of children? To millions of Americans, that assertion sounds very persuasive. Two words sum it up: maternal instinct.

Do women have maternal instinct? What would it consist of? How would we tell? Those are hard questions. To start unraveling them, we need to recall several everyday facts that suggest that *even if* women have more innate baby care skills or propensities than men, the absolute amount of those innate traits is tiny.

First, girls and women—just like boys and men—need to be *taught* each iota of baby care by someone else: how to support the newborn's head safely, how to care for the umbilicus, how to bathe the newborn. That someone else needed to be taught by another someone else. Human knowledge about baby care is mainly passed on socially, not genetically. Hospital maternity wards are now stocked with piles of videotapes: "How to Dress Your Baby," "How to Burp Your Baby," and other riveting titles for today's first-time mothers.

Second, the technology of baby care has changed greatly over the last, say, two million years. It's no surprise that our genetic fund of reflexes hasn't yet caught up with disposable diapers and plastic wash basins. One constant, though, since the dawn of the mammalian class, is lactation and breastfeeding. Our *Homo sapiens* foremothers, long ago on the African savannah, all breastfed their babies. If there is any baby care skill that should come to women as easily as blinking their eyes, it is breastfeeding. But to a lot of women, at first, it feels exactly as easy as landing a jet on an aircraft carrier. The baby wiggles, the breast bobs, and there's no way the two will connect. In walks the nurse, or an experienced mother, and teaches you. Grab, jam— presto. After a week (eight feedings times seven days), you're a pro.

The large national apparatus of La Leche League testifies to the amount of advice many women need to accomplish this most primeval act of mothering. We're not stupid. We're just not hardwired for baby care the way we are for breathing, blinking, and walking.

Still, suppose maternal instinct didn't consist of innate knowledge, but innate predilection. Suppose that, on average, women are biologically built in such a way that they are more attracted to babies than men are, or more sensitive to their needs and emotions, or both. It is possible. How might we test for sex differences in that sort of baby sensitivity?

One group of researchers in the 1970s who worked on that problem came up with a theory they called "maternal bonding" (Klaus et al., 1972, cited in Eyer, 1992). It said that a mother was hormonally primed, just after the delivery of her newborn, to become deeply emotionally attached to it. The implication was that she was capable of becoming more attached than anyone else was *if* she took advantage of that brief window of opportunity. That attachment could make her a more skillful mother, and help her baby grow and mature better.

Newspapers, magazines, and broadcasters widely reported the results of those studies. Hundreds of thousands of Americans probably still believe the results. Beginning in the 1980s, however, careful reviews of the methods and data in those studies showed that they were, at best, very sloppy. As the psychologist Diane Eyer describes in *Mother-Infant Bonding: A Scientific Fiction* (1992) the whole line of bonding research now stands discredited. We just have no reliable evidence that maternal bonding, as defined here, occurs at all.[2]

However, other evidence suggests that women might make warmer, more attentive parents than men. In her popular book *In a Different Voice* (1982), the psychologist Carol Gilligan wrote that she had detected two different styles of moral reasoning. One, which emphasized personal relationships and the responsibility to give care that grew out of them, turned up more often in girls and women; the other style, which concentrated on abstract rights and duties that people have regardless of the relationships between them, turned up more often in boys and men.

Conceivably, grown-ups who care more about particular people than about abstract rules might make more devoted caretakers. Enthusiasts of the book have put more weight on it than it can probably safely bear, however. Gilligan herself wrote that she intended the book to be merely suggestive. She used small samples and, in one of them, included no men at all. More troubling, though, is that many researchers who have read the answers given by the children in a famous hypothetical example (about whether a man should steal life-saving medicine for his wife that they cannot afford) find that they cannot tell the boys from the girls at all. They say it is hard to tell whether there are two styles of moral reasoning and, if so, whether the girls used one more than the boys did (Epstein, 1988).[3]

A 1984 survey of sixty-one studies of moral reasoning found that in most studies, men and women did *not* use different levels of abstraction. Other researchers have found that both men and women talk about rights, and personal relationships, and the importance of finding solutions that would be good for society as a whole (Walker, cited in Epstein, 1988). So far, then, we have no strong evidence of significant differences between women and men in their styles of moral reasoning.

Even if the so-called bonding research and research on moral reasoning have failed to turn up persuasive evidence of a unique predilection in women to take care of babies, surely biology must tell us something. Males and females have different biochemistry, right? Surely some of those differences might make women more interested in baby care than men are?

Some readers will have heard of oxytocin, a short chain of amino acids found in the blood and in the nervous system. Scientists first learned that it plays a role in reproduction in female mammals. It promotes uterine contractions during labor, helps shrink the uterus after delivery, and promotes the flow of milk from the mammary gland. In animals such as rats, voles, sheep, and monkeys, it seems to affect behavior, too; it encourages mothers to pay attention to their babies and to take care of them (Burbach, Adan, and deBree, 1992).

Aha! Could oxytocin be, in essence, a maternal-instinct hormone? Even in human beings? Maybe so, maybe not. Before conservatives leap for lapel pins that say, "Oxytocin Rules!," there are a few more things they should know.

First, very little research has been done on the effects of oxytocin on the behavior of human beings. Since we already know about striking differences between the maternal behavior of humans and that of rats, voles, and sheep, we can't draw analogies about oxytocin with any confidence at all. After all, the inventors of the bonding theory dreamed it up because of something sheep do. If a mother sheep is separated from her newborn lamb for several hours right after birth, when reunited, she refuses to take care of it at all. Human mothers, however, do nothing of the kind. Theorists who rush to proclaim oxytocin the foundation of the traditional sexual division of labor may wind up looking like the bonding researchers. That is, well, sheepish.

What's more, male animals have oxytocin, too. Researchers have found that it is essential for penile erection and male mounting behavior. In fact, it helps regulate many different kinds of sexual and social behaviors in both male and female animals: sexual receptivity, aggression, calls of distress at being separated from members of their species, grooming, and displays of affection between mates. Scientists' best guess now is that oxytocin is a chemical that promotes reproduction *and* ties of affection between male and female mates and their offspring (Pedersen et al., 1992). That is, it's an emotional-attachment hormone. Moreover, the male and female animals studied so far have similar amounts of it (Arletti, Benelli, and Bertoli, 1992, p. 180).

So people who are tempted to say that oxytocin proves that women are uniquely capable of hands-on parenting should watch out. They may just be falling for the latest, but incorrect, form of biological determinism.

Aggression

There has been a great diversity of opinion on the subject, but the generally accepted rule is pink for the boy and blue for the girl. The reason is that pink being a more decided and stronger color is more suitable for the boy; while blue, which is more delicate and dainty, is prettier for the girl.

—*The Infant's Department,* a children's wear trade journal, 1918, quoted in Paoletti, 1989

The flip side of believing that women are naturally tender is believing that men are naturally belligerent. I suspect that many Americans hold this belief with even more confidence than their belief in maternal instinct. Nearly everything in our everyday experience seems to confirm it: movies, Nintendo games, even the news on television. It's one reason that many people find it hard to imagine putting millions of men in charge of babies. It helps cement our current—and ancient—sexual division of labor.

Are men really innately more aggressive than women? The evidence is weaker than you might think. One problem is that the ground of the discussion keeps shifting. What has sounded scientific to one generation sounds silly to the next. Right now, if you asked people what the scientific basis of men's supposedly greater aggressiveness is, few would hesitate. They would say, "Testosterone."

Even people who should know better rush into pronouncements of that sort. For example, my sister, Karin, produced the first grandchild in our family, named Connor. At a family get-together when he was eighteen months old, we watched him try to climb my parents' staircase. He couldn't quite pull himself up the first polished wooden step, but he kept trying over and over again—grinning, panting, and determined.

My father, a doctor, shook his head and laughed. "Wow, that testosterone is really something. You girls never did that."

I sputtered something like, "Dad, you've got a sample size of three: me, Karin, and Connor. And I never read anything about testosterone and climbing."

My sister's next child, Sarah, was supernaturally precocious in her physical development. When she was six months old, she was pulling herself up to a standing position. One day when Sarah was eight months old, my sister walked into the kitchen and found her on top of the refrigerator. She had scaled the kitchen drawers, pulled herself onto the counter, climbed up the cereal boxes, and vaulted on top of the refrigerator. When my father heard that, he dropped his pipe. He hasn't said a word since about testosterone.

For many people, though—especially those who haven't met my niece—the scientific answer to lots of muddled questions about men's inner nature is still "testosterone."

Scientists have devoted a lot of effort to finding connections between that hormone and aggression. They've defined aggression narrowly, to mean a propensity to act violently, fight, or dominate others. The peculiar thing is that they have found *no evidence* that testosterone causes aggressive behavior. Instead, in work with animals, scientists have learned that *after* aggressive behavior or a sudden rise in an individual animal's social status, its level of testosterone often rises (Maccoby and Jacklin, 1974, p. 246). A plunge in its social status is often followed by a drop in its testosterone level. Conceivably, then, changes in behavior and status may cause changes in testosterone levels. Both male and female animals experience those changes. Currently, there is no evidence that it works the other way around.

Scientists have also studied testosterone in people. Six projects in the 1970s carefully measured aggressive behavior in men and their blood levels of testosterone. To measure aggressive behavior, they used psychological tests, arrest records, and prison records. Four of the six studies found no correlations at all. In the two that did find a correlation, it wasn't clear which came first—slightly higher levels of the hormone or slightly higher level of aggression (Fausto-Sterling, 1985). Conspicuously, none of those studies included women. Even if they had made dramatic findings, then, we wouldn't have been able to conclude anything, strictly speaking, about sex differences.

Researchers have not even been able to confirm the everyday stereotype that males act more aggressively than females. Many researchers have studied young children, in the hopes of observing their behavior before it is shaped by adults. Unfortunately, the studies have used many different definitions of aggression. In the 1970s, one review of twenty-four studies of children between one and five years old determined that twelve studies had found no sex differences at all in aggressive behavior. Eleven had found that boys were more aggressive and one found that girls were (Maccoby and Jacklin, cited in Fausto-Sterling, 1985).

We also need to consider one odd catch in this research. The observers scoring the children's behavior *knew* which were girls and which were boys. It turns out that can make a difference. In one study, male and female college students watched a videotape of a baby playing with a jack-in-the-box. The jack jumped three times, first startling the baby, then agitating it, then making it cry. Students who had been told that the baby was a boy said that "he" was angry. Students told that it was a girl said that "she" was scared (Conway and Conway, cited in Fausto-Sterling, 1985).

It's possible, then, that stereotypes influenced observers in the studies of older children, too. It may be harder than many researchers expect to design a valid study of possible sex differences in aggression.

Let's say here, for the sake of argument, that men are more likely than women, on average, to resort to physical violence during an argument, when they are frustrated, or when they are angry. (Now we are *not* wondering whether there is an *innate* difference; we are just imagining that there is an observed difference.) As I noted in chapter 1, studies on battering do suggest that, in the family, men are more likely than women to start a physical fight with their partner.[4]

We need to pose a question, clearly and precisely, that seldom gets asked: If all primary caretakers of children were men, would that make them more likely to hit their children than they are now, or less likely?

The answer is not at all clear.

Men would have more opportunity to hit their kids, since they would be around them all day, but it's not clear whether they would be more or less inclined to hit them. Would men feel more or less anger and frustration than they do now? Would they abuse alcohol and other drugs more or less? We don't know what fraction of the feelings that contribute to men's battering and child abuse comes from the pressures of holding down exasperating jobs. Staying home might *prevent* the average guy from losing his temper.

Economic dependency on their wives would influence the behavior of many men, too. Other things equal, we would expect it to decrease the amount of child abuse by men that wives could detect. Of course, thousands of women who are economically dependent on male partners abuse their children. (Possibly less than they would if they were economically independent.) Economic factors alone are certainly no cure-all. Still, the average breadwinner wife might disapprove of child abuse more than the average breadwinner husband. We don't know. Even if so, we're not home-free: that would still leave men with carte blanche to inflict hurts on their children that were subtle and hard for their wives, or others, to detect.

What are we left with? A complicated picture: a gaping absence of evidence about innate male aggression and a little economic theory that says we're not sure what difference it would make anyway.

We can add one more nugget of data. One recent study found that if a man takes responsibility for the daily, hands-on care of a child under the age of three, he is much less likely to commit sexual abuse against any child in the future (cited in Pruett, 1988, p. 48).[5] Of course, it's true that the things that lead men to sexually abuse children may be quite different from those that lead them to beat, burn, and shake them. However, sexual abuse is exactly the sort of harm that can be very hard for another adult—such as a breadwinner wife—to detect. If hands-on male care reduces the incidence of that kind of abuse, that is good news. It suggests that the average man who becomes a full-time father might feel less willing to hurt his children *in other ways, too,* than he would if he weren't so involved in their care.

Traditional Cultures

When people make the "other cultures" argument, they say: If men were meant to raise children, there'd be an island somewhere, or a mountaintop kingdom, where they did just that. It's similar to the "other animals" argument, and just as wrong.

It is true that in all the societies that anthropologists and historians know about, women do more than half the work of taking care of babies and very small children. However, in half the nonindustrial societies that have been studied, men have very close relationships with their children. In at least thirty-two of them, men give lots of direct, daily care to their infants and toddlers (Coltrane, 1988).

What are those intensive-fathering societies like? A recent review of studies of ninety nonindustrial, traditional cultures found that in many of them men and women do similar work. For example, both men and women gather food and they go hunting together for small animals. Often, parents in those cultures discipline their children in an easygoing way. Typically, these groups do not go to war often. Grown-ups do not think it is important to teach military skills to boys.

For example, among the Semang people on the Malay Peninsula, who earn their living by hunting and foraging, men take part in *all* family and child-rearing activities. When Margaret Mead studied the Manu, in New

Guinea, who fish and practice simple agriculture, she found that men took a big share of responsibility for infants from the moment of birth. The Mbuti people, or so-called pygmies, of the Ituri Forest in central Africa are hunter-gatherers. Men and women have equal status and, on the whole, do the same tasks. Fathers help take care of very young children. One anthropologist noticed this custom, which every young child experienced:

> The adult male who has been sharing the familiar leaf bed with [the child's] mother, and whose body smell, sound, taste, appearance, and rhythm [the child] knows almost as well, and which has been found to be every bit as secure and safe, begins to fondle the child as its mother does. He takes it to his breast and holds it there. With everything else so familiar, the child explores for milk, but instead of milk is given its first solid food. [Turnbull, cited in Coltrane, 1988, p. 1073]

Fathers in the Trobriand Islands, in the southwestern Pacific, traditionally had a great deal of responsibility for child care. In 1927, the anthropologist Bronislaw Malinowski described a typical father's duties:

> He has to carry them about when on the march the mother is tired, and he has to assist in the nursing at home. He tends them in their natural needs, and cleanses them, and there are many stereotyped expressions in the native language referring to fatherhood and its hardships, and to the duty of filial gratitude towards him. A typical Trobriand father is a hard-working and conscientious nurse and in this he obeys the call of duty, expressed in social tradition. The fact is, however, that the father is always interested in the children, sometimes passionately so, and performs all his duties eagerly and fondly. [Quoted in Katz and Konner, 1981, p. 171]

In all those societies, birth rates are high and parents have no alternatives to breastfeeding. Why don't frequent pregnancies and the demands of nursing result in very separate spheres for men and women? No one knows for sure. Maybe, in those societies, given the climate, natural resources, and technological gear, there are no productive tasks that are easier for men to do, on average, than for women. We also have to remember, though, that culture is an autonomous force. Societies living in similar ecological settings, with similar technologies, have gone in different directions. For example, the Chiricahua, an Apache people living in what is now Arizona, had close father–child relationships, but the Comanche, of the western plains, Texas, and New Mexico, had distant ones (Coltrane, 1988, p. 1074).

The lack of warfare, or relative lack of it, in societies with very caring fathers is probably an important factor. Some anthropologists perceive a pattern in societies that need warriors. Often, the men sleep and eat in a men's house, apart from the women and children, and develop an aloof and belligerent style (Whiting and Whiting, 1975, cited in Coltrane, 1988). In most such societies, fathers have little contact with young children. With preteens, fathers' only child care tasks may be to perform rituals and mete out punishment.[6]

Unfortunately, that observation only pushes the question to another level. Why do some people live in peace? Would that we knew.

This picture suggests that two factors may be paramount. Apparently, a very high degree of male involvement in baby care can arise in a society whose economy has few important tasks that men can do more easily than women *and* in which warfare doesn't touch the life of the typical man.

Does that sound like any place you know?

One researcher, Scott Coltrane, asked a more probing question: Is there a relationship between men's responsibility for the care of children and women's power outside the home? He analyzed data from ninety traditional societies to find out. In chapter 1, I asked that same question and proposed that women would not be able to join men as full and equal partners until men joined women in raising children. The best available data confirm my thesis. Coltrane (1988) found a strong and statistically significant correlation between men's responsibility for taking care of children and women's participation in community decisions and access to positions of authority.

In many traditional societies, all over the world, where women share children with men, men share power with women.

Fathers in Rich Countries

Q: Why did you decide to record again?
A: Because this *housewife would like to have a career for a bit! On October 9, I'll be 40 and Sean will be 5 and I can afford to say "Daddy does something else as well." He's not accustomed to it—in five years I hardly picked up a guitar. Last Christmas our neighbors showed him "Yellow Submarine" and he came running in, saying, "Daddy, you were singing . . . Were you a Beatle?" I said, "Well—yes, right."*

—John Lennon, in *Newsweek* interview, September 29, 1980

Americans' ignorance about fathers in traditional cultures who take care of their babies helps perpetuate our own sexual division of labor. However, men in the Ituri Forest and the southwestern Pacific are not the only fathers who raise children. Many men in the United States, Europe, and other high-technology places do, too. Because almost no one outside their own families knows about their work, though, stereotypes go unchallenged. Also, Americans' fears about the psychological effects of a stay-at-home father and breadwinner mother go unchallenged. Remember how James Dean's character in *Rebel Without a Cause* flinched when his father came into the room wearing a frilly apron? The director intended the father's domesticity to signal lack of purpose and authenticity to his 1950s audience. I suspect that many Americans still have mental images of that sort squirreled away. Those images fortify the habits of thought and feeling that say that only women belong at home with children.

How many men are now putting in a large share of the time necessary to raise their kids? It is hard to say. I had very little trouble finding sixty-five such men to survey for this book. What was very striking, though, was that hardly any families with a househusband-father knew another family with one. That suggests that such families are a small minority. It also suggests that they have formed very few organizations.[7]

Psychologists and physicians have done lots of research on such families. The studies have looked at fathers in two-parent families who are the main, hands-on parents, fathers who share child care about equally with their wives, divorced fathers with custody, and homosexual fathers raising their children alone or with a male partner. All the studies have found that the children are as healthy and happy as children in traditional families.

Let's start with the research on children raised by men in two-parent families. Six separate studies have been done in four modern countries.

Kyle Pruett, a Yale University physician, followed seventeen fathers in New Haven, Connecticut, who were raising their children while their wives worked, beginning in 1983. The parents ranged across the economic spectrum. Some received welfare, most were middle class, and some were professionals. All the children were firstborns, between two and twenty-four months old when the study began. Pruett (1991) found that the babies were "active, vigorous, and thriving." Most scored above average on tests of their strength, dexterity, persistence, language skills, and emotional attachment to their parents.

Pruett revisited the families when the children were between three and seven years old. In more than half the families, the father had stayed in charge of hands-on child care. In another one-third of the families, fathers had begun to share child care equally with their wives. In three families, the mothers had stepped in to become the primary hands-on parent. The children continued to score above average on tests of problem-solving and social skills. They showed "zest for life, assertiveness, a vigorous drive for mastery and the usual childhood worries" (Pruett, 1991, p. 84).

Of course, one good criticism that could be made of this study is that it doesn't reveal how well the *average* man would do as a primary parent. That is, these men were probably a little unusual. They decided to be stay-at-home dads, but the vast majority of fathers do not. Scientists call that problem "selection bias." It is a problem in all the research on children raised by men.

However, Pruett was aware of selection bias. He interviewed the parents to ferret out unusual qualities. He couldn't find any. None of the men was an ardent feminist. Two-thirds of them had decided only during the pregnancy or afterward to take on baby care. Eight of them were unemployed, and said that was why they chose to be the primary parent. Of course, most unemployed men don't make that choice. So the decision of these eight is still a mystery. Careful work with a very large sample of stay-at-home fathers could be revealing.

There is another reason, though, why the selection bias in this body of research shouldn't bother us much. We can expect that the men who choose to be stay-at-home fathers in the next few decades will tend to be more child-oriented than the average man. They will, after all, be bucking convention. That means we don't have to worry about the performance of the truly average guy until further in the future, when conventions have changed, and the effort and social cost involved in being a househusband are much lower. By then, men's ability to perform well in the nursery might not even seem like an interesting question. (Just as today, unlike in the early 1960s, no one wonders about women's ability to perform as physicians or pilots.)

Researchers in Sweden have also studied babies raised by men in two-parent families. They tracked fifty-two male–female couples expecting their first baby and compared babies whose fathers stayed home alone with them for over one month with babies whose fathers stayed home for only two weeks. The scope of this study was limited, because most of the highly involved fathers were home for only a few months. Still, the study found no difference between the two groups of babies. All of them had normal physical, cognitive, and emotional development (Lamb, Frodi, Hwang, and Frodi, 1982).

One study at the University of Michigan looked at a group of fifty-nine families, most of them white and middle class, in the Ann Arbor, Michigan, area in 1978. The children ranged in age from two to twelve. In twenty of the families, the father took care of the children. In nineteen families, the mother and father shared child care about equally, and in twenty of the families, the mother was the primary parent. The study's main finding was that the children raised by their fathers were happy and normal. The preschoolers' attitudes toward what sorts of work men and women should do were the same as the attitudes of preschoolers raised by their mothers found in other studies. Apparently these children generalized from their knowledge of the wide world around them, and used rigid categories, in the same way that other preschoolers are known to.

One interesting difference did turn up. The father-raised kids were much more likely than children raised by women to think that they had control over what happened to them, especially bad things, such as flunking a test. Psychologists call that quality a strong "internal locus of control." Young people who have that quality tend to be more responsible and self-motivated (Radin, 1994).

In 1988, the researchers tracked down these families again. They found thirty-two of the original fifty-nine. The children were then between fourteen and sixteen years old. In some ways, care from their fathers had made a difference in the children's lives and in some ways it hadn't. It did not affect children's grades, as they reported them. But teenagers whose fathers had taken care of them during their preschool years were more likely to expect to go to graduate school than teenagers from traditional families. Both the girls and boys had more flexible views about what sorts of personality traits and jobs were appropriate for men and women than other teenagers did. They were more likely to approve of stay-at-home fathers and work-for-pay mothers (Williams and Radin, 1992).

Research done in Berkeley, California, confirms those findings. A psychologist there followed forty families in which the father and the mother equally shared the care of their child. In interviews and observation sessions, the psychologist found that the children were happy and healthy. They showed no anxiety, insecurity, separation anxiety, cognitive lags, or aggressiveness. Many of their attitudes toward gender were traditional. However, both the boys and the girls sometimes played at traditional female tasks. For example, when it came time for one little boy's father to diaper the new baby, he ran for his doll so he could change a baby, too. One two-year-old boy sometimes fantasized about the feminine side of his father. He would quietly snuggle up to him and pretend to be breastfeeding from him. The boy knew perfectly well who was who; it was just a tender game he had invented for himself.

Between the ages of four and nine, these children showed unusually flexible attitudes toward what jobs they might do when they were grown up. One boy, for example, said he wanted to be a day care provider. Their notion of the burdens of fatherhood was also different from that of typical children. One day, a four-year-old boy cried out, "Mommy, Mommy, what am I going to do? How am I ever going to be a zookeeper and a daddy at the same time?" (Ehrensaft, 1987, p. 1).

Research in Australia has also found that fathers can raise healthy children. One psychologist interviewed and observed fifty families who lived near Sydney and who had at least one preschooler. He mainly wanted to see how the parents had decided to give the father major child care responsibilities. He didn't give any formal tests to the children, but concluded that the arrangement hadn't harmed the children in any way (Russell, 1982).

In Israel, the psychologist Abraham Sagi worked with sixty Jewish families in a large, middle-class suburb of Haifa. In fifteen of the families, the father had primary responsibility for the children. In twenty families, the parents shared equally. In the rest, the mother was the primary parent. All the families had two children, and one was between three and six years old. Sagi gave the children the same tests as the Michigan study used (translated into Hebrew).

Sagi's results were a little different from those just cited. He found that the involved fathers had a big impact on their children. Their children saw themselves as having much more control over events in their lives than other children did. Both girls and boys were more empathic, assertive, and self-confident than other children. What might have caused the difference between the American children and the Israeli children? Sagi's tests on the Israeli fathers showed that they were emotionally warmer, more involved in making decisions about the children, and more likely to take care of them when the mother was home than highly involved American fathers were. They seemed to be more child-oriented. It is also possible that their views about gender were less stereotypical, and so they passed on an extra measure of assertiveness and self-confidence to their daughters (Sagi, 1982).

What are children raised by their fathers like as adults? Do the men stay home and bake muffins? Do the women all run for the Senate?

Very few studies of highly involved fathers and their families began long enough ago to tell us what their children are like as adults. One team of researchers studied a group of children, starting at age five, who were raised by their fathers, and looked at them again when they were thirty-one years old. On tests of their emotional makeup, those grown-ups were more sensitive and empathic than average grown-ups (Koestner, Franz, and Weinberger, 1990).

We see one other glimmer, but only indirectly, in the parents of the father-raised children. What could have caused those nontraditional parents to choose a family arrangement no one else in the neighborhood had chosen? All the researchers whose work is described here—in the United States, Sweden, Australia, and Israel—were very interested in that puzzle. They found that highly involved fathers were more likely than noninvolved fathers to believe that their own fathers had been warm, close, and loving, even if they had had no hands-on child care responsibilities. Also, on average, the more hands-on responsibility the grandfather had had, the more hands-on responsibility the father had. Both nontraditional mothers and fathers were more likely to have had a mother who worked for pay, at least part-time.

We can't conclude anything definite from those findings. But it's possible that hands-on fathers may pass on to their sons an appreciation of the rewards of taking care of young children.

What about men who raise children with no woman in the house? Can they manage?

Consider, first of all, divorced fathers who have custody. Their experience matters to us because if more men become highly involved parents, the percentage of divorced men who have custody of their children may rise. Researchers in the Dallas–Fort Worth area studied such fathers in 1979. They interviewed and videotaped sixty-four white, middle-class families whose children ranged in age from six to eleven years old. They concluded that the fathers with custody were competent parents.

Compared to the boys living with both parents, the boys in their father's custody showed more warmth, social skills, self-esteem, maturity, and independence. The girls, though, showed less warmth, self-esteem, and independence than girls living with both parents. Among children in their *mother's* custody, however, girls had better social skills than their brothers. Those findings may mean that it's hard for some single parents after a divorce to do right by both their sons and their daughters.

Second, consider homosexual fathers. They may be raising a child without a woman in the house because they are single or because their partner is male. If more Americans start to accept men as primary parents, it might become easier for men in male–male couples to raise children. Unfortunately, most research on gay fathers has been very narrow. Most studies asked whether the father's sexual life had any impact on his children. Studies on male–female couples in which the fathers raised the children asked no questions about the couples' sexual lives. That said, here are the results: a recent review of the scholarly literature found that the children of the gay men studied were no more likely to be homosexual, have social problems, or suffer sexual abuse by their fathers than children of heterosexual men. It concluded that "the evidence to date suggests that home environments provided by gay and lesbian parents are as likely as those provided by heterosexual parents to support and enable children's psychosocial growth" (Patterson, 1992, p. 1036).

We have now reviewed all the scholarly literature on children raised by their fathers. There is no hint in the results that men are less tender or competent at bringing up children than women are. However, because so few young people contemplating parenthood know about this research, or know any men who are primary parents, few contemplate the arrangement that might make sense for them: putting Dad in charge of the baby.

At the beginning of this chapter, I conceded that masses of women still believe that men can't parent effectively. Millions of men are delighted to agree. They believe prehistoric men were too busy sharpening spears to take care of their children, that male animals hunt all day and leave their babies behind, that men are clumsy with words, that women are gifted with so-called maternal instinct, that men are too aggressive to take care of babies, that men in traditional societies fish or plow or smoke pipes all day and leave their children behind, and, finally, that no men in the rich countries manage to juggle PTA meetings, soccer practice, and trumpet lessons, while managing to get dinner on the table most nights, as so many skillful mothers do.

Those beliefs are received ideas. In criticizing them here, I have made the same kind of argument repeatedly. Good scientific evidence for significant differences between women and men in many traits related to child rearing just doesn't exist. That is, many of our popular beliefs about sex differences are myths.

Do I belong to that wing of feminists who hold that all differences between the behavior of men and women result from cultural training? No. I admire researchers who are exploring the links between biology and social behavior. It is some of the most exciting work being done in science. I will not be surprised if someday a careful study with a large, random sample, good controls, and a design that eliminates the influence of mischievous stereotypes turns up a small difference in the average performance of girls and boys, or women and men, in a cognitive, emotional, or behavioral trait that is related to child rearing. It won't come as bad news to me.

First, I know that a small difference in average scores means that the overlap between females and males is very large. Second, I believe that any difference that might be found is far less relevant now than it was in the past. The technology and social organization of modern life have changed the value to us of hundreds of traits. Great physical strength counts for very little, except for professional entertainers such as athletes. Nearsightedness isn't crippling; in fact, it's easily fixable. The ability to puzzle out abstractions hidden in complicated symbolic systems—an alphabet, a wiring diagram, a topographical map—is very valuable. Yet it's something we didn't even know we could do 10,000 years ago.

I think that any small sex differences that may turn up in traits related to child rearing will be swamped—really submerged—by the facts of modern life: formula, breast pumps, and baby bottles; small families who live near thousands of others; capital-intensive rather than labor-intensive warfare and, one hopes, not much of it; new ways of learning and training people (if your father refuses to teach you, you have other sources); and the transformation of the labor market that gives the work that women can do just as much clout—once again, after a long derailment—as the work that men can do.

Masses of women know in their marrow that they can do nearly everything that men can do. Every day, more men agree. It's time for all of us to return the favor.

9

Government and Employers

The year the Sears Tower was capped off I applied for an apprenticeship with the iron workers. The men who were applying formed groups, and sent someone from each group to talk to me. They threatened me. They said, "You may get this job because of the government, but you won't leave it alive. We'll be on a site with you some day, and we'll take care of that." At another job every morning the men came in, punched the time clock and then spat on the floor in front of me.

— Former welder, a woman, quoted in LeBreton and Loevy,
Breaking New Ground

When putting up Chicago's new Metcalfe Federal Building, for instance, [Julia] Stasch [president of the construction firm Stein & Co.] made sure women worked 54,000 hours, or roughly 7% of the total. At the towering USG Building nearby, 75 women, or roughly 6% of the workforce, collected $1 million in wages. "She does it because she believes it's fair and moral and right," explains Chairman Richard Stein. "It's also good business."

— *Business Week*

IN THE UNITED STATES IN THE 1930S, MANY BUSINESSES ROUTINELY fired female office workers when they got married (Goldin, 1990). In a 1992 survey of women working in the construction trades in Chicago, over half the respondents said that, in at least one instance, men had refused to work with them (LeBreton and Loevy, 1992).

It is easy to see how such treatment has hurt women. Discrimination against women by bosses and co-workers, along with failure by government officials to eliminate it, hurts women's bargaining power relative to men's. It holds down women's earnings, keeps women penned into female-

190

dominated occupations, and makes it more likely that in the typical male–female couple the woman will earn less than the man. Thus when parental care for the baby is essential, she will be the parent who stays home.

Discrimination against women and official connivance in it, therefore, perpetuate the traditional sexual division of labor in the home. They perpetuate women's poverty, their second-class citizenship, and domestic violence. The last twenty-five years of scholarship, activism, and legal reform have made those points clear to everyone.

However, what is not clear to most people is that many reforms suggested recently for the workplace will not, by themselves, improve women's bargaining power. They won't make a dent in the traditional sexual division of labor. That means that they won't close the gap in economic well-being between women and men, as their advocates promised. Also, we have something to learn from the experience of European countries with generous social programs, programs that many liberals and feminists in the United States envy. Their experience shows that governments and employers can open the door, but real change will not happen until women walk through it. Women will not walk through it until they train up, marry down in income, and give men lots of solo time with babies.

The Government

TAXES

As you probably already know, the United States has a progressive income tax and married couples file jointly. Progressive means that if you earn more money, you pay more tax. Filing jointly means that the wife and husband add their incomes together and then look at the Married Couple Table in the IRS booklet to find out how much tax they owe.

When a wife and husband add their incomes together, they often discover that they fall into a higher tax bracket together than either would fall into alone. The first earner's income is taxed in a low bracket and part or all of the second earner's income is taxed in the higher bracket. In effect, the second earner faces a higher income tax rate than the first. That matters because taxes can discourage a person from working. The higher the tax, the stiffer the discouragement.

Who is being taxed at the higher, more discouraging rate? In the abstract, we could consider either the wife or the husband as the second earner. In the typical couple in the United States, however, the husband earns more than (usually twice as much as) his wife. There is little question in the typical couple that if one of them is going to choose to stop working for pay, it will be the wife.

If the couple has a baby, this question becomes pressing. The cost of having both the wife and husband work for pay suddenly skyrockets, because they have to arrange for someone to care for the baby. All the options are expensive. They can care for the baby all by themselves, by working different shifts. Then they won't see each other much, though, which is emotionally costly. They can get a relative to provide care for free. Relatives are the main source of care for roughly 17 percent of all children under five years old with an employed mother (Hofferth et al., 1990). Many relatives get paid for babysitting, but even if they don't, that care still costs the family something because the relative could be earning money elsewhere.

The couple can put the baby in a center that charges them nothing or very little. In the United States, though, such places are rare. In 1990, only 4 percent of families reported getting some aid from government, employers, or nonrelatives to pay for child care (not counting the 1988 Child Care Income Tax Credit, which I'll discuss later) (Hofferth et al., 1990, p. 183).

Finally, they can pay a relative, a babysitter, an informal family child care provider, or a child care center. However, paying for child care *greatly* increases the cost of holding down a job. Many American women do not have high enough wages to make the effort, time, and unpleasantness of a paying job seem worthwhile after paying for child care, transportation, other work-related expenses, *and* the taxes levied on the second earner in a married couple filing jointly.

Does the income tax system have to tax married couples jointly? The short answer is no. Sweden introduced separate taxation for married couples in 1971. Income tax there is highly progressive. The wife falls into the tax bracket appropriate for her income, and pays that tax. The husband falls into the tax bracket appropriate for his income, and pays that tax. Because taxes are high, the first earner loses a big chunk of each paycheck. There is a big incentive for a second member of the family to work for pay. Because the second earner pays tax in a bracket lower or equal to the first earner, the system doesn't discourage the second earner. After that tax reform, many more Swedish wives began to work for pay (Sundström and Stafford, 1992).

Did the change affect their bargaining power? There is some evidence that it did. Earnings by wives in Sweden are high relative to their husbands', especially when we compare them to wives' earnings in other countries. Researchers have also found that husbands in Sweden do more housework than husbands anywhere else in the world (Juster and Stafford, 1991).

More and more European countries are seriously considering ending the compulsory joint taxation of married couples. Officials recognize that this change will help them achieve one of their social goals: to encourage married women to work for pay (Bakker, 1988).

Thus, as long as the U.S. government makes joint taxation of married couples compulsory, it will buttress the traditional sexual division of labor in the home. Social Security taxes have a similar effect. The way they are levied now, they tax low earners at a higher rate than high earners and so penalize the second earner in a married couple.

MANDATED BENEFITS

Some jobs pay only wages. Some jobs pay wages and benefits, which can include disability insurance, discounts on the company's products, and free tickets to the ball game. States and the federal government require companies—usually just big companies, say, those with fifty or more employees—to give certain benefits to their employees. Liberals, feminists, trade unionists, and others have worked hard for many years to enact mandated benefits they think would be good for employees. They were afraid that companies wouldn't offer them otherwise, wouldn't offer them to a big enough pool of employees, or wouldn't offer them on good terms.

For example, the 1978 federal Pregnancy Discrimination Act required companies to provide insurance for pregnancy and childbirth if they provided insurance for disability. The law required that the maternity insurance be as generous as the disability insurance. Before the law was passed, most companies treated pregnancy and childbirth much more stingily than other sorts of medical conditions that required hospital stays.[1]

However, when economists hear the phrase "mandated benefit," two questions immediately pop into their minds: Who will pay for it? And how? Economic theory suggests several possibilities, but only empirical research will reveal the answers for each particular mandated benefit.

For example, buying more generous insurance for pregnancy and childbirth costs something. The average cost of a normal delivery in 1989 was $4,334. Roughly 17 percent of all the married women in the country between the ages of twenty and thirty have a child in any given year (Gruber, 1992). So for every young married woman in the country, the average annual expected cost of childbirth is $767. Will that expense come out of the company's shareholders' pockets, out of consumers' pockets through higher prices for the products or services the company sells, out of the pockets of employees in the form of lower wages, or out of the pockets of women in general in the form of reduced hiring of women between the ages of twenty and forty, since they are the people most likely to incur the expense of maternity? If the mandated benefit were to reduce employment of women of childbearing age, many activists who had fought for the mandate would be disappointed. So would the rest of us. Companies would be hiring less qualified people just because they were cheaper to insure.

On the other hand, if the mandated benefit were to lower the wages of employees, especially those who benefited from the new insurance, activists might be surprised, but they might not be upset. Whether or not they would be upset would depend on what goals they had in mind when they were advocating the mandate. If the goal was to correct some sort of flaw in the job and insurance markets that deprived women of maternity insurance, then the mistake will have been corrected. If, however, the goal was to spread the cost of maternity benefits widely over the whole population, and so to improve equity, then that goal would not have been achieved.

So who does pay for mandated maternity benefits and how? According to recent research, the new expense comes out of the wages of women and men who are roughly between the ages of twenty and forty (Gruber, 1992). Why men, too? Because the policies also cover employees' spouses: young male employees have young wives who are likely to get pregnant. The mandate does not hurt women's chances of getting paid employment, but it does not improve equity or make big corporations swallow the expense.

That leaves two important questions: How are mandated benefits for maternity or other things likely to improve women's well-being and bargaining power? And how are they likely to affect the division of labor in the home?

It's hard to say. More insurance may result in better medical care for pregnant women and women in childbirth.[2] Also, a woman who has maternity insurance of her own, through her own job, will be less dependent on her partner than a woman who has maternity insurance only through her partner's policy or who has no insurance at all. Of course, many women who get maternity coverage because of the mandate get it through their husband's employment-provided insurance. Separation *will* strip them of their maternity insurance (after a short optional extension period) unless they can sign up for coverage at their own job, or get a job that covers it. (The cocka-mamie linkage of insurance to people's jobs makes those women more dependent on their bosses and co-workers than they would be under a sensible insurance system, but that's a different story.)

All in all, mandated maternity benefits by themselves seem unlikely to greatly increase women's bargaining power or to have a big impact on the traditional sexual division of labor.

What about the Pregnancy Discrimination Act? It also addressed maternity leave. If more women get generous maternity leaves, that might enable more women to go back to their paying jobs after giving birth. As I've stated again and again, women with high earnings and good job advancement have better negotiating positions at home than other women. So generous, mandated maternity leaves sound good.

Or do they? Remember what we learned earlier about the emotional dynamics of taking care of a newborn baby. In many couples, the mother has a head start over the father in emotional attachment to their baby. That extra bit of attachment hurts her bargaining power. It may also make her more likely to gatekeep.

What happens in a couple when the mother has six weeks of job-guaranteed maternity leave and the father has none? Most likely, she will take the six weeks and he will take little or no time off from work. That six-week period could firmly solidify the head start she has in emotional attachment. It can also put her far ahead of him in baby care skills and self-confidence. This tipping process can happen even in a nontraditional couple determined to share child care fifty-fifty or to make the father the primary parent. I suspect that this happens in thousands of couples who naively expected that the husband would do plenty of child care.

Long maternity leaves, therefore—and even more so long, paid ones—may actually do serious damage to mothers' bargaining power in the home, *if they are not matched by equally long, paid paternity leaves.* Chances are they will very strongly reinforce the traditional sexual division of labor.

What about the Family and Medical Leave Act? It became law in August 1993. It enacted a mandated job benefit, too: companies with fifty or more employees must allow up to twelve weeks of unpaid leave to any employee who wants it for a family medical emergency, childbirth, or adoption. Who pays for this mandated benefit and how? We don't know.

Who are the workers most likely to use family leave? If no one can predict, then employers may just spread the cost over the whole workforce, by slightly lowering every worker's pay. However, we do have some information about which workers are likeliest to use family leave. That information is only patchy and anecdotal, but it strongly suggests that the answer is women. Newspapers report that at big and small companies all over the country, the vast majority of those who use family leave are women (Brott, 1994; Chira, 1993).

Why aren't men taking leave? Fathers interviewed for those newspaper articles give two reasons for their reluctance. First, they made more money than their wives, so it was economically sensible for their wives to stay home. Second, they were afraid they would be stigmatized at work if they took time off to take care of their children.

If the Family Leave Act increases women's ability to remain in their jobs, that will be good for women's negotiating position. However, if it increases the perceived legitimacy of time off to take care of family matters for women relative to men, that is bad for women's negotiating position. It is hard to tell how those two possible effects will balance out.[3]

CHILD CARE SUBSIDIES

Many Americans who care about women's well-being and about children have fought long and hard for government subsidies to child care, without much success. Right now, the federal government gives out only skimpy subsidies. It allots small amounts of money to some child care centers for low-income children through the Title XX, Head Start, and Child Care Food programs. Since the late 1970s, however, those programs have accounted for a smaller and smaller share of federal subsidies to child care. The government has replaced them with the Child and Dependent Care Tax Credit, which parents of children or other dependents claim on their federal income tax return. This tax credit now accounts for roughly 45 percent of all federal subsidies to child care (Robins, 1991).

For our purposes, the Child Care Tax Credit has a big flaw: it is nonrefundable. That means that if Hortense owes $5,000 in taxes and has a credit of $1,000, Hortense pays only $4,000 in tax. If Beth owes $700 in taxes and has a credit of $1,000, Beth doesn't pay any tax, but doesn't get any refund either. If the tax credit were refundable, then Beth would get a refund of $300. It is easy to see that the nonrefundability of the tax credit means that rich Hortense gets much more benefit out of it than poor Beth does.

A nonrefundable tax credit inevitably benefits high-income people much more than low-income people. In fact, even though federal spending on child care has increased 65 percent since 1977, nearly all the new benefits have gone to middle-income and upper-income families, through the tax credit (Robins, 1991).

State and local governments also subsidize child care, partly through direct spending and partly through tax credits, most of which work like the federal tax credit. Their spending comes to roughly 20 percent of federal spending on child care. All in all, total government spending on child care in 1985 came to roughly $5.9 billion (Robins, 1991).

How much of this money do families actually see? Again, the single largest subsidy any parents are likely to get is through the federal Child Care Tax Credit. In 1988, the average credit paid out per family was $423 (Robins, 1991, p. 20). For families with incomes high enough to benefit fully from the credit, it amounts to at most a 20 percent discount on their child care expenses.

Here is the important question: How does that spending affect women's economic well-being and their bargaining power? Probably less than you think.

The nonrefundability of the tax credit, the main form of subsidy, pretty much guarantees that it won't benefit women very much. First, single mothers are much poorer than the average family. Second, a woman married to a man who is threatening to leave the family, or to a man she would like to leave, will be much poorer *after* the separation. That means that the tax credit will be *worth less to the woman and her children after the separation* than it was worth to the intact family. Therefore, the tax credit does not increase her bargaining power very much while she is in the marriage. In all likelihood, child care subsidies in the United States are not putting any pressure on the traditional sexual division of labor in the home.

Another weakness of government child care subsidies is that it isn't clear why the government should favor child care by nonparents, by paying for it, over care by parents, by not paying for it (except possibly as a way of counteracting the tax system's bias in favor of couples with a stay-at-home spouse). A *child allowance* scheme gets around those objections. A child allowance is money that the government pays directly to parents of young children. They can spend it on anything they want. Many European countries have child allowances. Strictly speaking, of course, a child allowance is not a child care subsidy. It is a *child* subsidy (see Fuchs, 1988).

Can we imagine a true child care subsidy that would dramatically melt down the traditional sexual division of labor in the home? The most dramatic example would be a federal subsidy to child care providers who employ *men* as child care workers and to families in which the *father* is the primary parent. We could call it affirmative action for men. It would ease men's transition into this previously nearly all-female enclave. It would help them break down the glass wall between them and their children.

Would such a subsidy increase women's well-being and bargaining power? Absolutely. In some couples, it would create a big incentive for the man to stay home with the kids. Those would be couples who strongly want a parent, not a hired person, to care for the children and where the woman and man have nearly equal earning power. If the subsidy were large enough, it would even be sensible for the man to stay at home if his earning power was *bigger* than the woman's, because the subsidy would be equal to or larger than the difference in their salaries. It would replace the income they lost by making her the breadwinner. Such an arrangement would definitely increase the wife's bargaining power. Moreover, if the Poppa subsidy were completely portable, it would also protect the homemaker father from the sort of vulnerability that housewives suffer now. If he separated from his wife and kept the children, he would still receive his subsidy as long as he was taking care of them. If he got a paying job, he would get subsidized child care if he found a male child care provider.

Of course, this example is extreme. It does show, though, how far away our current programs are from nudging men into child care. Until governments nudge men in that direction, their programs will at best remain neutral toward the sexual division of labor. At worst, they will reinforce it.

CHILD SUPPORT ASSURANCE

Chapter 1 noted that when the typical married woman separates from her husband, her income drops significantly. She no longer benefits from her husband's income. She loses the economies of scale that come when two adults live together. Also, if she has custody of children, she has high expenses. This combination of hardships means that her standard of living falls a lot.

If all custodial parents received child support payments that covered a fair percentage of the cost of taking care of children, divorce would be much less devastating for them. For that to happen, noncustodial parents would have to give part of their paychecks to their ex-partners, or the government would have to send a guaranteed amount of child support to custodial parents, or both. When both happen, you have a child support assurance system. That is, even in cases where the father is elusive or broke, child support is still assured because the government will pay it.

This system should not sound far-fetched. Wisconsin has it. The federal Family Support Act of 1988 required all states to set up something roughly like it by 1994. Whether the federal government will enforce the act remains to be seen.

Some critics object to changing the child support system by claiming that the fathers who don't pay can't pay. "You can't get blood from a stone," they say. However, recent research shows that they are wrong. In 1983, the income of the average noncustodial father was $19,000. That is only 14 percent below the income of the average American man between the ages of twenty-five and sixty-four. The average white noncustodial father earned $22,000—he wasn't rich, but he could certainly help to support the children he had brought into the world. (Some stones *are* bloodless, though. Noncustodial fathers who have never married have very low incomes: $7,700 on average in 1983. Their children are the ones who most need a government guarantee of support [Garfinkel, McLanahan, and Robins, 1992].)

Another objection that critics often make is that vigorous enforcement of child support might lift mothers and children out of poverty, but only by impoverishing fathers. Again, recent research shows that this view is wrong. The poverty rate of single, custodial mothers is much, much higher than that of noncustodial fathers (29 percent versus 5 percent for white parents and 44 percent versus 26 percent for black parents [Garfinkel et al., pp. 16–17]). If the system now operating in Wisconsin were extended nationwide, it would destroy much more poverty than it would create.

Wisconsin's child support assurance system increases women's bargaining power in several ways. First, consider the dynamics of an intact couple. Any threat the man makes to leave is not as scary as it would be in a state without child support assurance, because the woman knows that if he leaves, she will at least get a little help from his paychecks, through withholding, or from the government. Because child support assurance covers everyone, rich and poor alike, it isn't stigmatizing, as Aid to Families with Dependent Children is for so many recipients. The assurance also makes her freer to leave an unhappy or abusive relationship.

Second, consider what happens after a divorce or separation. The guaranteed child support that she gets increases her bargaining power relative to other potential romantic partners she might meet. She has a little more income than she would otherwise (her earnings plus the child support). That makes her a little more attractive. She is also less desperate to get another partner, because she is a little more self-sufficient. That means she can be choosier about new romantic partners.

Research on divorced mothers in Wisconsin bears this out. In the mid-1980s, mothers who received high, regular payments of child support remarried later than other mothers (Yun, 1992). They also married men whose incomes were significantly higher than those of second husbands of women getting low child support. Of course, income is a poor measure of the quality of a man's character. However, for the typical divorced woman with young children, given today's sexual division of labor, it is a good measure of the desirability of any particular man as a second husband, other things equal.

Child support enforcement and assurance systems, therefore, have a surprisingly large effect on women's bargaining power. States that do not guarantee child support are reinforcing the traditional sexual division of labor with a vengeance. They are making women desperate to remarry whoever they can find. They are releasing fathers from their responsibility not only to give their children hands-on care but even to pay for their food and clothing. Note that the federal Family Support Act of 1988 did *not* require states to guarantee payment of child support if fathers can't or won't pay. When Congress passed the bill in that form, it lost an opportunity to redress a cruel injustice.

CUSTODY OF CHILDREN

After a couple with young children are divorced, the mother usually gets physical custody of them. Either the wife and husband agree that the mother will have custody and the court agrees, or the wife and husband disagree, but the court awards the children to the wife.

In the past, the rules worked differently. In the nineteenth century, courts routinely awarded children to their father. In this century, most states adopted the tender years rule, which said that during their tender years, children need to be with their mother. That rule grew out of the belief that fathers were unlikely to give loving, skillful care. Now, in most states, courts make custody decisions according to the "best interests of the child." If that sounds vague, it's because it is.

The vagueness of the "best interests rule" creates a problem, one that has given rise to melodramatic plots in dozens of TV shows and movies. Suppose a divorcing husband doesn't want custody of the children but says he does. The wife, who in nearly all couples did most of the child-raising work, will, in most couples, very strongly want to continue to live with her children. In negotiating the terms of their divorce, the husband may be able to persuade the woman to give up something she wants in order to persuade him to let her have the children. The husband may even be able to get the wife to give up most of her share of the family's savings and property. (Of course, most couples who get divorced don't have much money or property to negotiate over; the average divorcing couple has a lower income than the average married couple.) That negotiating tactic would be used mainly by upper-income fathers, or nonprimary parents, which is to say, their lawyers.

Outside of TV and movies, do couples run into this problem? Very little good evidence about what happens inside private divorce negotiations is available, and that evidence is mixed. Nonetheless, even if it is rare, whenever someone holds children hostage just to hog more than his share of the family assets, something very distasteful is going on. The vast majority of primary parents gouged by that tactic are women.

States that keep the best-interests-of-the-child rule are, therefore, in a small number of cases, helping to make divorced women poorer than they would be under a different system of awarding custody. That relative poverty makes them less likely to find an appealing second romantic partner, as noted in the discussion of child support. It also hurts their bargaining power with future romantic partners. It may also cause real hardship for some divorced mothers and their children.

Some scholars have proposed a better rule. They say that courts should make a strong presumption in favor of awarding custody to whichever parent has provided most of the hands-on care of the children (Chambers, 1984). In traditional couples, that would prevent the father from gouging the mother in return for letting her keep the children. In couples in which the father was the primary parent, it would prevent courts from acting on old-fashioned stereotypes and taking the children away from him.

A primary-parent rule would not help couples who had truly shared the work of child raising fifty-fifty. Their custody fights will be very painful, no matter what rules the courts adopt. In other couples, though, a primary-parent rule would protect the parents who most need a presumption in their favor: the ones who probably earn less money and whose bargaining power is weakened by their strong emotional attachment to their children. It is an elegant solution. It is now the law in California.

SCHOOLS

Governments run schools. Most American children go to them. The evidence reviewed in chapter 7 on the big differences in the housework most parents assign to their daughters and their sons suggests that many parents expect their daughters and their sons to do different things when they grow up. In theory, schools could either debunk or reinforce those notions.

Some research—which varies in quality—does suggest that many teachers, schoolbooks, and school atmospheres may be discouraging girls more than boys from achieving their highest potential for intellectual achievement and leadership. The American Association of University Women gathered much of that research together in its book *How Schools Shortchange Girls* (1992). So did Myra and David Sadker in *Failing at Fairness: How America's Schools Cheat Girls* (1994). Until we eradicate sexism from our schools, they will reinforce the traditional sexual division of labor. They will be teaching girls to tiptoe quietly into second-class citizenship.

Reformers have suggested many ways to make schools better at teaching girls. (See the AAUW, *How Schools Shortchange Girls: Action Guide.*) Would those reforms make public schools uncomfortable for traditionalists? Possibly. But parents who believe strongly that women should mainly raise children and men should mainly do everything else can send their children to private schools. Nor can they persuasively argue that only the rich have recourse to private schooling. Hasidic Jewish parents, who have lower incomes than average, believe intensely in strictly segregating boys and girls and manage to send them to private schools.

DISCRIMINATION, SEXUAL HARASSMENT, AND BIGOTRY AT WORK

Lawyers who represent plaintiffs in sexual discrimination cases still have plenty of work to keep them busy. They also tell hundreds of startling stories. Some discrimination has become refined and ingenious. However, lots of it is still boneheaded and blatant. Better government enforcement, higher penalties, or both would decrease the amount of discrimination faced by women in the workplace. Higher incentives for private lawyers to bring sexual discrimination lawsuits would also make more schools and employers examine their policies and practices to avoid being sued.

Many businesses indulge in, or let their male workers indulge in, openly sexist behavior. For example, until recently the managers of Lucky Stores supermarkets had a policy of not posting openings in management-track jobs. Instead, they whispered the news into the ears of favored men in the store. Store officials said they knew women didn't want those jobs because the jobs were too demanding and would get in the way of their family responsibilities. A lawsuit forced Lucky to post the job openings. Since then, women have snapped up 58 percent of the management-track jobs. This did not take place in the dark days of the 1950s; the lawsuit was settled in December 1993 (Gross, 1993).

Until government agencies take the obvious steps to eradicate sexual discrimination, harassment, and exclusion in the workplace, government officials will remain accomplices to men's illegal bigotry. They will, without a doubt, be reinforcing the traditional sexual division of labor in the home.

Other federal and state laws have a big impact on women's bargaining power relative to men's. Access to affordable, safe abortion means that an unwanted pregnancy need not interrupt a woman's education or paying work. Affordable, safe contraceptives also let her plan the timing of her pregnancies so that she can make the most of her opportunities to study, train, and work for pay. In the past, unwanted pregnancies propelled some young men into the labor market before their education was finished, so that they could support a new wife and baby. Nowadays in the United States, young men are unlikely to leave school because they have become parents. Young women still do, much to their detriment.

Of course, all these issues—discrimination and sexual harassment at work and access to abortion and contraception—are even more urgent for women who live in poor countries.

UTOPIAS IN THE EASTERN HEMISPHERE

One last bit of news is both encouraging and discouraging. It is encouraging because it shows that dramatic government programs can have a big impact on women's participation in paid work and in the amount of housework men do. It is discouraging because it shows how difficult it is for government programs alone to lever men into doing lots of child care.

Let's start with Sweden. As was noted at the beginning of the chapter, its personal income tax is based on separate, highly progressive taxation of wives and husbands. That encourages both wives and husbands to work for pay. All families with children receive a generous child allowance, with increments that increase for third, fourth, and fifth children. The government heavily subsidizes child care by providing public day care centers (although it is starting to privatize them [Stevenson, 1993]). Children of mothers who work for pay for twenty hours or more a week are eligible for a spot in a child care center.

The government also runs an unusual parental leave program. It guarantees that any parent who stays home with a new baby for up to a year will receive 90 percent of her or his salary during that period. The program was extended in 1974 to cover fathers, and certain incentives were added to make it more attractive to men (Gustafsson and Stafford, 1994). Finally, official policies give part-time workers full social benefits, job security, pension rights, and eligibility for the parental leave program (Sundström, 1991).

To many feminists in the United States, that combination of programs sounds like paradise. The Swedish government's stated intention was to increase fertility in Sweden and make it possible for women to keep their paid work while having more babies. It has been successful. In the late 1980s and early 1990s, Sweden achieved something remarkable: the highest participation rate of women in the labor force in all of Europe *and* the highest total fertility rate, second only to Ireland, where very few mothers of young children work for pay (Sundström and Stafford, 1992).

The Swedish regime has achieved something else remarkable. Swedish men do much more housework than men in other rich, industrialized countries. (Norwegian men come close. What's interesting is that Norway has family-related programs that are similar to but slightly more modest than Sweden's.) One study that gathered data from nationally representative samples in the 1980s found that American men did 13.8 hours of housework a week, Soviet men did 11.9 hours, and Swedish men did 18.1 (Juster and Stafford, 1991).

Why are Swedish men unique? Economists who have studied the issue concede that it's possible Swedish men like housework more than other men do. However, they point out that Sweden's generous array of government programs give Swedish women an alternative to economic dependency on a man that women nowhere else in the world enjoy. If a Swedish woman is unhappy with the contribution her male partner is making around the house, she can leave and take her kids. Once gone, she still enjoys her child allowance, public child care, adult vocational education, parental leave, and so on. In other words, her threat point is much lower than that of most other women (Juster and Stafford, 1991). That gives her more bargaining power in the marriage and more leverage to persuade her husband to do housework.

What about the hands-on work of raising children? How much do those world-champion Swedish men do? Sweden has good national data on who uses its parental leave program, since the government pays out guaranteed salaries to parents on leave. The vast majority of parental leave is taken by Swedish women. In 1987, men took only 7.5 percent of all leave days taken (Sundström and Stafford, 1992), in spite of strenuous government efforts since 1974 to encourage fathers to take leave.

Another clue comes from figures on part-time work. In 1989, 85 percent of Swedish women between the ages of sixteen and sixty-four worked for pay. However, roughly 38 percent of them were working only part-time. In contrast, only 6 percent of Swedish men work part-time (Sundström, 1991).

It is no mystery why the patterns for men and women are so different. Women started pouring into the labor market in Sweden in the 1970s, after two conspicuous changes: the number of public day care spots quadrupled and parental leave was introduced. Women who work part-time are overwhelmingly women with young children. Thus, men are working full-time because they are breadwinners; women are working part-time in order to raise their children.

In spite of the remarkable bargaining power that their generous social programs give them, Swedish women are still the primary parents of their children. Why haven't they budged their male partners into child care, even though the typical married Swedish woman earns 39 percent of total after-tax family income (Sundström, 1991)?

I suggest that it is precisely because they earn *only* 39 percent of after-tax family income. In fact, research by the Swedish government has found that the willingness of husbands to take parental leave depends mainly on their *wives'* earnings (Sundström and Stafford, 1992). High-earning wives, because of their bargaining power and their ability to support their families at a comfortable middle-class standard of living, find that their husbands are willing to stay home to raise the children for significant lengths of time.

Sweden's utopia has one other drawback. The programs are very expensive. In the 1991–92 fiscal year, total government spending on parental benefits came to roughly $2.8 billion. That amounted to 1 percent of Sweden's GNP (Sundström and Stafford, 1992). Because the programs are expensive, they are vulnerable. In fact, slow economic growth and rising budget deficits have persuaded the government to dismantle or cut back many of the social benefits that made Sweden special (Stevenson, 1993).

For women, that is bad news. This change reveals that although the social-welfare system reduced women's dependence on the men they lived with, it didn't reduce their dependence on the men who run the country one bit. I say "men who run the country" on purpose. Without a doubt, women do not make up half the people in the top echelons of Swedish government, academia, or business. They are too busy raising their children.

What about other countries famous for giving lots of help to parents of young children? Surely, somewhere, those policies must lever men into doing significant amounts of child care?

Consider France. It offers a generous set of programs that include child allowances (which kick in at two children and provide increments for third and subsequent children), housing allowances that mainly benefit families with children, government-provided day care, highly subsidized care for some babies, paid leave for mothers of newborns, a cash benefit to working parents to help them pay their babysitter, and stipends for parents of three or more children who are staying at home to raise them. All children get government-paid health insurance, which includes preventive treatment and care from public health nurses specializing in pediatrics. The government also runs a child support allowance system. Of all these programs, the child allowance is the most expensive. In 1988, it cost the government roughly $80.1 billion (Bergmann, 1993, p. 71).

French children undoubtedly benefit from all the resources being devoted to them. What is the effect on women? It is true that a high percentage of French women work for pay: roughly 50 percent of them, including 72 percent of women with a child under three years old (Combes, 1993). Those wages probably give French women more bargaining power relative to their male partners than women there had in the past.

However, France's family programs do not encourage men to devote significant amounts of time to child care. Instead, they discourage men. For example, mothers of newborns get sixteen weeks of paid leave for childbirth and the care of a newborn. Fathers get only four days.

What are the goals of French family policy? Mainly to increase the fertility rate and to direct resources toward children (as well as to integrate all children into the dominant French culture). The obsession of certain

French intellectuals and politicians with their slow rate of population growth has become famous. Giscard D'Estaing said in 1978 that "a society no longer capable of assuring the replacement of generations is a condemned society" (quoted in Teitelbaum and Winter, 1985, p. 122). In 1984 Jacques Chirac said, "In demographic terms, Europe is vanishing" (p. 123).

To professional demographers, it is obvious that Europe is nowhere close to vanishing. However, fear of population decline has motivated French leaders to put into place incentives that will encourage French women to have more children. Thus, the child allowances pay *nothing* for the first child, and especially reward families who have three or more children. The stipend for stay-at-home parents is available only to those with three or more children.

Policies like these that are designed to encourage births are called pro-natalist. Because the French are so generous to children after they are born, we can also say that their policies are genuinely pro-child. However, they are not pro-woman. That distinction is crucial. As long as policymakers and ordinary French citizens think of primary parenting as mainly women's work, women will not be fully integrated into the highest echelons of French life. Even in the land of *liberté, égalité, fraternité,* women will remain second-class citizens.

I could give many more examples. Fear of population decline lies behind the family policies of Germany, the Netherlands, and other Scandinavian countries. Rivalry within a country between different social groups can also lead to pro-natalist policies. In the Netherlands, Catholics have competed with Protestants for dominance for centuries. For a long time there, married women were forbidden to work. Many programs encouraged mothers to stay at home. Why? Each side hoped to beat the other by simply outpopulating it (Gustafsson and Stafford, 1994).

Even in Israel, which many observers consider a very child-friendly country, it was mainly rivalry between Jews and Arabs and the Arabs' much higher rate of population growth that prompted Jewish leaders to adopt pro-natalist policies (Teitelbaum and Winter, 1985).

Recall also the kibbutzim. They are famous for their efforts to re-engineer family life. In some, children sleep in a separate children's house at night to expunge the bourgeois notion that they are the property of their parents. However, kibbutzniks have never laid a finger on the sexual division of labor. All child care workers are women. Nowadays, the job of *metapelet* (child care worker) is so low in status that most kibbutz mothers don't even want to do it. Young unmarried women or female volunteer guest workers work as *metaplot.*

Israeli government officials and ordinary citizens assume that primary parenting is women's work. For example, many child care centers are located next to large factories and public institutions. All the centers are open to children of mothers who work next door, but most do not let fathers enroll their children (Sagi and Koren-Karie, 1993). A male employee who happens to be the primary parent is simply out of luck.

There is a big difference, then, between policies that are pro-natalist, policies that are pro-children, and policies that are pro-women. Policies that are pro-natalist or pro-children may actually hurt women's negotiating position, and, therefore, their relative well-being.

What policies *are* pro-women? Those that are pro–primary father, pro–househusband, and pro–male child care worker. No country has yet enacted such policies. Sweden made a weak attempt, but its failure to lure men into child raising shows the limits, and vulnerability, of government incentive schemes.

For men to go into primary parenting on a large scale, women will have to ardently want it. We will know that women ardently want it when hundreds of thousands of them take the necessary steps: they will train up, marry down, and give men lots of solo time with their babies. Thousands will become primary breadwinners. Government can open the door, by eradicating tax penalties, free rides by noncustodial parents, prejudice in schools, discrimination at work, and so on. But real change will not come until women walk through that door, by redefining motherhood for themselves.

Employers

Owners and managers of companies, not the government, set most company policies. As a result, women's advocates have worked hard for decades to persuade owners and managers to adopt new policies that would make it easier for women to combine working with pay and raising children. However, from a negotiating perspective that is exactly backwards. What women need are policies that make it easier for men—relative to how easy it is now for women—to combine working with pay and raising children.

Why? Think back to the egalitarian couple in chapter 5, Gloria and Phil. If they ever disagree about who should take a leave of absence from the office to raise their child, Phil can still say in good faith, "Are you kidding? *Me* ask for half-time work for two years to raise the baby? That would totally blow my credibility. But you, they expect you to scale back."

Phil is right. We hear lots of smarmy repetitions of the new nostrum, "But our family leave is equally available to mommies and daddies." That's nothing but garglewater. Men know where their costs and benefits lie at work. To change their behavior, we have to change those costs and benefits.

Let's see how our much-touted workplace reforms of the 1980s and 1990s stack up against that standard.

FLEXTIME

Flextime lets employees come to work early and leave early, or come to work late and leave late. Managers pick a core time, say from 11 A.M. to 3 P.M., when they expect all employees to be at work. Flextime lets employees do family work, such as taking children to school. It also may let them avoid rush-hour traffic. That may save time. If it reduces traffic congestion, it also benefits people who don't use flextime. If it doesn't reduce productivity at work, then everyone benefits (Moss and Curtis, 1985).

Managers who haven't adopted flextime yet may be hesitating because they are unimaginative or because flextime would reduce productivity at their company. We can't tell without some research. It is safe to say that the average firm that hasn't yet adopted flextime faces a higher cost of adoption than the average firm that has adopted it. The places that adopted it and kept it expected *and* discovered that it didn't cost them much. The firms that haven't adopted it include places that expect it would be expensive and are wrong, and places that expect it would be expensive and are right. After all, at some businesses, all the workers need to be there at the same time. Think of a baseball team or a symphony orchestra.

How does flextime affect women? If it gets adopted in more companies or occupations where women work than where men work, then, from a negotiating perspective, it's bad for women. It would make women more flexible, on average, than men. If managers are more likely to let women than men use flextime, then it's bad for women for the same reason. Finally, if men take flextime but don't use it to do housework or child care, then it won't thaw out the sexual division of labor in the home at all.

What actually happens? We have barely a clue. No one has gathered data from nationally representative samples on the adoption, cost, utilization, or benefits of flextime. Scholars have done a few experiments in government agencies to see how employees use it. The best research found that most men who used flextime did *not* spend the extra time doing housework or child care (Presser, 1989, p. 534; Winett and Neale, 1980). However, those studies were done ten to fifteen years ago and were limited in scope.

In the future, if more women train up and marry down, flextime could make it slightly easier for their male partners to be primary parents while continuing to work for pay. Right now, though, we have no reason to think that it is helping to melt down the traditional sexual division of labor.

Part-Time Work

Advocates of family-friendly employment policies want more companies to offer good part-time jobs. It's easy to see why. Millions of primary parents of young children would rather have a part-time job than a full-time job or no job at all. In the United States in 1988, 18.4 percent of all workers worked part-time, including 26.8 percent of women and 11.4 percent of men. Part-timers are disproportionately likely to be teenagers, women with young children, and people over sixty-five years old (Blank, 1990).

Why can't more workers go part-time for a while? Why aren't more interesting jobs available on a part-time basis? Unimaginative managers and ossified routines are partly to blame. Recent newspaper articles make that clear. For example, Millie Kallik made partner at the big Manhattan law firm of Simpson, Thacher & Bartlett in 1992, even though for the previous twelve years she had worked at the firm only three days a week. She was apparently the first part-timer to be promoted to partnership at a major New York law firm (Margolick, 1992). Kallik's area of practice is probate law; she handles wills and estates. For a long time, that was the only department in big law firms that employed women lawyers in significant numbers. It is a sedate area. There are no rush jobs. So why didn't probate produce a part-time partner a long time ago? What about other relatively slow-moving areas of practice, such as real estate, divorce, or bankruptcy? Managers didn't think of them or didn't want to change their routine.

Consider also Cathy Pratt. She is president of the First National Bank of Chicago in Highland Park, Illinois. So is Kathy Weidner. They share the job and each works half-time. Why not? Frequent communication makes the arrangement work. Why didn't it happen long ago? No one thought of it, and no one wanted to change the routine (Kunde, 1994).

Ossification isn't the only barrier to more good part-time jobs, though.

What some people want is a part-time job that pays proportional salary and full fringe benefits. That is, they want two-thirds the salary for doing two-thirds the work, plus full benefits. Clearly, the company would then be paying them more than it pays full-timers, relative to the amount of work they do. Not many companies will offer jobs like that.[4]

It can also be hard to measure the amount of work that part-time employees are doing. If the manager sees workers in the office constantly, she concludes that they're at least working eight hours a day. With part-timers, so-called face time doesn't give the manager a good proxy for employees' level of effort. If firms come up with a more objective measure to replace face time—such as number of cases carried, or widgets built per month—it will be easier to calculate part-timers' pay (Schwartz, 1992).

Should part-timers be paid purely proportionately to the amount of work they do? Not all of them. For many jobs, they will receive *less* than proportionate pay, unless union rules or government regulations require otherwise. That is because professionals in many lines of work—litigators, tax lawyers, consultants, business executives—get paid a premium for being available around the clock. Fanatical dedication is worth something extra. That means part-timers won't, and shouldn't, get a proportional piece of the round-the-clock premium. The premium may explain why part-time work for some professionals is either paid surprisingly poorly or is scarce (if pay per hour or per case is a bit sticky for some reason).[5]

Would more and better part-time jobs improve women's bargaining power? Clearly, a woman who can easily shift from full-time work to part-time work and then back to full-time is more likely to stay in the labor force, have good earnings, and maintain her negotiating position at home.

How would those reforms affect the sexual division of labor in the home? It is hard to say. More continuity in the labor force, and more bargaining power for women at home as a consequence, would slightly thaw out the sexual division of labor. However, if women are more likely than men to accept new opportunities to work part-time work, that is bad for women's bargaining power. It makes them the flexible parent. Right now, women are in fact much more likely than men to snap up an opportunity to work part-time or to happily accept a compulsory shift to part-time work (Fuchs and Jacobsen, 1991).

Obviously, the real challenge is to attract large numbers of men into shifting from full-time work to part-time work. Men cannot contribute significantly to child care—much less do half the nation's child care—until millions are working for pay part-time, are staying at home full-time, or are employed as child care workers.

What will make men willing to risk conflict and stigma at work by requesting part-time work? They will do it when their wives make it a condition of fatherhood *and* have the bargaining power to back up the proposal.

THE FLEXIBLE CORPORATION

Companies, government offices, and nonprofit firms are experimenting with other changes that will make it easier for employees to mesh their jobs with their family responsibilities.

Some consulting firms, for example, are reducing the amount of travel they ask of their employees and are telling them not to work weekends. Managers at CSC Index, in Cambridge, Massachusetts, and Gemini Consulting, in Morristown, New Jersey, expect that those policies will help them recruit top business school graduates and reduce turnover (Shellenbarger, 1993). If more high-paying jobs offer those terms, women may be able to bargain men into taking them.

A few firms are also trying to give more help to so-called trailing spouses, the people who uproot themselves in order to follow their partner after a relocation. Sprint Corporation, Ciba-Geigy, Monsanto, and CARE, the international relief agency, have all started to give more money and guidance to trailing spouses. Managers at several of those firms admit that the issue started to seem important to them only after the ranks of trailing spouses started to include men (Lublin, 1993). Obviously, the more help trailing male spouses get, the more leverage career-devoted women will have in persuading men to relocate with them.

More companies are also using telecommuting. According to one recent survey, about 5 million employees in the United States work at home on a personal computer that is linked by modem to the computer network at their company. They are mostly white-collar workers. More than half are men. Telecommuters typically work at home only one to three days a week. Managers and employees say that more time at home makes supervision hard, reduces camaraderie, and provokes resentment in nontelecommuting colleagues (Calem, 1993).

How does telecommuting affect the sexual division of labor in the home? Some news articles have described mothers who telecommute several half-days a week in order to spend the rest of those days with their young children. Basically, they save their commuting time. Telecommuting can, therefore, increase the amount of productive time a part-timer gives to the job, which benefits both the firm and the employee. It could open up more challenging, high-paying jobs to part-timers. As noted earlier, though, that by itself will probably have little impact on the division of labor in the home.

Companies will invent more mild innovations of this sort in the coming years. Tough global competition has made jobs less secure, even for highly trained professionals. One way firms can compensate workers for that insecurity is to offer more flexibility. *The Economist,* not usually seen as a radical feminist magazine, has called for "a new understanding between employees and companies," which will include "job-sharing, sabbaticals, subsidised education, flexible hours, telecommuting, creches [child care centers], [and] paternity as well as maternity leave" (July 17, 1993, pp. 13–14).

These proposals may be good for both employees and businesses.

New Ideas

Government and employer policies that really do encourage men to become primary parents look very different from the milquetoast changes most people have proposed so far.

For example, consider affirmative action for men who raise children. Federal law requires all large employers to keep careful track of their recruiting, hiring, and retention of people from disadvantaged ethnic groups, women, and disabled people. Many organizations set goals to hire and retain a certain number of employees from those targeted groups. Managers create incentives so that supervisors under them will make an effort to meet the goal. At many universities, for example, a department that hires an African-American professor is deemed to have used up only half a hiring slot. If the department's budget has room for only one new professor, that means it has room for *two* new African-American professors. Most department chairpersons like to have more people to boss around. So the half-a-slot rule acts as an incentive.

Affirmative action for men who raise children would work like this. Say the department's old goal was to hire four new women. Now it raises its goal to six. However, if the department hires a man who is a primary parent, that relieves it of the duty of hiring one of those six women. Primary-parenting men can count against no more than two newly hired women.[6]

How would this new policy affect women? The department would still be obligated to hire four new women. That hasn't changed. However, now it has a choice of hiring two additional women, or two primary-parenting men. Think about those men. For every man who is a primary parent, especially if he is middle- or upper-middle class, chances are there is a wife who is the main breadwinner and extremely career-devoted. Affirmative action for primary-parenting men gives highly career-devoted women more bargaining power. They can say, "Don't tell me you can't afford to be the primary parent. Universities and big companies are *falling all over themselves* to hire guys like you."

Is this scheme a crackpot fantasy? No. Consider it a limbering-up exercise. A break for men who raise children, over and above the breaks for women who raise children, will abruptly change the incentives that men face at work. Policies that offer such juicy breaks to men who raise children are the only government and employer policies that will really make a tangible, immediate difference in the sexual division of labor in the home.

10

A Future World

I HAVE ARGUED THAT WOMEN CANNOT CATCH UP WITH MEN IN INCOME, wealth, leisure time, political power, or cultural influence until the sexual division of labor in the home has disappeared. Sixty million adults who specialize in science, politics, or business will always outperform, on average, 60 million adults who cannot specialize as intensely because they moonlight in running a household and raising children. Notice that "on average." Very energetic, very talented, very driven, and just plain lucky women will excel at their paying work even though they are primary parents. The *average* woman won't, however. She will be stuck with a large slab of vulnerability, risk of battering, poverty, and marginalization. It will be larger than the slab of unpleasantness on the plate of the average man.

It is time, therefore, to explore in detail what I mean by an end to the sexual division of labor. This point is easy to misunderstand. Many people who hear about this book say, "Oh, so all the husbands will do half the child raising in their family."

That's wrong. A scheme like that would make Procrustes look considerate. (He stretched or sawed off parts of his guests to make them fit his iron beds.) Not all fathers can do half the child raising, or want to, or should. Much more to the point, some fathers can do lots more, and want to, and should. People give the incorrect answer, I think, because they can't boost their imaginations over the hump of the present to imagine a future in which there really exists no sexual division of labor.

So what *does* it mean? It means that there is no chain link connecting sex to occupation. People's sex tells you nothing about their occupation. People's occupation tells you nothing about their sex.

Right now, the chain link is tight. If you hear that Robin is a homemaker, you figure that Robin is female. If you hear that Leslie flies EA-6A jets for the navy, you say, "Geez, why'd his parents stick him with a name like that?" In the future world that we are imagining, those thumbnail descriptions of Robin and Leslie will give you no clues. For example, if today you hear that Robin operates a photo processing machine, works in advertising, or is an accountant, you can't be sure that Robin is female. Odds are 50 percent yes and 50 percent no (*Employment and Earnings,* 1993, table 21). In those occupations, the Ice Age is over, the glaciers have retreated, and sex does not mean destiny.

When the sexual division of labor has disappeared, men will be doing half the total amount of child-raising work. Roughly half the primary breadwinners will be women and roughly half will be men. Roughly half the homemakers will be women and roughly half will be men. Also, it will mean that roughly half the primary parents—the ones who stay home when Junior is sick, who carpool to soccer practice, who cook chili for the bake sale—will be men. Those men will be economically dependent on their wives. They'll do what millions of women have done for so long: they'll focus on their children.

Readers with a philosophical bent may see this notion as the latest bloom on the rosebush of classical liberal theory. Henry Maine, a nineteenth-century English legal scholar, and others after him thought that they detected a slow trend in the history of human societies. In many deeply traditional places, a person's social position is fixed at birth. Each person is assigned a status based on things that can't be changed, such as birth order, clan, color, and caste. That status rules the person's whole life: the food he'll eat, the clothes he'll be allowed to wear, the training he'll get, and the work he'll do as an adult. Caste still rules the lives of millions of people in India in that way.

When cities arise, industry begins, migrations start, and foreigners arrive, the old ways break up. The classic liberal thinkers of the 1700s and 1800s watching that process begin in Europe hoped for a day in the distant future when a person's social position would be limited only by his or her talent and effort. We call that idea equality of opportunity.

In the United States today, the statuses attached to a baby at birth still rule its life and destiny much more than they should. However, I can say "should," without you blinking, only because the sensibility of the classical liberals has so influenced our own. I don't consider myself a classical liberal. Yet, I say "should" with passion. John Stuart Mill did, too, in 1859: "The family, justly constituted, would be the real school of the virtues of freedom" (p. 518).

Philosophers mining other veins of theory have reached the same conclusion. John Rawls's 1971 book, *A Theory of Justice,* changed the way nearly everyone thinks about moral philosophy. In 1989, the political scientist Susan Moller Okin plugged one gaping hole in his theory by applying it to the family. She asked, What would it take to make families just? What would it take so that it really wouldn't matter to you—behind the veil of ignorance, not knowing where and to whom you'll be born—whether you'll be male or female, a husband or a wife? She answered that, in a just society, "in its social structures and practices, one's sex would have no more relevance than one's eye color or the length of one's toes" (p. 171). That is, women and men would have an equal opportunity to enjoy the rewards of raising children. Women would not be forced, more than men, to bear the costs.

Will It Happen?

Could we get to the point where men were doing half the child raising? Yes. Will it happen? No one knows. I suspect, though, that it's likelier than many people think. Let's take a closer look at several changes that would probably have to precede and accompany that kind of transformation.

As I have said, women have to train up. If women study and enter well-paid fields, then the average young woman will earn as much as the average young man. On average, wives will earn as much as husbands (if women marry men their age). Can women make that sort of leap? Absolutely. In the recent past, millions of women have greatly increased their level of schooling. African-American women are the leading examples. In 1952, the median African-American woman had 8.1 years of schooling. In 1975, the median was 12.4 years. In contrast, over that period, white women in the United States increased their median years of schooling only from 12.1 to 12.6 years (Wallace, Datcher, and Malveaux, 1980). This unheralded, stupendous achievement, in only twenty-three years, suggests that if all young women in the United States imitated the grit and high aspirations shown by black women, then by the year 2020 the typical young American woman would have a master's degree (median of 17.1 years of schooling).[1]

Already, the average young, white, unmarried, college-educated woman earns nearly as much as her white male classmates (Fuchs, 1988). That is

because highly educated women have poured into traditionally male-domi-
nated fields. If they continue to train up and move into those fields, then,
without a doubt, earnings equality for young women will be within reach.

What will that change imply for the typical marriage? It does not guarantee that in every marriage the wife will earn as much as her husband.
Whether she does depends on how people choose their romantic partners.
Once young women earn as much as young men, there are two possibilities.
One is that men and women will choose partners whose expected earnings
are the same as theirs—that is, they marry across. The other possibility is
that half the men and women choose partners whose expected earnings are
lower than theirs, and half choose partners expected to earn more—that is,
half the women marry up and half marry down. Consider figure 10.1.

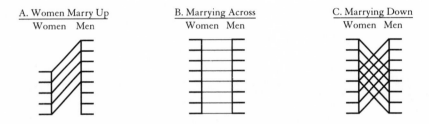

Figure 10.1. Marriage Ladders

In figure 10.1, people at the top of each ladder have high expected earnings. They are computer inventors and movie stars. People on lower rungs
earn less. In Ladder B, people have a very strong tendency to marry partners
who earn as much as they do. They marry across.

In Ladder C, women on the top earnings rung marry men on rungs below
them. Men on the top earnings rung marry women on rungs below them.
Roughly half the women are marrying up and roughly half are marrying down.

Ladder A shows the situation we have now. Women earn less than men.
There are no women on the top rung. In order for men on the top rung to
marry, they have to marry down. Virtually all women marry up. The lowest-
earning men do not get married at all. This behavior has been widespread in
human societies for thousands of years. Scholars call it "female hypergamy"
(*hyper* means "up"; *gamy* means "marriage"). When women are not allowed
to own productive resources, such as land, cattle, or factories; are not allowed
to earn wages or salaries; specialize in having and raising large numbers of

children so that it is impractical for them to earn salaries; or are discouraged from acquiring skills that are valuable in the labor market, they will have much lower incomes than men. On average, therefore, they will have to marry up. (Or, high-earning men don't get married.)

When young women earn as much on average as young men do, the traditional marrying-up system will come under pressure. If women choose to marry across, as so many professional women do today, and men consent, then in millions of marriages, the expected earnings of the husband and wife will be roughly equal. Wives who don't want sole responsibility for raising their children will have to do a lot of fancy negotiating to persuade their husbands to take on half or more of the work.

If, on the other hand, millions of women choose to marry down, as a few women do today, and they find partners who consent, then in millions of marriages the wife will earn more than the husband. The husbands may be as intelligent, healthy, attractive, and competent as the wives. They simply choose not to maximize their incomes. They might be men who would enjoy an upper-middle-class style of life but who aren't prepared to make the bruising competitive effort that earning that kind of money requires. They might vaguely or explicitly imagine a future in which they focus on taking care of children. They might work in a low-paying field, such as music, counseling, or community organizing.

(As noted in chapter 3, the scenario I am describing here is not a major departure from positive assortative mating, in which like marries like. That is, I am using "marrying up" and "marrying down" in a narrow sense, to refer only to expected income. In this scenario, women need not marry men who are less intelligent, less healthy, less competent, or who come from significantly lower socioeconomic backgrounds than they do. Such a change on a large scale would really be dramatic. Women would have to make two changes: they would have to stop marrying men like themselves and men who earn more money. If current patterns held, such marriages would also be more likely to break up than marriages of likes. That scenario is less probable and less desirable than the scenario described here.)

Something else will need to happen before men take on half the total amount of child care in the United States. High-earning women will have to change their own attitudes toward homemaking. Kathleen Gerson, in her study *Hard Choices: How Women Decide About Work, Career, and Motherhood* (1985), found that very few of the forty-six women she interviewed wanted a househusband. The women who worked full-time and earned high salaries thought that achievement in paying work was very important. They didn't respect homemaking.

A woman who feels that no intelligent person who deserves to be her husband should be a homemaker, or even a part-time wage earner who focuses mainly on children, is going to get what she wants. The supply of men who agree is large. She is going to get a man who will refuse to do significant amounts of child care. To bargain him up to doing half the parental child care, she will have to hire out so much child care that half of the remainder is very little. Note that, today, nearly all the people hired to do child care are female. The sexual division of labor in those two-career couples, or in a society in which all women are either computer inventors or nannies, has not changed one whit. (The sexual division of labor is the same as that in a society in which all adult women work for pay half-time and do all the traditional women's chores at home. That is, quite like our own.)

Therefore, for high-earning women to marry men who will do lots of child care, they have to root out from their own hearts the internalized devaluation of homemaking that so many now feel.

Of course, men will also have to change their attitudes. At least, half of young men—those who become primary parents—will have to adopt a new attitude. There is no doubt that for millions of young men to accept economic dependence on their wives, a basic shift in their outlook will be necessary. As I mentioned in chapter 7, David Gilmore explored the meaning of manhood in scores of cultures around the world in *Manhood in the Making* (1990). He found that in many cultures, adults rigorously train boys to take on the role of a man: "building up and buttressing the family or kindred . . . no matter what the personal cost" and "standing between his family and destruction, absorbing the blows of fate with equanimity" (pp. 43, 48). When men do their job properly, they acquire wealth and income that give them power over women. However, accumulating or enjoying that power is really not the main drive instilled in boys. The main drive is unwillingness to slack off, to slink back into the protected, warm nest of the mother, to become dependent. In places where women have eight children and breast-feed them, they cannot be soldiers, deep-sea fishermen, or roving, dauntless providers and protectors. In places where someone has to do that work, boys will be psychologically molded for it. They will suffer self-contempt and gruesome social punishment if they fail. Thus, they will fear and avoid dependence on women.

For our purposes, Gilmore's story is optimistic. Boys fear dependence on women only because of lifelong, intense psychological and social manipulation. They are not innate breadwinners. They are not innately averse to primary parenting or homemaking.

In the United States, millions of men have already fled the rigors of supporting their children or of acquiring status among their peers by building up their family's resources. They include not only so-called deadbeat dads but the men Barbara Ehrenreich described in *The Hearts of Men* (1983), who resent being locked into the rat race. They want a different sort of life. It may be a small step for millions of young men to add to a hesitant view of breadwinning a positive—or at least not aversive—view of raising children.

For that to happen, I suspect another change is necessary. Men who choose primary parenting as the focus of their twenties and thirties have to believe that raising children properly is challenging. In fact, raising children properly *is* much more challenging now than it was a hundred years ago. Back then, most parents had large families and raised their boys to be unskilled laborers and factory workers and their girls to be passable homemakers, with just enough training to raise unskilled laborers, factory workers, and passable homemakers. They didn't give lots of attention to each child. They couldn't. They had too many of them.

Now, the typical woman in the United States has one or two children. For children to get by in today's world, they need special character traits, literacy, mathematical skills, and sophisticated social skills that take years of effort to instill. Good parents give each child lots of attention.

Men will not only have to think that raising children right is challenging; they'll have to think that it is worthy. That is, that is an appropriately manly way to "build up the family" and "absorb the blows of fate with equanimity." In some cultures, as individuals and as a group, adults dote on children; they pour most of their surplus into them. They cherish them almost as though they were holy. The ancient sages of the Babylonian Talmud wrote, "The world exists only because of the innocent breath of schoolchildren" (Shabbat 119b, quoted in Grishaver, 1990). To me it is conspicuous that they wrote "schoolchildren." Children who are learning are the preservation of this world.

When more people believe that, more men will go into primary parenting. As more men become fifty-fifty fathers and primary parents and bring the glittery aura of male status to the job, more people will think that raising children is challenging and worthy.[2] That change, in turn, will make children better off. It will increase the political clout of people trying to steer more of our society's surplus toward children. Schools, libraries, and child support assurance programs will all get more money. More talented people will want to teach, heal, and work with children.

In order for hundreds of thousands, and later millions, of young men to become fifty-fifty fathers and primary parents, another change is necessary. The job conditions will have to improve. Mainly, primary parents will have to face less economic vulnerability than they do now. That means the laws and social customs surrounding separation and divorce will have to give much more protection to the lower-earning spouse. More couples might use marriage contracts to list the duties of the spouses to each other during and after marriage. Contracts like that are actually a very old institution. They are part of traditional Jewish and Islamic law and appear in many other cultures. Laws about alimony should take into account that homemakers forgo accumulating market skills when they specialize in household work that benefits the higher-earning spouse. State and federal law should guarantee child support. There is simply no other civilized way to operate. (Otherwise, selfish people litter the landscape with offspring like so many cast-off puppies, expecting former lovers, or the government, or no one in particular to support them.) Child allowances can also increase the bargaining power within marriage of the primary parent.

Breaking down the social isolation that stay-at-home parents now suffer would also be a big improvement. One option is co-housing. In a co-housing development, many families share a central kitchen, a dining room, a laundry room, and play areas. The grown-ups take turns cooking, so once a month each one cooks for thirty people. That arrangement frees up time. Some people spend it socializing. Parents and kids who live in co-housing say it is the kind of neighborhood they have always dreamed of (see, for example, Chan, 1994).

One important job condition will improve as more men take primary responsibility for raising children and more women become breadwinners. There will be less battering. That change will take place all by itself.

Why? As I mentioned earlier, men are more likely than women to start a physical fight with their romantic partner (Strauss and Gelles, 1990, p. 98). Men are also more likely to inflict serious injury on women than women are on them.

We face two possibilities. I'll call the first one the Bashing Man hypothesis. Suppose that men in typical couples start a fight mainly because they are men (whatever that might mean and however remediable or irremediable it may be in the short or medium term), rather than mainly because their economic advantage makes them think they can get away with it. How can we best curb their propensity to use violence? Men who are homemakers will be economically dependent on their wives. They will suffer hardship if their female providers leave them.

How likely is it that economic calculations along those lines can influence angry people, who may have been drinking or using illegal drugs (as we know is often the case in domestic violence)? On the margin, economic considerations do affect how angry people behave. After all, how many men punch their bosses? Even their female bosses?

There is a second possibility. Call it the Bashing Breadwinner hypothesis.[3] Suppose men start fights with their wives during conflicts because the men earn the money, which makes them feel invulnerable to economic hardship should their wives leave. What if putting women into the breadwinners' shoes turns *them* into bashing breadwinners? Then the incidence of battering wouldn't fall.

Remember, though, that women in fights with men are more likely to suffer serious injury than the men are. That problem in itself could act as a big disincentive to a female breadwinner and prevent her from initiating fights. In fact, she is a bashable breadwinner. (Only on average. Large women, women with military or martial arts training, weight training aficionados, and very scrappy women might not be bashable. If more women enter those categories, then women's average physical vulnerability will fall.)

In this bashable breadwinner scenario, which is the most realistic one in the short term, women are constrained from starting a physical fight by their likelihood of being badly hurt. Men are constrained from starting a fight by their economic vulnerability. The result is that there is much less battering.

Now consider those female breadwinner–male homemaker couples who have children. Remember that in a typical couple the presence of just one child increases a woman's relative probability of being abused by 50 percent. What happens in a nontraditional couple?

Meet Nita and Mando Peach, our last hypothetical couple. They have two young children. Nita sells insurance against virtual-reality software crashes. Mando works part-time at a bodypainting salon in the local mall. Mostly, he takes care of their children. They have a slightly below-average income. Sometimes life is stressful. Occasionally they fight. Once Mando threw the toaster at the window; neither broke.

Even so, having children did *not* raise the odds of violence in their family as much as it did in the families of some of their neighbors, in which the wives are primary caretakers of the kids. Why? Nita is not likely to start a fight because, as it happens, Mando is more able to hurt her than she is to hurt him. Mando is inhibited by the fact that if he ever hit or threatened to hit Nita, she could walk. She could *more easily walk* than could her female neighbors who are primary-parent moms.

Why is that? What about those cute children? (They are Peaches.) Three things make walking out easier for Nita than it is for primary-parent moms. First, it is easier for her to leave *and* take the kids. She can support them on her own salary. Mando has never contributed more than 30 percent of the family's income. Nita's threat (implicit or explicit) to leave with the kids is credible.

Second, she can leave and *not* take the kids. That option is easier for her than it is for primary-parent moms, because she is probably a little less emotionally attached to her children than they are to theirs. Even if she feels much more emotionally close to them than the typical breadwinner father would, she is probably a little less close than the typical primary parent. (This may sound harsh. A small difference, though, could matter a lot on the margin.) Her threat to leave without the kids (implicit or explicit) is more credible than it would be coming from a primary-parent mom.

Something else makes it easier for her to leave and not take the kids. Mando is a skillful parent. She knows it and he knows she knows it. He has been nursing the children through ear infections and stomach flus, cooking dinners, and hosting birthday parties for years. He cannot credibly threaten incompetence, as can so many husbands of primary-parent moms. He is vulnerable. Even though they have two kids, even though the ruckus and bills are sometimes stressful, he is unlikely to lose his temper and hit Nita.

From the standpoint of eliminating battering, then, it is men who belong at home.

As the changes I've discussed take place and more people become aware of them, more young men will be willing to devote themselves to their children for several years. As more men devote themselves to raising children, political activists will find it easier to persuade legislators and judges to enact more encouraging, homemaker-friendly laws. The feedback loop will be good for women, for children, and for men who want to raise children.

We are left, therefore, with a matching problem. How do the newfangled young women find the newfangled young men? This question is fascinating. Somehow, young men planning to throw themselves into the race to become CEO find young women who are happy to devote themselves to the men's careers, rather than their own. Do those young women send out subtle signals in the way they dress or behave, in the fields they study, or in the extracurricular activities they pursue? Or do the young men screen dates by picking up clues to their attitudes toward homemaking and being a helpmeet? Do networks of friends and relatives help? All the above.

Career-devoted women looking for a husband who will raise the children can use the same clues and the same help. Right now, though, their search is harder. The supply of such men seems smaller than the supply of women willing to raise children.

We will know that lots of women are sincerely interested in marrying down when new social customs arise. In chapter 7, I mentioned that my law school classmates from Texas threw parties for women from a nearby women's college. When women in professional schools throw parties for men from nearby colleges that are several notches down the scholastic-prestige scale, we'll know they're serious. Will any men come to the parties? A community organizer once told me, "If people didn't come to your meeting, it's not because they're not interested. You didn't put up enough signs." If women put up enough signs, men will come. If they throw a great party, men will also come back.

Other ways to meet the right kind of men are obvious. A few possibilities are college classmates majoring in low-paying fields, such as literature or education; men in one's religious congregation who are less driven to succeed in public life but who are bright and kind; men whom relatives and friends know; and even men who have signed up with a matchmaking service. In situations where it is hard for compatible people to find each other, matchmakers or marriage brokers often set up business to help. Maybe more people in the United States will use them in the future.[4]

The Crystal Ball

Now that we understand the prerequisites for an end to the sexual division of labor in the home, can we imagine in detail a U.S. of A. in which it has happened? In which men really do half the child raising? To do so, we need to grapple with several puzzling questions.

SPECIALIZATION IN THE HOME

Economists like specialization. Specialists do their special task faster and with less effort than a nonspecialist. If the task requires skill, they do it better, too. Wherever speed, ease, and polish are important, there will be some specialists.

In a future without a sexual division of labor, will most couples share breadwinning and household work fifty-fifty, or will most couples consist of a breadwinner and a homemaker? (Note that even in the breadwinner–homemaker scenario, the average homemaker might work part-time and contribute as much as 30 percent of the family's income in some years, but still specialize in household work and child care.)

I said earlier that this choice depends in part on whether women marry across in income or half the women marry down. However, if the practical realities of housework and child raising create pressure for one member of each couple to specialize in them, that will influence who marries whom. More high-earners will marry down in order to form a partnership with someone willing to specialize in homemaking.

Right now, many people feel that the practical realities of working for pay create pressure for one person to specialize in homemaking. They call for more flexibility by employers. I'm all in favor of more flexibility by employers. However, I don't think people have seriously considered the practical realities of housework and child raising. That topic is taboo. It is easy to see why. The only escape most women can envision from 100 percent responsibility for child raising is an arrangement where their husband does, maybe—imagine!—50 percent of the child care. Employed women whose husbands do 30 to 50 percent count themselves lucky. They put up with chaos at home, a shortage of time, and the sense that they are always juggling flaming torches on a tightrope. Some books, such as Faye Crosby's *Juggling* (1991), reassure women that there is nothing wrong with them for aspiring that high. (Here, of course, I've argued that lots will stay wrong unless women aspire much higher.)

In truth, though, it's not just that there are big gains from specializing in particular household tasks. There are big complementarities *between* many household tasks. For example, in our family my husband does all the grocery shopping and I do most of the cooking. We each do our task faster, easier, and better because we've built up knowledge and skills. When I shop, I have trouble finding things. When he cooks, that means he buys a store-cooked chicken. Because we specialize, we're both better off. However, we would both be even better off if *one* of us did *both* the shopping and the cooking. When I happen to go shopping, I notice things that I'd like to cook—such as vegetables for soup—and I buy them. My husband shops from a list on which, at best, I've collaborated distractedly. He rarely improvises. In a sense, grocery shopping and cooking go together as one big job to specialize in.

Why do we separate them? We have other values that override the gain we'd get from combining the jobs. My husband likes grocery shopping but knows nothing about cooking. I'm a mediocre cook but I dislike shopping. So we lump the efficiency loss.

The point is that there is a small efficiency loss. Careful consideration of other household chores would, I think, reveal that it is efficient to combine them, too, into one big job to specialize in. For example, it is much easier to do the laundry while you're watching your kid than while you're dictating a memo. If that is true, then the practical realities of household work do create pressure for one person in the couple to specialize in homemaking. That includes primary parenting.

People who cherish values other than an efficient household will choose to share housework and child care. They will enjoy a special kind of partnership. My husband and I get tremendous pleasure out of sharing the minutiae of our daughter's day. He appreciates each tiny detail as much as I do because he spends as much time taking care of her as I do.

I like my arrangement, but I know I pay a price for it. I not only endure chaos and flaming torches; I also enjoy few of the niceties that good homemakers take justifiable pride in: clever Halloween costumes, a beautifully set dinner table, home-baked bread. Those niceties require the time and skill of a specialist.

My husband and I each wanted a partner who was vitally interested in books and ideas. We married across. I suspect, though, that thousands of other professionals marry across mainly because we are all in a messy transitional stage to another way of living. I suspect that when men are doing half the child care, more couples will choose to reap the gains of specialization that a homemaker gives his or her family. Breadwinner–homemaker couples will outnumber the oddballs who try to share parenting fifty-fifty.

WARTIME

If men are raising half the babies, whom do we draft? This is not a frivolous question. I hope that the United States does not get involved in a war of such magnitude and danger that it would be necessary to reinstitute the draft. However, it may.

Here are some possibilities. First, we can simply draft men. We know that such a draft worked in the past. We also know what its social impact was. One problem is that in a world without a sexual division of labor in the home, many draft-age men will be primary parents with young children. The social impact will be different. The main problem, though, is that drafting only men seems unfair. Why shouldn't women bear their share of the risks of war?

Second, we can simply draft breadwinners. That will closely imitate the social impact of previous drafts. People who have chosen the economically risky job of raising children will not be forced to also face the risks of war. However, it is an odd rule. Why pick on breadwinners? What about homemakers who are childless or whose children are grown up?

Third, we can draft a randomly chosen batch of adults who are in the right age range. The pool will be roughly half men and half women. The problem then, of course, will be that the military needs a certain number of draftees to fill physically arduous jobs, such as infantry, for which a lower percentage of women than men will qualify. (This problem also arises in a breadwinner draft.) Men will remain better suited for infantry jobs unless and until military planners redesign the infantry, make the gear much lighter, or both.[5] It is possible that a higher percentage of women than men will qualify for noninfantry jobs, by virtue of their aptitude and skills. If so, a half-female pool of draftees is fine. If not, it won't do.

Finally, we can draft a randomly chosen batch of adults who are in the right age range, but weight it so that more men than women will get drafted. For example, the federal government could announce that this year it will draft 100,000 men and 70,000 women. That way, women bear the risks of war proportional to their ability to contribute to the war effort. That draft will meet military needs and won't unfairly relieve women of the duties of citizenship. However, it might be a little hard to explain to the public.

Should homemakers who are raising young children get an exemption?

Probably. Otherwise, children will suffer terribly. However, in each couple, only one person should be allowed the exemption. Truly fifty-fifty couples will toss a coin or the draft board will pick one. To persuade the draft board of their good faith, primary parents will have to show a copy of the family's income tax return or something comparable. As always, some people will try to commit fraud.

On the other hand, if war darkens the horizon, more men will try to become primary parents.

IDLERS

A few economists and policy nabobs who read this book will shout, "Ack! Do we really want to encourage men *not* to work? The country will crumble!"

When they calm down, they'll rephrase: "Do we really want to weaken men's attachment to the labor force? Such a transformation would slow economic growth, hurt productivity, reduce savings and investment, weaken if not destroy U.S. dominance in global politics, and disseminate rot and flab of every kind."

I doubt it. Men are not stupid. More to the point, they are not less selfish than women. Men will start withdrawing time from the labor force to raise children only if they are very nicely compensated for it by their wives. Women will join and displace men at the high echelons of earnings, responsibility, and power before, and as, men shift toward more work in the home.

We won't have more idlers. Men at home *will* be working, thank you, and so will their wives.

BAD DADS: FATHERS WHO AREN'T IN FAMILIES

Many scholars who study families have noticed the growth in the percentage of fathers who are so-called bad dads. They don't live with their children and they don't send them any money. Currently, two-thirds of children in fatherless homes get no child support at all (Furstenberg and Condran, 1988).

Many men who have cut their ties with their children claim it happened because the mother excluded them. However, recent research done on separated and divorced couples in Pennsylvania suggests that in most cases, the men were not excluded, as they claimed. They just walked away (Furstenberg and Condran, 1988).

If so many men in the United States are choosing to live apart from their children and not even support them financially, how could we ever reach a situation in which men were doing half the child care? That question is serious and disturbing.

Several things are clear. First, the easiest men to recruit into involved fatherhood and child raising are those who are already in the good-dad camp. They are highly motivated husbands and would-be husbands. Many want to be emotionally closer to their children than their fathers were to them (Osherson, 1986).

Second, many men who separate from their children and then fail to pay child support don't have a strong emotional attachment to them. That may sound obvious, but it isn't. It's conceivable that fathers who don't visit their kids send them money instead. In fact, the opposite is true. Fathers who visit a lot also pay. Fathers who don't visit don't pay (Furstenberg and Condran, 1988). Note also that a high percentage of absent fathers are really, really absent. In the 1981 National Survey of Children, for example, almost half the kids in fatherless homes had not seen their biological fathers in the previous twelve months. One-sixth had seen them only once or twice in the previous twelve months.

That suggests a twist. Fathers who become more emotionally attached to their children might be less likely to leave them and fail to support them. As I have stressed, fathers who are present in the home when the baby is born can become very emotionally attached if they get lots of solo time. That implies that when more women allow and persuade men to do significant amounts of baby care, *fewer fathers will become bad dads.*

Third, we need to take into account the economic characteristics of fathers who become bad dads. Bad dadhood is not randomly sprinkled through the male population. As noted in chapter 9, the average absent father has an income that is 14 percent lower than that of the average American man. The average absent father who has never married has a very low income: only $7,700 in 1983 (Garfinkel, McLanahan, and Robins, 1992). Some scholars speculate that those men fail to stay with their children partly out of shame at their inability to support them decently. Much more effective anti-poverty programs would help. In addition, though, if more women marry down, a smaller percentage of low-income fathers will feel it is their duty to support their children. Some fraction of men who would otherwise become bad dads might be enticed into family life if they had an alternative to being a lousy breadwinner. They could be good househusbands.

It seems unlikely that millions of poor, unskilled young men will be scooped up by higher-earning women marrying down. Marrying down will not make bad dads a curious fossil for future generations to puzzle over. However, it could give many young men the opportunity to be the kind of father they do in fact want to be: present, loving, and loved.

A Trickle or a Surge?

Will men trickle into hands-on fathering or surge into it? If all it takes is a trickle, we can just sit back and watch. In some cases, though, a change that would make everyone happier and that everyone wants cannot happen gradually. It happens only because many people are making a surging effort or it doesn't happen at all.

An example: many of you have probably heard of the Dvorak Simple Keyboard (DSK). On the DSK, the most frequently used keys are close to each other. On a conventional keyboard, the frequently used keys are far apart. That slows down the typist. Slowness was valuable at the turn of the century when typewriter keys jammed easily. Now it isn't. During World War II, the navy trained hundreds of typists to use the DSK. It took about three weeks. They were able to type about 10 percent faster (Dixit and Nalebuff, 1991). So why are we still using the old keyboard?

The problem is that it is hard for just a few people to switch. If they make the effort of learning the DSK, what good is it? Everywhere they go, they find old-fashioned keyboards. A few independent-minded eccentrics will switch, but not many. If everyone agreed to make the shift at once, it would be worthwhile for nearly all of us. More precisely, if we thought that a significant percentage of people would install DSK, it would be worthwhile for a significant number of us, as individuals, to make the switch. Thus a large-scale switch to DSKs will happen only as a surge, and never as a trickle.

People aren't the only ones who face such problems. Penguins do, too. At feeding time, penguins stand at the edge of the ice, staring into the water, their stomachs growling, all waiting for one or two hardy colleagues to jump in. Each would be happy to be part of a large crowd of penguins swimming and gobbling up fish. However, no one wants to be first, because there may be walruses swimming under the surface. Walruses eat penguins. In particular, they eat the first one or two penguins that go into the water. So the penguins wait. Finally, a few penguins get knocked in or a few bravely dive in. Then hundreds more surge after them. After all, if you're too late, the fish will have all been eaten.[6]

So, is primary fathering like the DSK? Are men like penguins? I suspect so. Both situations are examples of a common problem that scientists call a critical-mass problem. The desired reaction will happen only if a certain number of people, penguins, or atoms are in the same place at the same time doing the same thing. If there are too few, nothing will happen, *even if every-one wants it to happen.*

The lesson for us is this: the fact that few men right now are fifty-fifty parents, primary parents, or househusbands *gives us absolutely no informa-tion about how many would like to be* (Schelling, 1978).[7] It's possible that if more men were, many more men would want to be. If men's attitudes toward doing lots of child care depend on other men's behavior in this way, then we have a critical-mass problem. Consider figure 10.2.

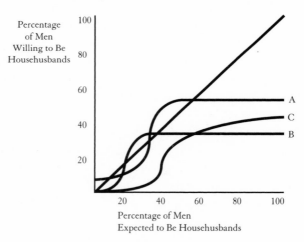

Figure 10.2. S-Curves

At any given time, people expect a certain percentage of men to become househusbands. That percentage is indicated on the horizontal axis. At the same time, a certain percentage of men are *willing* to become house-husbands. That percentage is indicated on the vertical axis. This graph says, in effect, that the percentage of men willing to become househusbands *depends* on the percentage expected to become househusbands. Also, vice versa. If only a tiny percentage of men are willing to become house-husbands, people will not expect a big percentage of them to become house-husbands, at least not for long, because experience will soon change their expectations. That means that for a given percentage of men to be house-husbands and stick with it, the percentage who are willing and the percentage who are expected have to be consistent with each other; the percentages have to be the same.

How exactly do men's attitudes and people's expectations depend on each other? There are many possibilities. The curves A, B, and C illustrate three possibilities or, if you like, three possible worlds. We don't know yet which world we live in. Possibly none of them. In C, even if every man in the United States had good reason to suspect that all his buddies were going to become househusbands (find where line C extends out to 100 percent on the horizontal axis), only 45 percent of men would actually want to become househusbands (reading across to the vertical axis). Soon, because people learn from experience, people will expect only 45 percent of men to become househusbands. Under that condition (find where line C extends out to 45 percent on the horizontal axis), only about 25 percent of men want to become househusbands (reading across to the vertical axis). Many men drop out of househusbandry. The househusbands left behind feel marooned. Men are stuck in a vicious circle, with more dropping out and, with each dropout, fewer wanting to stay. When only 25 percent of men are expected to become husbands (find where line C extends out to 25 percent on the horizontal axis), only a minuscule number of men are willing to do it. In scenario C, therefore, there is no stable situation in which significant numbers of men are willing to be househusbands.

Consider curve B. It crosses the 45-degree line, where the number of men expected to be househusbands equals the number who want to be. That sounds promising. In fact, it is. Notice that curve B crosses the 45-degree line twice, once at 15 percent and once at 30 percent. At 15 percent, what happens? If just a few men drop out, many fewer men want to be househusbands. We crash back to minuscule numbers. If, on the other hand, a few more men join in, significantly more men want to become househusbands. We zoom up to the next crossover point. Thus, the 15 percent point is not stable.

What about the 30 percent point? There, if a few men drop out, it doesn't matter. The curve is flat, which means that 30 percent of men still want to be househusbands. Similarly, if a few more men join in, it doesn't matter. Exactly 30 percent of men are househusbands, 70 percent are doing something else. The top crossover point is stable. It is a social arrangement that will stand the test of time.

To reach the stable point where significant numbers of men are house-husbands, all we have to do is make a surging effort past the difficult beginning stages. In the beginning stages, even though 20 percent of men are expected, only 10 percent or so of men want to be househusbands. A big surge could carry us up and over. A trickle never will.

Now consider curve A. It describes the only world bedeviled with a critical-mass problem in which half the men could become househusbands. In curve A, if 50 percent of men are expected to be househusbands, then 50 percent of men really and truly want to be househusbands. It, too, is a stable social arrangement that will stand the test of time.

Notice, of course, that instead of househusbands we could have said primary-parent fathers or fifty-fifty fathers. The reasoning is the same.

Scholars call curves like this S-curves, because of their shape. When people disagree about the likelihood of large numbers of men becoming househusbands, or primary fathers, or fifty-fifty parents, they are, whether they know it or not, arguing about the shape of the S-curve that describes the real world.

Which of these S-curves do we face? We don't know. We don't even know for sure whether we face a critical-mass problem. If we do, then curve A is what we hope for. Even in that best-case scenario, we have lots of work ahead to get over the hump in the beginning stages. As Thomas Schelling (1978) wrote, "Getting over the hump from one stable equilibrium to another often requires either a large perturbation or concerted action" (p. 165). In this case, it may take both.

WHO JUMPS FIRST?

Where will we first see primary-parent fathers and fifty-fifty fathers in large numbers? Probably in the United States first and then in western Europe. My impression is that a larger percentage of young American women than women in other countries have begun to work in traditionally male fields and earn high incomes. They also seem to hold less traditional ideas about family life than women in other countries do. Japanese women, for example, have terrific educations but live in an old-fashioned environment. Recent research has found that most college students there still have mothers who are full-time homemakers and fathers who are breadwinners. That childhood experience shapes their attitudes. Young Japanese men, in particular, have remarkably conservative views; they typically disapprove of women pursuing careers and believe that they belong at home (Kawashima, Yeh, and Takai, 1994).[8] To budge them anytime soon, Japanese women will probably need both a large perturbation and a large concerted action.

In what sorts of families will we first see primary-parent fathers and fifty-fifty fathers in large numbers? Probably in families with higher than average incomes. A woman with a high income has the most scope for marrying down and still marrying a man who is an attractive match, in the conventional sense. She can also compensate her husband for taking on a job that, in the early decades of the transformation, may be slightly stigmatizing in his social circle. She can let him buy lots of things he wants and still have money left over for herself, to spend or save. Women may not explicitly or consciously compensate their husbands like that. Still, some probably will.

Of course, fifty-fifty fathering is much less of a leap for a man than taking on chief responsibility for child raising. A woman who marries across, uses moral language, is devoted to her work, honestly isn't willing to have a baby on any other terms, and chooses a relatively child-oriented man has a decent chance of bargaining him into fifty-fifty parenthood. That is most likely to happen in upper-middle-income or middle-income couples who can afford to hire out lots of child care. Then there is less to split.

Another set of fathers has already begun to share child raising fifty-fifty. They are men working full-time with average and below-average incomes who are married to women who also work full-time. Both parents dislike hiring out child care on principle or dislike the sort of care they can afford, so they do all the child care themselves. That means the husband and wife have to work different shifts.

In the couples doing this whom I interviewed, each spouse earned from $20,000 to $35,000. One father, for example, worked as a chef at a seafood restaurant at night and the mother worked as a wire operator at a stock brokerage during the day. Both parents felt terribly pressed for time. Also, they missed each other. Neither had any ideological commitment to involved fatherhood. The husband's income was close to the national average but, because it didn't meet their goals, they had decided to sacrifice time and togetherness for a higher family income. If the real incomes of less-educated Americans fall further, or if well-educated Americans' income falls, more of us may get a taste of this hectic and lonely style of family life.

What about working-class couples? Will those men ever become fifty-fifty fathers or full-time fathers? Several things make it hard for them. For one, less-educated, lower-income men in the United States have more conservative views about work, women, and men than privileged men have (Rubin, 1994). Working-class women also have a harder time breaking into the occupations of their brothers and husbands, such as construction, than middle-class women do. Their families also earn too little money to buy high-quality child care. They do it all themselves, get a relative, or settle for care that makes them nervous. They are also more likely than middle-class parents to object on principle to hiring out child care (Rubin, 1976).

I suspect, though, that if middle- and upper-class people transform their lives at home, their new attitudes will trickle down to working-class and poor families. It has happened before. Middle- and upper-middle-class women were the first to go to high school and college, the first to switch to having only a few children, and, among white women, the first to work for pay outside the home. Within a few decades, working-class women in the United States and Europe adopted every one of those new fashions (Stacey, 1990). Moreover, new sexual and marital behaviors are still trickling down. Young working-class women do things today that never occurred to their mothers, such as indulging in premarital sex and living in their own apartments before marriage (Rubin, 1994). They are imitating the behavior that young middle-class women pioneered in the 1970s.

It's possible, then, that training up, marrying across or down, and giving solo time with babies to men could catch on, after a time lag, among less privileged young women, too. They face the toughest obstacles, but they have the most to gain.

MORE THAN A FEW GOOD MEN

If transforming the division of labor at home requires a surge, not a trickle, then we need lots of men to bravely step forward. Who will they be?

It's impossible to say. We can't rule anyone out. Women surprise themselves, and rise higher in the business world than they ever expected. Men surprise themselves, and discover they don't have to prove the things that once seemed so important.

One couple I interviewed makes this point clear. I have changed their names, but nothing else.

Meg graduated from an Ivy League college in the early 1980s with a major in biochemistry. She felt disgusted with the careerism of many of her fellow students, and she didn't know what she wanted to do next. She decided to work as a waitress in New York City while she figured it out. However, finding an apartment was hard. She finally happened upon an opening in the apartment of a young man named Kohope. The rent was reasonable. She moved in.

Kohope was an immigrant from Eritrea, north of Ethiopia. He drove a cab for a living. Meg had never known anyone like him. He had grown up in a small village herding sheep and goats. He ran away when he was eleven. For the next two years, he lived as a street urchin in Masawa, the Red Sea port. He became friends with a British marine pilot and his wife, who then informally adopted him. At the age of thirteen he went to school for the first time. At the beginning, he didn't even know the alphabet. He studied hard and in three years he struggled his way up to the seventh grade.

Then his British friends moved away. At sixteen, he was on his own again. Eventually, he found work on a Greek merchant ship. On a trip to the United States, he jumped ship in North Carolina, and made his way to New York City. He was determined to work, save money, and go back to school.

As Meg heard Kohope's stories and Kohope heard her stories, they began to fall in love. One day she mentioned offhandedly that her biochemistry degree could get her into medical school. Kohope was amazed.

"Wow! You could be a doctor?" he said. "The world needs doctors." From that moment on, everything was different. They got married. She applied to medical schools and was admitted to a top school as an M.D.–Ph.D. student. Kohope studied high school textbooks and got a GED (high school equivalency certificate). Then, because his relatives insisted on it and Kohope himself thought it was natural, they began trying to conceive a baby. They had talked at length about that decision. They both knew that while Meg was in medical school, he would have to be the primary parent. She had to study. Her tiny stipend as a Ph.D. student would be enough to live on, but not enough to hire out child care.

For the next four years, Kohope raised their son and did the housework. He also took courses at a local community college. He worked part-time, too, as a clerk in the student center, but their 1992 income was still under $10,000.

After finishing her degree, Meg applied to residency programs in her specialty. Kohope applied to four-year colleges. Now, Kohope is majoring in engineering at an Ivy League college. Meg is a resident at a university hospital. Their income is higher, and they have hired a cousin from Eritrea to work as their nanny.

Kohope and Meg's experience illustrates many of the points discussed in this book. Kohope had never dreamed of becoming a primary parent or a househusband. He was a very ambitious man from a traditional culture in which women wait on men. Meg married down, in every conventional sense. However, Kohope was just as smart and competent as she was, and shared her respect for education. They married for love. That love and their commitment gave them tremendous trust, which enabled them to make valuable long-term trades. Working together, they are both building up and provisioning their family.

In 1993, the psychologist Terri Apter wrote a book called *Working Women Don't Have Wives*. She took it as a given that working women would never have a partner at home devoted to helping them succeed at work. She, too, mistook a transition for a destination. Women *can* have a romantic partner who is devoted to helping them succeed at work, but for that to happen, things need to change. Women need to climb high in the business world or train up. They need to open their minds to the possibility of marrying a man whose expected income is lower than theirs. They need to imagine a future in which they will economically support their husband and children.

Most important, they need to redefine motherhood in their own hearts. They need to give their partners long stretches of solo time with the baby. They need to accept that at times their children will prefer to snuggle with Daddy, because they are most accustomed to him. They also need to give up control over what happens at home: what the baby eats for lunch, how she gets toilet-trained, the state of the living room. It won't be easy. It is, however, the price of not doing the work. If they don't want to work the second shift, they have to let someone else be the supervisor.

To marry the person who will do that work and do it well, ambitious women need to embrace something else, something their grandmothers knew but that many of us have forgotten: raising children and keeping a house really is a job to be proud of.

When millions of women begin to make those decisions, the sexual division of labor in the home will begin to melt away. The dream of real equality that so many women have dreamed for thousands of years will finally be within reach.

Notes

Chapter 1. Women's Predicament

1. Conversation with John Previ, Labor Force Branch, U.S. Bureau of the Census, August 26, 1993.

2. Wage discrimination by employers has also held down women's hourly earnings. Academics have confirmed the everyday experience of millions of women by uncovering evidence of pervasive and significant wage discrimination in the recent past (see, for example, Zabalza and Tzannatos, 1985). Discrimination is bad. However, occupational segregation pushes down women's earnings much more (see Fuchs, 1988). Studies have found that occupational segregation accounts for between 10 and 30 percent of the earnings gap between men and women who are working full-time (see Sorenson, 1989; Sorenson herself, using 1984 data and controlling for many relevant characteristics of workers, found that it explained 23 percent of the gap [p. 74]).

3. NCS interviewers talk to a nationally representative sample of people who live in 59,000 housing units all over the country. They talk to them once every six months for a period of three and a half years. If new people have moved into the apartment, the interviewers talk to them. They ask detailed questions of each person over fourteen years old, in private, about all crimes that they experienced in the last six months, along with questions about their income, occupation, educational background, and whether or not they have a job. The survey done from 1979 to 1983 included over 1,900,000 interviews (see Sandberg, 1991).

   To readers who know even a little about battering, one drawback of the NCS leaps instantly to mind. Interviewers asked people what crimes they had suffered, not whether anyone had beaten them or hurt them. Some people do not consider battering a crime, or don't think of it primarily as a crime. That means NCS data may understate the total amount of domestic violence in its sample. Much more troubling, though, is the possibility that some kinds of people (Southerners, vegetarians, who knows) may be more likely to think that battering is a crime than others. If so, that bias might distort findings that link economic factors to battering. For example, it is possible that, for some reason, more highly educated women are *less* likely to report battering to the NCS than other women. That could account for the apparent drop in battering as family income rises. However, NCS battering victims actually tend to have higher educational backgrounds and higher family incomes than victims in other major domestic violence surveys (Sandberg, 1991, p. 38). That suggests NCS data might actually underreport the amount of abuse in poor families. If they do, then poor women are at even greater risk than the NCS suggests.

4. Weitzman interviewed 228 women and men who had gotten divorced in Los Angeles County between 1968 and 1977. See pp. xix–xxi of Weitzman (1985).

5. In order to adjust people's incomes to calculate their standard of living, Duncan and Hoffman used the official U.S. government poverty standard. It takes into account how people's needs vary with their sex and age and the economies of scale that larger families enjoy (see Duncan and Hoffman, 1985, p. 490).

6. For example, Annemette Sørensen (1992) used data from the Panel Study of Income Dynamics to generate a sample of people who got married between 1969 and 1982 and whose marriages broke up between 1970 and 1984. She made a meticulous effort to see how different assumptions about the size of economies of scale can influence estimates of the economic consequences of divorce. Sørensen ran her calculations twice, using different assumptions about the size of economies of scale. She found that, one year after a separation or divorce, white women's standard of living fell 26 percent (20 percent if economies of scale were small) and black women's standard of living fell 31 percent (28 percent). Men's experience was very different. White men's standard of living rose 26 percent (44 percent) and black men's rose 22 percent (35 percent) (pp. 278 and 279). She did not consider the effects of remarriage.

7. Martha Minow, a professor at Harvard Law School and a specialist in family law, contributed this insight in telephone conversations with me in 1992.

Chapter 2. How Women Negotiate

1. Thanks to John G. Treble in his review of Shoshana Grossbard-Shechtman's book *On the Economics of Marriage,* in the *Economic Journal,* May 1994, p. 693, for reminding me of this example.

Chapter 3. BATNAs, Babies, and Bedrock Facts

1. This definition, and much of what follows, draws heavily from Lax and Sebenius (1986).

2. Or they come from a culture very different from that of most Americans, such as the extremely unassertive Senoi Semai of Malaysia, described in Gilmore (1990).

3. The cough syrup example came from conversations with Gillian Hadfield, professor of law, University of California at Berkeley, while she was a visiting fel-

low at the Hoover Institution at Stanford University, during the 1992–93 academic year.

4. Thanks to Gary Becker, Department of Economics, University of Chicago, for this point and for the point about feedback loops, which follows.

5. Thanks to Shoshana Grossbard-Shechtman, Economics Department, San Diego State University, who suggested that I make this point prominently (and who would like it made even more prominently than this). See Grossbard-Shechtman, 1993.

6. Biologists and others may recognize the outwaiting game as a descendant of the theory of the war of attrition developed by the biologist Maynard Smith. The animal that can wait longest has many advantages (for example, Smith and Price, 1973). When a woman says that her husband never cleans, waits for weeks until she gives in, and is an utter beast, she is, technically speaking, correct.

Chapter 4. A Traditional Marriage

1. My sources include Alpert (1988); Beer (1983); Cowan and Cowan (1992); Ehrensaft (1987); Gerson (1985); Griswold (1993); Kimball (1983 and 1988); Lamb, Pleck, and Levine (1985); Lewin (1993); McAdoo (1988); McDuff (1989); Marcus (1992); Martin (1993); Millman (1991); Pesquera (1985); Pruett (1990); Radin (1988 and 1994); Rubin (1976 and 1994); Snarey (1993); Staples and Johnson (1993); Taffel (1994); Terkel (1988). Also, research from England: Burgoyne (1990); Pahl (1983).

In my survey, I sent questionnaires to sixty-five couples in which the father did as much child care as the mother or more. I included several gay and lesbian couples sharing the care of their children. The questionnaire drew heavily from General Social Survey questionnaires used by the National Opinion Research Center, to find out the economic, ethnic, religious, educational, and occupational background of my respondents. These couples ranged from fifty-fifty sharers of child care to couples in which the mother was a breadwinner and the father was a full-time homemaker and planned to remain one indefinitely. I have used many details from the background, experiences, and negotiations of those couples in the last hypothetical marriage, that of Amy and Dave.

2. What about the possibility that men grieve as deeply but don't show it? Men do seem to mourn the loss of a child differently from women, so it's possible. Men are more likely than women to report difficulty working, to abuse alcohol, and to withdraw from other people. In interviews, some also tensely answer that they are experiencing no symptoms of grief at all, leaving researchers with the suspicion that the men are suffering, but don't want to talk about it (see Zeanah, 1989).

However, in one study that tried to directly measure parents' feelings of emotional attachment to their third-trimester fetuses, women reported significantly stronger attachment than men (see Zeanah, Carr, and Wolk, 1990).

We have another scrap of evidence about this point. All over the world, it is much more common for a father to abandon his child than it is for a mother to. However, it is also easier for fathers than for mothers to do so. A father has nine months to disappear. The mother can either seek an abortion or go to term. If she goes to term, once the baby is born, she may face legal—even criminal—liability for child neglect or abandonment if she skips out as the father did. She can give the child to relatives or put the child up for adoption, formally or informally, but she may face social stigma if she does. All this means that mothers' lower rate of child abandonment may partly reflect lower opportunity and higher cost, rather than only higher emotional attachment to their children.

3. With the following exceptions: it has become slightly easier for male couples to adopt, and some foster and adoptive couples include a father who does a lot of hands-on child raising.

4. From the National Long Term Care Survey, begun in 1982. See Select Committee on Aging, U.S. House of Representatives (1988, p. 18).

5. The Health and Retirement Survey randomly sampled 13,000 people in the United States between the ages of fifty-one and sixty-one. See National Institute on Aging press release, June 17, 1993, also available from the Survey Research Center, Institute for Social Research, University of Michigan.

Chapter 5. Two Transitional Marriages

1. The odds are low, but not zero. In 1993 I interviewed several husbands who worked part-time in order to spend more time with their children at home. These men included Silicon Valley computer programmers and engineers.

2. The towel example comes from Taffel (1994).

3. This analysis of Solomon's use of game theory comes from Brams (1990).

4. An unexpected blow by fate can also cause tipping in a would-be egalitarian couple. For example, an unusually difficult delivery can create pressure for the mother to become the primary caretaker. While she is recovering, her partner will almost certainly work for pay, even if he gives her lots of help with housework and baby care when he can. Their arrangement will tip if she can handle baby care and housework long before she can return to her paying job.

Also, a disabled or seriously ill newborn can create an emotionally charged atmosphere. Mothers are much more likely than fathers to feel guilt in such situations (see Zeanah, 1989). Also, relatives and acquaintances may visibly disapprove of the mother, but not of the father, returning to work with a sick baby at home. The combination of internal and external pressure, plus the enormous caretaking workload, may make the couple shelve their nontraditional plans and make Mom the primary parent.

5. Gayle Kimball also suggests solo time for men who want to be highly involved fathers in *50-50 Parenting* (1988).

Chapter 6. A Nontraditional Marriage

1. One couple I interviewed showed how strong an emotional impact solo time can have on a father. Here I'll call the couple Ben and Linda. Ben was an engineer who wrote computer software; Linda managed the production of technical documents at a big research company. Both parents believed strongly that babies need parental care, not care by a hired person. Linda planned to stay home full-time for several years after their baby was born. Ben earned more money than Linda and was not interested in becoming a full-time or even half-time parent. Just before the birth, though, Ben unexpectedly lost his job. Linda would have to support the family on her income, after her maternity leave ended. So, three months after their son was born, Ben became a full-time parent at home.

Months later, Linda began to worry that her income was not enough to meet her goals for the family. Ben said that she could ask for a raise. She asked Ben to go back to work, at least part-time. Ben was horrified. "Who will take care of Tommy? No one can do it as well as I can!"

Linda and Ben faced a serious conflict, in part because Ben had become even more emotionally attached to the baby than Linda had. They compromised by hiring a babysitter for twenty hours a week and getting Tommy's grandfather to babysit for two hours a week. Ben did part-time work from a home office. That way, he could peek in on Tommy whenever he wanted.

2. Several fathers I interviewed said they felt self-conscious when they were outside during a weekday with their children.

One man said he wasn't used to pushing a stroller. "I feel like people are saying, 'Look, his wife made him take the kids downtown.'" He was a part-time college student; his wife supported the family by working at three different nursing jobs. He said when he took his kids to the park, the other children seemed to like him but the mothers seemed to recoil from him. One problem, he admitted, was that he looked "a bit out of the ordinary," like a "biker-type person." He wore his hair down to his waist, had a biker goatee, and always wore sunglasses.

Another father who worked part-time struggled with feelings of guilt because he wasn't supporting his family as he had been raised to do. His wife earned more than he did. He was grateful when his boss asked him to wear a beeper. Then, when he was out pushing the stroller at 3 P.M. on a weekday, people would see it, know he was employed, and not think he "was a bum."

Sometimes, women give men they don't even know unsolicited advice. A father in Philadelphia told me that mothers at the playground told him from time to time that his child needed warmer clothes. He knew that his child was comfortable, though. He wondered, Would they assume a mother with a lightly dressed child was incompetent? He doubted it, and resented the treatment a little bit.

The most dramatic meddling I have heard about happened one day a stay-at-home father took his children out for an ice cream cone on a weekday afternoon. A complete stranger came up to him, started a conversation, and admitted several minutes later that he was relieved to discover that the man really was the children's father. He had been afraid that he might be a kidnapper! The father was certain that mothers did not get that sort of treatment at ice cream shops (see Kimball, 1988).

3. Some househusbands and highly involved fathers feel real distress about their status. One father who was a struggling, unpublished writer told me that he was "plagued by feelings of self-contempt." Taking care of his baby and trying, not very successfully, to write seemed very unmanly to him. Yet it was what he really wanted to do. Another father, who was an artist and househusband, said, "I feel very isolated most of the time." He had to work hard to meet people and make friends. He had recently started to take a class at night, mainly to meet people.

4. See, for example, *Full-time Dads: The Journal for Caring Fathers,* available from P.O. Box 577, Cumberland Center, ME 04021; books and pamphlets from the Father's Resource Center, 430 Oak Grove Street, Suite 105, Minneapolis, MN 55403; and the Fatherhood Project, 330 Seventh Avenue, 14th Floor, New York, NY 10001.

5. Fathers I interviewed had a wide range of experiences with play groups and with mothers' groups. Some fathers tried one, and quit immediately. Some quit later. One father joined several groups for new mothers, but found each time that after only a few months the mothers all went back to work or moved away. One father, in contrast, loved the group that he found, a large, townwide mothers' group in the San Francisco Bay area. After a few months, he became president of the whole group.

Chapter 7. A World in Transition

1. Some psychologists believe that it is unlikely that large numbers of women will ever consider lower-earning men attractive. They include researchers who are applying ideas about natural selection and adaptation to psychology. They note that for 99 percent of human existence, our ancestors were hunter-gatherers. Those researchers ask, What things would have made men and women valuable mates in that environment? Might natural selection have worked in favor of women and men who chose mates who were valuable, and thus, on average,

more successful than other mates? If so, then it's possible that most of us today are still walking around with an innate psychological propensity to find attractive the same traits that made members of the other sex successful as mates in the Pleistocene.

These psychologists speculate that the following traits made Pleistocene men valuable as mates: willingness and ability to provide for women and children; willingness and ability to protect them; and willingness and ability to do hands-on parenting, such as feeding and teaching the children. As evidence for their theory that women have an innate propensity to find men like that attractive, they cite data gathered from 200 small, nonurban societies that show that men's attractiveness to women depended mainly on their skills and prowess, not their physical attractiveness. Other studies have found that women are attracted to men who are ambitious, intelligent, and hardworking; men who express their feelings and so show that they are willing to make an emotional investment; and men who seem to enjoy playing with small children (Ellis, 1992).

As further evidence of an innate psychological mechanism, psychologists cite research on the dating and marriage preferences of women medical students and other highly successful women. Some studies have shown that those women do not behave like their male classmates, who put a high value on physical attractiveness, but instead want partners who are as successful or even more successful than they are. That is, their preferences do not seem to reflect the fact that they don't need a provider and protector (see Ellis, 1992).

I am delighted that psychologists are researching links between evolutionary theory and psychology. The fact remains, however, that all the evidence they cite can be explained more simply by an economic theory. Women in the 200 nonurban societies preferred men who would in fact be valuable to them. They lived in places where everyone followed a traditional sexual division of labor. The women medical students' preferences have been shaped in part by their cultural environment, where the vast majority of women are still looking for men who will be providers because they plan to raise children. We know that people's cultural environment shapes their marriage preferences in ways that seem unlikely to be innate. For example, in 1940 nearly all American Jews who got married chose other Jews. In the last few years, only half have. Only a very few women used to marry younger men; now 20 percent do.

In order to know whom women are going to marry in the future when more women earn high incomes, we are just going to have to wait and see.

2. Note that there is another reason for even a career-oriented woman to prefer a man who is a few years older. A privileged man's old-boy network becomes more valuable as he becomes older, to his *wife's* career as well as to his own. As more women enter the high echelons of business, politics, science, and so on, the difference in value between the old-boy and old-girl networks will decline, as

may the degree of sex segregation of the networks. That change will make career-oriented women more confident about marrying down in age.

3. Women are overrepresented in low-paying helping and social-change jobs for other reasons, too. Some mothers train their daughters more than their sons to help relatives and tend the sick. Martha Minow, a professor at Harvard Law School, suggests it's no coincidence that many women feel fellowship with underdogs; that feeling may grow as their own critique of women's position in society becomes sharper. Also, discrimination in hiring or promotion and repugnant environments in some traditionally male firms, such as investment banks and manufacturing companies, might result in a concentration of women at nonprofit, lower-paying firms, where they can confirm their supervisors' stereotypes by helping the needy.

4. Of course, in some workplaces it is not enough for women simply to summon the gall to ask for a raise. According to my law-professor friend, who has requested anonymity, the first woman hired after her cohort did ask for something extra during her hiring interview: a laser printer and a wooden desk. The senior faculty members who learned of her request told her that it was impossible and that her request was in poor form. She is still living it down. Nearly all the senior faculty members are male. It does seem possible that some unconscious derogation of women may have been partly responsible for the difference in treatment between the man who got $5,000 extra and the woman who was denied her laser printer and wooden desk.

5. Families earning over $70,000 may think they are under financial pressure. However, most are not struggling to survive, but to satisfy high and relatively new expectations about consumption. Amy Dacyczyn, publisher of the *Tightwad Gazette,* makes tart comments about middle-class Americans' ability to spend money without noticing. She argues that forty years ago parents practiced a thousand humble economies which today have been forgotten: mixing milk from powder, making soup from the water that vegetables steamed in, getting a haircut at a barber school (see Dacyczyn, 1993).

6. As the example of Dave helped show in chapter 6, the outwaiting game always hurts the impatient partner, whether the impatient one is a man or a woman, in a male–female couple, or in a same-sex couple. The biological clock ticks in lesbian couples, too. It disadvantages the older woman, the woman who most wants to raise a child, and the woman who most wants to carry a child. Thus a young woman who isn't particularly interested in giving birth has some leverage over an older woman who would like to give birth. That leverage might matter, because lesbians face negotiations that in some ways are more complex than those in male–female couples. If neither woman has a child yet, then they must not only decide whether and when to have a child, but which partner will

be the birth mother, how they will conceive (that is, whether they will use alternative insemination), and who the father will be.

The leverage of younger, less maternal partners may be counteracted by the strong ethos of egalitarianism that underlies many committed same-sex relationships and the fact that in most such unions, both partners usually work for pay even when they are raising children (see Weston, 1991). That is, both preserve a good BATNA. Data on lesbian and gay male couples are scarce, so we don't know whether it is egalitarian feelings that lead both partners to continue earning money or whether the risk of splitting up (which may be even higher than male–female couples' risk) makes each hesitant to become dependent on the other.

Gay male couples are different. They don't face a rapidly ticking clock. However, one man may want children more intensely than the other. Most gay men raising children fathered them in a relationship with a woman (see Patterson, 1992). However, in a growing number of states men can now adopt a child, regardless of the sex of their partner. A gay male couple who are free to adopt must decide—that is, negotiate—whether and when to adopt. Other things equal, the man who is impatient or very devoted to parenthood may find that he needs to concede a few things to his partner to persuade him to go along.

7. Goldscheider and Waite's data came from three National Longitudinal Surveys of Labor Market Experience, funded by the U.S. Department of Labor, each of which covered 5,000 people in a national probability sample. The surveys started with young men (ages fourteen to twenty-four), young women (same ages), and mature women (ages thirty to forty-four), in the late 1960s. Each person has been interviewed annually or every other year since then. See Goldscheider and Waite, Appendix A, p. 211.

8. There is one interesting exception. Children in two-parent black families do roughly 20 percent more chores than children in comparable nonblack families (see Goldscheider and Waite, 1991, p. 161). However, they may be one of those rare exceptions that actually proves the rule. More black parents and grandparents than white parents and grandparents grew up in very small towns or rural areas. Today's black two-parent families may be continuing the old, rural pattern of expecting lots of help from children. If that explains their kids' behavior, it may fizzle out with the next generation. Their children may behave like nonblack urbanites and suburbanites when they start their families and expect few chores from their own children.

9. For example, see Ehrensaft (1987); Beer (1983); and Kimball (1983; 1988).

10. None of the studies I've seen on involved fathers in two-parent couples did the statistical work necessary to distinguish between the effects of education and religion, nor did they have samples big enough to make such an analysis valid.

Another problem is that none of those studies started with random samples of households.

11. For example, see Abraham Ain, "Swislocz: Portrait of a Shtetl," and Abraham Joshua Heschel, "The Eastern European Era in Jewish History," in *Voices from the Yiddish,* ed. Irving Howe and Eliezer Greenberg (Ann Arbor: University of Michigan Press, 1972).

12. Hammudah Abd al Ati argues this position with great energy in *The Family Structure in Islam* (American Trust Publications, 1977), especially in pp. 178–82.

13. One difficulty comes from the traditional Islamic legal requirement that a husband support his wife economically. What happens if he is poor? May his wife divorce him, since he cannot fulfill his duty to support her? Abd al Ati writes in *The Family Structure in Islam* that, according to the one Muslim school of thought, *"[i]f she has the means, the wife must support herself and also her poor husband,* who is not responsible for repaying anything of what she has expended. But the great majority among the Muslim jurists grant the wife *a right of choice.* She may bear with him and keep the marital bonds, if she so desires. Otherwise, she may seek separation from him, and the court shall agree with her request" (p. 160, emphasis added).

As more Muslims enjoy the fruits of a modern economy and education for women, more Muslim jurists may conclude that they have no religious–legal objections to couples in which wives support husbands who aren't poor, but simply earn less (or have lower potential earnings) than the wives.

Chapter 8. Myths That Hold Us Back

1. This story explaining sexual divisions of labor among hunter-gatherers is only one of many possible stories we could tell. Psychologists, theologists, feminist theorists, and others tell many different sorts of stories. Our story here has the virtue of simplicity. It contrasts with explanations that propose biological, divinely ordained, or otherwise innate differences in receptivity to babies, or propensity to look after them, for which we have no direct evidence. It also contrasts with explanations that posit psychological differences acquired in early childhood, such as those proposed by Nancy Chodorow (1978), for which we have no direct evidence.

2. According to Eyer, the original 1972 study by Klaus et al. purporting to find maternal bonding looked at twenty-eight babies: fourteen who got special treatment and fourteen in a control group. Babies in the treatment group had sixteen extra hours of contact with their mothers right after birth. Some of the measures of attachment used were not convincing. For example, mothers who stood closer to their babies than other mothers did during a pediatric exam

were rated as more emotionally attached. The authors also rated as more attached new mothers who didn't leave their babies in another person's care even once for an hour or two during the baby's first month. It's not hard to think of other explanations for differences between women in those behaviors: trust in doctors, habits of acquiescence to authority, the qualifications of other available caretakers, and so on.

Strictly speaking, since no men were included in that study we couldn't conclude anything from it about *sex differences* in sensitivity to babies. Most remarkably of all, however, the so-called bonded babies scored higher than the other babies on only four out of seventy-five tests. Statistically, that does not suggest a large effect.

3. Gilligan based her book on four studies. In the first, she asked twenty-nine women to discuss how they had decided whether or not to have an abortion. Since no men were asked to discuss anything, we can't draw any conclusions about sex differences from that material. In a second study, eight boys and eight girls talked about a famous moral dilemma: Should Heinz steal medicine that he can't afford to buy from a pharmacist in order to save his fatally ill wife? Sixteen children is a small sample. In the third study, Gilligan interviewed twenty-five college sophomores chosen from those who had signed up for a Harvard course on moral and political choice. In the fourth, she interviewed 144 people about their moral decisions and their reactions to hypothetical situations. Other researchers, however, have found that people's moral decisions in answering hypotheticals are different from their decisions in similar, real-life situations (see citations in Orbell, Dawes, and Schwartz-Shea, 1994).

4. Also, in every country that reports homicide rates to Interpol, male killers outnumber female killers. That is evidence for our popular belief that in any given social environment, men are more violent than women, or at least are more successful killers (ICPO-Interpol General Secretariat, 1990).

5. The paper cited there, though, seems to be the wrong one. Dr. Pruett was not able to supply the correct citation in time for publication here.

6. For example, fathers are typically distant and stern among the Mundurucu of the Amazon (who conducted routine raids against neighboring villages for heads); among many herding peoples of Africa, such as the Rwala Bedouin (who were extremely warlike), the Masai, and the Dodoth; and among the Bantu peoples of sub-Saharan Africa, who combined herding with agriculture (see Coltrane, 1988, and Katz and Konner, 1981).

7. Lesbian and gay male parents, in contrast, have thriving organizations. They may be few in number, but they get lots of support by sharing their experiences with similar families.

Chapter 9. Government and Employers

1. Jonathan Gruber (1992) has found that at least 50 percent of women who were covered by work-based group health insurance in 1977 had less coverage for childbirth than for other in-patient hospital care or had no coverage at all. Since many states had already passed their own maternity mandates by 1977, that figure understates the lack of coverage that American women faced before activists started working on this issue.

2. Mandated insurance might also result in the overuse of some procedures. The rate of caesarean deliveries doubled between 1975 and 1981, just when mandated insurance of maternity expenses was taking effect all around the United States (see Gruber, 1992).

3. Does paid family leave work differently from unpaid leave? Probably not. The federal law required only unpaid leave. Companies that offer paid leaves will most likely offer it to both men and women, to avoid blatant sexual discrimination. The main hurdle, then, is to persuade men to take what is offered.

    We should note one thing about paid family leave that few advocates acknowledge. As a way of helping families with young children (and frail elderly relatives), it is regressive and inequitable. Employees with high salaries get high pay during their leave, but employees with low salaries get low pay during their leave. This matters because only 3 percent of poor children live in two-parent households in which both parents work. A fairer system would not make extra money for family needs dependent on people's employment status or their pay (see Fuchs, 1988).

4. In some European countries, firms are required to give full benefits to part-time workers. The result in Italy has been to drive part-time work completely out of the official economy. Union leaders sought that rule to make part-time work scarce, in order to protect the full-time jobs of their members. As a result, women with young children are crowded into the underground, unregulated labor market (see Del Boca, 1988).

5. Those long hours raise a related question. Why on earth are so many professionals expected to work them? Some researchers think that employers in companies where partners share income, such as law firms, worry that if they promote a slacker to partnership, their income will suffer. It's hard to weed out slackers who are pretending to be hardworking for a few years. So the partners make all the young employees work hours that are so horribly long, no slacker could endure the deception long enough to fool anyone. This combination of adverse selection and information problems could explain why so few prestigious law firms offer a forty- or fifty-hour workweek, much less a true part-time or slower track (see Landers, Rebitzer, and Taylor, 1993).

6. Thanks to Jeremy Bulow, professor at Stanford Business School, for the plan for affirmative action for men in academia.

Chapter 10. A Future World

1. As of March 1991, the median years of schooling completed for all American women 25 years old and older was 12.8 years (see *Current Population Reports,* 1992, table 1). The Bureau of Labor Statistics stopped publishing figures on median years of schooling completed in 1992.

   The figure of 17.1 years equals 12.8 years plus the 4.3 years by which black women increased their schooling by 1975. Obviously, when young people surge into high school and college, that will raise the median years of schooling in a young population much more than in an old population. Black Americans in the 1950s through the 1970s had a lower average age than white Americans had then, and than all Americans have now. That's why we can't say that by 2020 the median years of schooling completed for *all* American women 25 years old and over would be 17.1.

2. Changes in the laws and rules governing adoption that make it easier for men to adopt, whether they are single or living in male–male couples, will also increase the number of men who are raising children.

3. Thanks to Meg Meyer, research fellow in economics at Nuffield College, Oxford University, for pointing out the possibility of a breadwinner effect on the propensity to start a physical fight.

4. Note that some men are willing to take radical steps to find a housewife. Consider the mail-order bride. She comes from a poor country, has traditional ideas about wifely duties, and has very little bargaining power once she is here. She isn't fluent in English, knows no one, and doesn't understand how our laws and officials work.

   Will career-devoted women ever consider mail-order grooms? Probably not, because men from poor countries are likely to have ideas about manhood and provisioning their family like those that David Gilmore described. Mail-order grooms also present serious problems. First, marriages between people from very different cultures and class backgrounds are, on average, more likely to break up. Second, it sounds as though the mail-order-bride business is shot through with unethical practices and exploitation. We don't need to start subjecting poor, foreign men to that mistreatment. Matchmakers in the United States would do a better job for both women and men.

5. Note that some fire departments forced to hire women have found that they are unexpectedly valuable precisely because they are smaller and lighter on average than male firefighters. First, they can stay inside a burning building using an air pack longer than men, because their lung volume is smaller. Second, they can safely walk across the weakened upper floors of a burning building because they are lighter. (I learned this from Shauna Marshall, formerly an attorney at Equal Rights Advocates in San Francisco, who litigated the sexual and racial discrimination case against the San Francisco Fire Department in the 1980s.)

The military may make similar discoveries about women in combat. Even if they do, though, it is likely that in the militarily ideal infantry force of the future, men will outnumber women.

6. Thanks to Ian Ayres, professor at Yale Law School, for telling me about the penguin effect, cited in Farrell and Saloner (1987).

7. Thanks to Thomas Schelling (1978) for this point.

8. Kawashima, Yeh, and Takai (1994) surveyed 1,200 undergraduate students at Stanford and at four prestigious universities in Yokohama. American women had the most liberal views about what work was proper for men and women; Japanese men had the most conservative views. According to Ms. Kawashima, the scholarly paper based on those data will be published only in Japanese.

References

Achebe, Chinua. [1958] 1976. *Things fall apart*. London: Heinemann.

Akerlof, George A. 1982. Labor contracts as a partial gift exchange. *Quarterly Journal of Economics* 97 (4, Nov.): 543–69.

Alpert, Harriet, ed. 1988. *We are everywhere: Writings by and about lesbian parents*. Freedom, Calif.: Crossing Press.

American Association of University Women. 1992. *How schools shortchange girls*.

Apter, Terri. 1993. *Working women don't have wives*. New York: St. Martin's.

Arkoun, Mohammed. 1993. *Penser l'Islam aujourd'hui*. Algiers: Editions Laphomic.

Arletti, Rossana, Augusta Benelli, and Alfio Bertoli. 1992. Oxytocin involvement in male and female sexual behavior. In *Oxytocin in maternal, sexual, and social behaviors,* ed. Cort A. Pedersen, Jack D. Caldwell, Gustav F. Jirikowski, and Thomas R. Insel, 180–93. New York: New York Academy of Science.

Association of American Medical Colleges. 1994. Section for Student Services. Fall Enrollment Questionnaire and Reported Graduates Report, Update, November.

Averett, Susan, and Sanders Korenman. 1993. The economic reality of *The Beauty Myth*. Working Paper No. 4521, November. Cambridge, Mass.: National Bureau of Economic Research.

Ayres, Ian. 1991. Fair driving: Gender and race discrimination in retail car negotiation. *Harvard Law Review* 104 (4): 817–72.

Badinter, Elisabeth. 1981. *Mother love: Myth and reality*. New York: Macmillan.

Bakker, Isabella. 1988. Women's employment in comparative perspective. In *Feminization of the labor force: Paradoxes and promises,* ed. Jane Henson, Elisabeth Hagen, and Ceallaigh Reddy, 17–44. New York: Oxford University Press.

Baldwin, James. 1961. *Nobody knows my name*. New York: Dell.

Becker, Gary S. 1991. *A treatise on the family*. Cambridge, Mass.: Harvard University Press.

Becker, Gary S., and Richard A. Posner. 1993. Cross-cultural differences in family and sexual life: An economic analysis. *Rationality and Society* 5 (4): 421–31.

Beer, William R. 1983. *Househusbands*. New York: Praeger.

Bergmann, Barbara R. 1993. Can we afford to save our children? Cost and structure of government programs for children in the U.S. and France. Economics Dept., American University, Washington, D.C.

Betcher, R. William, and William S. Pollack. 1993. *In a time of fallen heroes: The recreation of masculinity.* New York: Atheneum.

Blank, Rebecca. 1990. Understanding part-time work. *Research in Labor Economics,* vol. 11, 137–58.

Blau, Francine, and Lawrence Kahn. 1994. The impact of the wage structure on trends in U.S. gender wage differentials: 1975–1987. Working Paper No. 4748. Cambridge, Mass.: National Bureau of Economic Research.

Bok, Sissela. 1978. *Lying: Moral choice in public and private life.* New York: Pantheon.

Bradbury, Ray. 1983. A sound of thunder. *Dinosaur Tales.* New York: Bantam.

Brams, Steven. 1990. *Negotiation games: Applying game theory to bargaining and arbitration.* New York: Routledge.

Brott, Armin A. 1994. The Daddy track. *San Jose Mercury News,* Feb. 6, 1C.

Brown, Roger. 1986. *Social psychology.* 2nd ed. New York: Free Press.

Burbach, J. Peter H., Roger A. H. Adan, and Freddy M. deBree. 1992. Regulation of oxytocin gene expression and forms of oxytocin in the brain. In *Oxytocin in maternal, sexual, and social behaviors,* ed. Cort A. Pedersen, Jack D. Caldwell, Gustav F. Jirikowski, and Thomas R. Insel, 1–13. New York: New York Academy of Science.

Burgoyne, Carole B. 1990. Money in marriage: How patterns of allocation both reflect and conceal power. *Sociological Review,* November: 634–65.

Burros, Marian. 1994. Despite awareness of risks, more in U.S. become fat. *New York Times,* July 17, p. 1.

Business Week. 1992. When the only parent is Daddy. Nov. 23, 122.

Business Week. 1993. Julia Stasch raises the roof for feminism. Jan. 25, 102.

Calem, Robert E. 1993. Working at home, for better or worse. *New York Times,* April 18, sec. 3, p. 1.

Chambers, David L. 1984. Rethinking the substantive rules for custody disputes in divorce. *Michigan Law Review* 83 (1): 477–569.

Chan, Gilbert. 1994. On common ground. *Sacramento Bee,* July 24, J-1.

Cherlin, Andrew. 1992. *Marriage, divorce, and remarriage.* Cambridge, Mass.: Harvard University Press.

Cherlin, Andrew. 1993. Letter to author, Feb. 18, citing *Current Population Reports,* 1992, P-20, no. 461, and unpublished research by the U.S. Bureau of the Census.

Chira, Susan. 1993. Obstacles for men who want family time. *New York Times,* Oct. 21, B-4.

Chodorow, Nancy. 1978. *The reproduction of mothering.* Berkeley: University of California Press.

Cohen, Lloyd. 1987. Marriage, divorce, and quasi rents; or, "I gave him the best years of my life." *Journal of Legal Studies* 16 (2): 267–303.

Cohen, Raymond. 1991. *Negotiation across cultures: Communication obstacles in international diplomacy.* Washington, D.C.: U.S. Institute of Peace Press.

Coltrane, Scott. 1988. Father-child relationships and the status of women: A cross-cultural study. *American Journal of Sociology* 93 (5, March): 1060–1095.

Combes, Josette. 1993. France. In *International handbook of child care policies and programs,* ed. Moncrieff Cochran, 187–209. Westport, Conn.: Greenwood Press.

Connelly, Rachel. 1991. The importance of child care costs to women's decision making. In *The economics of child care,* ed. David Blau, 87–117. New York: Russell Sage Foundation.

Cooper, Joel, and Russell H. Fazio. 1984. A new look at dissonance theory. In *Advances in experimental social psychology,* vol. 17, ed. Leonard Berkowitz, 229–66. New York: Academic Press.

Cowan, Carolyn Pape, and Philip A. Cowan. 1992. *When partners become parents.* New York: Basic Books.

Crosby, Faye. 1991. *Juggling.* New York: Free Press.

Current Population Reports. 1987. Ser. P-70, no. 10: Male–female differences in work experience, occupation, and earnings: 1984. Washington, D.C.: U.S. Bureau of the Census.

Current Population Reports. 1991. Ser. P-60, no. 180: Money income: 1991. Washington, D.C.: U.S. Bureau of the Census.

Current Population Reports. 1992. Ser. P-720, no. 462: Educational attainment in the United States: March 1991 and 1990. Washington, D.C.: U.S. Bureau of Labor Statistics.

Current Population Reports. 1992. Ser. P-70, no. 32: What's it worth? Educational background and economic status: Spring 1990. Washington, D.C.: U.S. Bureau of the Census.

Dacyczyn, Amy. 1993. Tips for tightwads. *New York Times Magazine,* June 6.

Dartmouth College. 1992. The Women in Science Project at Dartmouth College.

Del Boca, Daniela. 1988. Women in a changing workplace: The case of Italy. In *Feminization of the labor force,* ed. Jane Jenson, Elisabeth Hagen, and Ceallaigh Reddy, 120–36. New York: Oxford University Press.

Devine, Theresa J. 1991. The recent rise in self-employment. Economics Department, Pennsylvania State University.

Diamond, Jared. 1991. *The rise and fall of the third chimpanzee.* London: Vintage.

Digest of Education Statistics. 1992. Washington, D.C.: National Center for Education Statistics, U.S. Department of Education.

Dixit, Avinash, and Barry Nalebuff. 1991. *Thinking strategically.* New York: Norton.

Duncan, Greg J., and Saul D. Hoffman. 1985. A reconsideration of the economic consequences of marital dissolution. *Demography* (4, Nov.): 485–97.

Eagly, Alice H., and Valerie J. Steffen. 1984. Gender stereotypes stem from the distribution of women and men into social roles. *Journal of Personality and Social Psychology* 46 (4): 735–54.

The Economist. 1993. Low-paid, with children. July 31.

Ehrenreich, Barbara. 1983. *The hearts of men.* Garden City, N.Y.: Anchor Press/ Doubleday.

Ehrensaft, Diane. 1987. *Parenting together: Men and women sharing the care of their children.* New York: Free Press.

Ellis, Bruce J. 1992. The evolution of sexual attraction: Evaluative mechanisms in women. In *The adapted mind: Evolutionary psychology and the generation of culture,* ed. Jerome H. Barkow, Leda Cosmides, and John Tooby. New York: Oxford University Press.

Employment and Earnings. 1993. 40 (1, Jan.). Washington, D.C.: U.S. Bureau of Labor Statistics.

England, Paula. 1992. *Comparable worth: Theories and evidence.* New York: de Gruyter.

Entwisle, Doris R. 1985. Becoming a parent. In *The handbook of family psychology and therapy,* vol. 1. Homewood, Ill.: Dorsey Press.

Epstein, Cynthia Fuchs. 1988. *Deceptive distinctions: Sex, gender, and the social order.* New Haven, Conn.: Yale University Press.

Eyer, Diane E. 1992. *Mother–infant bonding: A scientific fiction.* New Haven, Conn.: Yale University Press.

Farrell, Joseph, and Garth Saloner. 1987. Competition, compatibility and standards: The economics of horses, penguins and lemmings. In *Product standardization and competitive strategy,* ed. H. Landis Gabel. New York: North-Holland.

Fausto-Sterling, Anne. 1985. *Myths of gender: Biological theories about women and men.* New York: Basic Books.

Fee, Joan, Andrew Greeley, William McCready, and Teresa Sullivan. 1981. *Young Catholics.* New York: Sadlier.

Frank, Robert H. Undated manuscript. What price the moral high ground? Economics Department, Cornell University.

Fuchs, Victor R. 1988. *Women's quest for economic equality.* Cambridge, Mass.: Harvard University Press.

Fuchs, Victor R. 1990. Are Americans underinvesting in children? In *Rebuilding the nest: A new commitment to the American family,* ed. David Blankenhorn, Steven Bayme, and Jean Bethke Elshtain. Milwaukee Family Service America.

Fuchs, Victor R., and Joyce P. Jacobsen. 1991. Employee response to compulsory short-time work. *Industrial Relations* 30 (3): 501–13.

Furstenberg, Frank F., and Gretchen A. Condran. 1988. Family change and adolescent well-being: A reexamination of U.S. trends. In *The Changing American Family and Public Policy,* ed. Andrew J. Cherlin, 117–33. Washington, D.C.: Urban Institute Press.

Garfinkel, Irwin, Sara S. McLanahan, and Philip K. Robins, eds. 1992. *Child support assurance.* Washington, D.C.: Urban Institute Press.

Geertz, Clifford. 1973. *The interpretation of cultures.* New York: Basic Books.

Gerson, Kathleen. 1985. *Hard choices: How women decide about work, career, and motherhood.* Berkeley: University of California Press.

Gilligan, Carol. 1982. *In a different voice: Psychological theory and women's development*. Cambridge, Mass.: Harvard University Press.

Gilmore, David D. 1990. *Manhood in the making: Cultural concepts of masculinity*. New Haven, Conn.: Yale University Press.

Goldin, Claudia. 1990. *Understanding the gender gap: An economic history of American women*. New York: Oxford University Press.

Goldscheider, Frances K., and Linda J. Waite. 1991. *New families, no families? The transformation of the American home*. Berkeley: University of California Press.

Greeley, Andrew M. 1990. *The Catholic myth: The behavior and beliefs of American Catholics*. New York: Scribner's.

Greenberg, Blu. 1981. *On women and Judaism: A view from tradition*. Philadelphia: Jewish Publication Society of America.

Grishaver, Joel Lurie. 1990. *Learning Torah*. New York: UAHC Press.

Griswold, Robert. 1993. *Fatherhood in America*. New York: Basic Books.

Grodzins, Morton. 1957. Metropolitan segregation. *Scientific American* 197 (4, Oct.): 33–41.

Gross, Jane. 1993. Big grocery chain reaches landmark sex-bias accord. *New York Times,* Dec. 17, 1.

Grossbard-Shechtman, Shoshana. 1993. *On the Economics of Marriage*. Boulder, Colo.: Westview Press.

Gruber, Jonathan. 1992. The incidence of mandated maternity benefits. Economics Department, Massachusetts Institute of Technology.

Gustafsson, Siv, and Frank P. Stafford. 1994. Three regimes of childcare: The United States, the Netherlands and Sweden. In *Social protection and economic flexibility: Is there a tradeoff?* ed. Rebecca Blank and Richard Freeman. Chicago: University of Chicago Press.

Harrell, Thomas W. 1993a. The association of marriage and MBA earnings. *Psychological Reports* 72: 955–64.

Harrell, Thomas W. 1993b. Women with MBAs marry up while men with MBAs marry down. *Psychological Reports* 72: 1178.

Herrnstein, R. J., and Charles Murray. 1992. But we're ignoring gifted kids; those low SAT scores reflect too many years of "dumbing down". *Washington Post,* Feb. 2, p. C-3.

Hill, M. Anne, and Mark R. Killingsworth, eds. 1989. *Comparable worth: Analysis and evidence*. Ithaca, N.Y.: ILR Press of Cornell University.

Hill, Martha S., and F. Thomas Juster. 1985. Constraints and complementarities in time use. In *Time, goods, and well-being,* ed. F. Thomas Juster and Frank P. Stafford. Ann Arbor: University of Michigan Press.

Hochschild, Arlie, with Anne Machung. 1989. *The second shift*. New York: Avon Books.

Hofferth, Sandra L., April Brayfield, Sharon Deich, and Pamela Holcomb. 1990. *National Child Care Survey, 1990*. Washington, D.C.: Urban Institute Press.

hooks, bell. 1990. *Yearning: Race, gender, and cultural politics.* Boston: South End Press.

Hrdy, Sarah Blaffer. 1981. *The woman that never evolved.* Cambridge, Mass.: Harvard University Press.

Hrdy, Sarah Blaffer. 1987. Sex-biased parental investment among primates and other mammals: A critical evaluation of the Trivers-Willard Hypothesis. In *Child abuse and neglect: Biosocial dimensions,* ed. R. Gelles and J. Lancaster, 97–147. New York: Aldine.

Hrdy, Sarah Blaffer. 1988. Empathy, polyandry, and the myth of the coy female. In *Feminist approaches to science,* ed. Ruth Bleier, 119–46. New York: Pergamon Press.

Hyde, Janet S. 1981. How large are cognitive differences? A meta-analysis using Ω and d. *American Psychologist* 36: 892–901.

Hyde, Janet S. 1984. How large are gender differences in aggression? *Developmental Psychology* 20: 722–36.

ICPO-Interpol General Secretariat. 1990. *International crime statistics, 1987–1988.* Saint-Cloud, France.

Jasso, G., and P. H. Rossi. 1977. Distributive justice and earned income. *American Sociological Review* 42: 639–51.

Jenson, Jane, Elisabeth Hagen, and Ceallaigh Reddy. 1988. *Feminization of the labor force: Paradoxes and promises.* New York: Oxford University Press.

Johnson, Dirk. 1993. More and more, the single parent is Dad. *New York Times,* Aug. 31, 1.

Juster, F. Thomas, and Frank P. Stafford. 1991. The allocation of time: Empirical findings, behavioral models, and problems of measurement. *Journal of Economic Literature* 29: 471–522.

Kahneman, Daniel, and Amos Tversky. 1979. Prospect theory: An analysis of decision under risk. *Econometrica* 47 (2, March): 263–91.

Katz, Mary Maxwell, and Melvin J. Konner. 1981. The role of the father: An anthropological perspective. In *The role of the father in child development,* ed. Michael E. Lamb. New York: Wiley.

Kaufman Associates. 1992. Unpublished survey of Stanford MBA Class of 1982. Menlo Park, Calif.

Kawashima, Yoko, Christine Yeh, and Yoko Takai. 1994. Institute and Japanese women's forum collaborate on research. Stanford University, Institute for Research on Women and Gender, *Newsletter* 18 (2): 10.

Kimball, Gayle. 1983. *The 50-50 marriage.* Boston: Beacon Press.

Kimball, Gayle. 1988. *50-50 parenting: Sharing family rewards and responsibilities.* Lexington, Mass.: Lexington Books.

Klaus, M., P. Jerauld, N. Kreger, W. McAlpine, M. Steffa, and J. Kennell. 1972. Maternal attachment: Importance of the first postpartum days. *New England Journal of Medicine* 286 (9, March): 460–63.

Kleiman, Devra G., and James R. Malcolm. 1981. The evolution of male parental investment in mammals. In *Parental care in mammals,* ed. David J. Gubernick and Peter H. Klopfer, 347–87. New York: Plenum Press.

Koestner, Richard, Carol Franz, and Joel Weinberger. 1990. The family origins of empathic concern: A 26-year longitudinal study. *Journal of Personality and Social Psychology* 58 (4): 709–17.

Kunde, Diane. 1994. Job sharing reaches executive ranks. *Dallas Morning News,* Jan. 12, 1-D.

Kung, S. W. 1962. *Chinese in American life: Some aspects of their history, status, problems, and contributions.* Seattle: University of Washington Press.

Lamb, Michael E., Ann M. Frodi, Carl-Philip Hwang, and Majt Frodi. 1982. Varying degrees of paternal involvement in infant care: Attitudinal and behavioral correlates. In *Nontraditional families: Parenting and child development,* ed. Michael E. Lamb. Hillsdale, N.J.: Erlbaum Associates.

Lamb, Michael E., Joseph H. Pleck, and James E. Levine. 1985. The role of the father in child development: The effects of increased paternal involvement. In *Advances in clinical child psychiatry,* vol. 8, ed. B. B. Lahey and A. E. Kazdin. New York: Plenum.

Landers, Renee M., James B. Rebitzer, and Lowell J. Taylor. 1993. Rat race redux: Adverse selection in the determination of work hours. Unpublished paper, Boston College Law School.

Lax, David A., and James K. Sebenius. 1986. *The manager as negotiator: Bargaining for cooperation and competitive gain.* New York: Free Press.

Lazear, Edward P., and Robert T. Michael. 1988. *Allocation of income within the household.* Chicago: University of Chicago Press.

LeBreton, Laurie Wessman, and Sara Segal Loevy. 1992. *Breaking new ground: Worksite 2000.* Chicago: Chicago Women in Trades.

Lewin, Ellen. 1993. *Lesbian mothers.* Ithaca, N.Y.: Cornell University Press.

Li Yu. [1657] 1992. *A tower for the summer heat,* trans. Patrick Hanan. New York: Ballantine Books.

Lublin, Joann S. 1993. Husbands in limbo. *Wall Street Journal,* April 13, 1.

McAdoo, Harriet Pipes. 1988. *Black families.* 2nd ed. New York: Sage.

Maccoby, Eleanor M., and Carol Nagy Jacklin. 1974. *The psychology of sex differences.* Stanford, Calif.: Stanford University Press.

McDuff, Mary Ann. 1989. Mexican American women: A three-generational study of attitudes and behaviors. Master's thesis, Texas Woman's University, College of Natural and Social Sciences.

McElroy, Marjorie B., and Mary Jean Horney. 1981. Nash-bargained household decisions: Toward a generalization of the theory of demand. *International Economic Review* 22 (2, June): 333–49.

Malinowski, Bronislaw. 1927. *Sex and repression in savage society.* New York: Harcourt Brace.

Manser, Marilyn, and Murray Brown. 1980. Marriage and household decision-making: A bargaining analysis. *International Economic Review* 21 (1, Feb.): 31–44.

Marcus, Eric. 1992. *The male couple's guide.* New York: HarperPerennial.

Margolick, David. 1992. At the bar. *New York Times,* Nov. 20, B-1.

Martin, April. 1993. *The lesbian and gay parenting handbook.* New York: Harper-Perennial.

Mill, John Stuart. [1859] 1991. *On liberty and other essays.* Oxford: Oxford University Press.

Millman, Marcia. 1991. *Warm hearts and cold cash: The intimate dynamics of families and money.* New York: Free Press.

Mortensen, Dale T. 1988. Matching: Finding a partner for life or otherwise. *American Journal of Sociology* 94, supplement: S215–S240.

Moss, Richard Loring, and Thomas D. Curtis. 1985. The economics of flextime. *Journal of Behavioral Economics* 14 (2): 95–115.

Muller, Carol B. 1992. Women in science: How long a rare species? *Directions,* Thayer School of Engineering, Dartmouth College.

Mullis, Ina, John Dossey, Eugene Owen, and Gary Phillips. 1991. *The state of mathematics achievement, executive summary.* Washington, D.C.: U.S. Department of Education.

Murasaki Shikibu. [ca. 1010] 1990. *The tale of Genji,* trans. Edward G. Seidensticker. New York: Vintage.

Narayan, R. K., trans. 1972. *The Ramayana.* New York: Viking.

National Conference of Catholic Bishops. 1993. Follow the way of love.

National Institute on Aging. 1993. Press release, June 17.

Okin, Susan Moller. 1989. *Justice, gender, and the family.* New York: Basic Books.

Orbell, John, Robyn Dawes, and Peregrine Schwartz-Shea. 1994. Trust, social categories, and individuals: The case of gender. *Motivation and Emotion* 18 (2): 109–28.

Osherson, Samuel. 1986. *Finding our fathers.* New York: Free Press.

Pahl, Jan. 1983. The allocation of money and the structuring of inequality within marriage. *Sociological Review* 31 (1): 237–64.

Paoletti, Jo. 1989. The Children's Department. In *Men and women: Dressing the part.* Washington, D.C.: Smithsonian Institution Press.

Patterson, Charlotte J. 1992. Children of lesbian and gay parents. *Child Development* 63: 1025–42.

Pedersen, Cort A., Jack D. Caldwell, Gustav F. Jirikowski, and Thomas R. Insel, eds. 1992. *Oxytocin in maternal, sexual, and social behaviors.* New York: New York Academy of Science.

Pesquera, Beatriz Margarita. 1985. Work and family: A comparative analysis of professional, clerical, and blue-collar Chicana women. Ph.D. diss. in sociology, University of California Berkeley.

Phelps, Edmund S. 1972. The statistical theory of racism and sexism. *American Economic Review* 62 (Sept.): 659–61.

Presser, Harriet B. 1989. Can we make time for children? The economy, work schedules, and child care. *Demography* 26 (4): 523–43.

Pruett, Kyle D. 1988. Father's influence in the development of infant's relationships. *Acta Paediatrica Scandinavica,* Supplementum No. 344, vol. 77: 43–53.

Pruett, Kyle D. 1990. The nurturing male: A longitudinal study of primary nurturing fathers. In *Fathers and their families,* ed. S. Cath and R. Corwitt. New York: Analytic Press.

Pruett, Kyle D. 1991. Consequences of primary paternal care: Fathers and babies in the first six years. In *The course of life: Middle and late childhood,* vol. 3, ed. S. Greenspan and G. Pollock. Madison, Conn.: International University Press.

Pruitt, Ida. 1945. *A daughter of Han.* Stanford, Calif.: Stanford University Press.

Radin, Norma. 1988. Primary caregiving fathers of long duration. In *Fatherhood today,* ed. Phyllis Bronstein and Carolyn Pape Cowan, 127–43. New York: Wiley-Interscience.

Radin, Norma. 1994. Primary caregiving fathers in intact families. In *Redefining families,* ed. Adele E. Gottfried and Allen W. Gottfried. New York: Plenum Press.

Raiffa, Howard. 1982. *The art and science of negotiation.* Cambridge, Mass.: Harvard University Press.

Rawls, John. 1971. *A theory of justice.* Cambridge, Mass.: Harvard University Press.

Review of legal education in the United States. 1992 (Fall). Chicago: American Bar Association.

Rich, Adrienne. 1979. *On lies, secrets, and silences.* New York: Norton.

Rigdon, Joan E. 1993. A wife's higher pay can test a marriage. *Wall Street Journal,* Jan. 28, B-1.

Rivera-Batiz, Francisco. 1992. Quantitative literacy and the likelihood of employment among young people in the United States. *Journal of Human Resources* 27 (2): 313–28.

Robins, Philip K. 1991. Child care policy and research: An economist's perspective. In *The economics of child care,* ed. David Blau. New York: Russell Sage Foundation.

Rose, Carol M. 1992. Women and property: Gaining and losing ground. *Virginia Law Review* 78 (2): 421–59.

Rousseau, Jean-Jacques. [1762] 1979. *Émile.* New York: Basic Books.

Rubin, Lillian B. 1976. *Worlds of pain: Life in the working class family.* New York: Basic Books.

Rubin, Lillian B. 1994. *Families on the fault line: America's working class speaks about the family, the economy, race, and ethnicity.* New York: HarperCollins.

Russell, Graeme. 1982. Shared caregiving families: An Australian study. In *Nontraditional families: Parenting and child development,* ed. Michael E. Lamb. Hillsdale, N.J.: Erlbaum.

Sadker, Myra, and David Sadker. 1994. *Failing at fairness: How America's schools cheat girls.* New York: Scribner's.

Sagi, Abraham. 1982. Antecedents and consequences of various degrees of paternal involvement in child rearing: The Israeli project. In *Nontraditional families: Parenting and child development,* ed. Michael E. Lamb. Hillsdale, N.J.: Erlbaum.

Sagi, Abraham, and Nina Koren-Karie. 1993. Israel. In *International handbook of child care policies and programs,* ed. Moncrieff Cochran, 269–90. Westport, Conn.: Greenwood Press.

Sahlins, Marshall D. 1972. *Stone Age economics.* Chicago: Aldine-Atherton.

Sandberg, Sheryl. 1991. Economic factors and intimate violence. Unpublished paper, Department of Economics, Harvard University.

Santrock, John W., and Richard A. Warshak. 1979. Father custody and social development in boys and girls. *Journal of Social Issues* 35 (4):112–25.

Schelling, Thomas C. 1978. *Micromotives and macrobehavior.* New York: Norton.

Schelling, Thomas C. 1980. *The strategy of conflict.* Cambridge, Mass.: Harvard University Press.

Schwartz, Felice N. 1992. *Breaking with tradition: Women and work, the new facts of life.* New York: Warner Books.

Select Committee on Aging, U.S. House of Representatives. 1988. Exploding the myths: Caregiving in America. Comm. Pub. No. 100-665.

Shellenbarger, Sue. 1993. Work and family. *Wall Street Journal,* March 15.

Sherman, Julia. 1978. *Sex-related cognitive differences: An essay on theory and evidence.* Springfield, Ill.: Charles C. Thomas.

Smith, John M., and G. R. Price. 1973. The logic of animal conflict. *Nature* 246:15–18.

Snarey, John. 1993. *How fathers care for the next generation.* Cambridge, Mass.: Harvard University Press.

Sørensen, Annemette. 1992. Estimating the economic consequences of separation and divorce: A cautionary tale from the United States. In *Economic consequences of divorce: The international perspective,* ed. Lenore J. Weitzman and Mavis Maclean. New York: Oxford University Press.

Sorenson, Elaine. 1989. The wage effects of occupational sex composition: A review and new findings. In *Comparable worth: Analysis and evidence,* ed. M. Anne Hill and Mark R. Killingsworth. Ithaca, N.Y.: ILR Press of Cornell University.

Sorenson, Elaine. 1991. *Exploring the reasons behind the narrowing gender gap in earnings.* Washington, D.C.: Urban Institute Press.

Stacey, Judith. 1990. *Brave new families: Stories of domestic upheaval in late twentieth century America.* New York: Basic Books.

Stacey, Judith, and Susan Elizabeth Gerard. 1990. "We are not doormats": The influence of feminism on contemporary evangelicals in the United States. In

Uncertain terms: Negotiating gender in American culture, ed. Faye Ginsberg and Anna Lowenhaupt Tsing, 98–117. Boston: Beacon Press.

Stamp, Peggy. 1985. Research note: Balance of financial power in marriage: An exploratory study of breadwinning wives. *Sociological Review* 33 (August): 546–57.

Staples, Robert, and Leanor Boulin Johnson. 1993. *Black families at the crossroads.* San Francisco: Jossey-Bass.

Statistical Abstract. 1993. Washington, D.C.: U.S. Bureau of the Census.

Stevenson, Richard W. 1993. Sweden facing rigors of welfare cuts. *New York Times,* March 14, 10.

Stone, Robyn I., and Pamela Farley Short. 1990. The competing demands of employment and informal caregiving to disabled elders. *Medical Care* 28 (6): 513–26.

Strauss, Murray A., and Richard J. Gelles. 1990. *Physical violence in American families: Risk factors and adaptations to violence in 8,145 families.* New Brunswick, N.J.: Transaction Publishers.

Sundström, Marianne. 1991. Part-time work in Sweden: Trends and equality effects. *Journal of Economic Issues* 25 (1): 167–78.

Sundström, Marianne, and Frank P. Stafford. 1992. Female labour force participation, fertility and public policy in Sweden. *European Journal of Population* 8: 199–215.

Swiss, Deborah J., and Judith P. Walker. 1993. *Women and the work/family dilemma.* New York: J. Wiley.

Taffel, Ron. 1994. *Why parents disagree.* New York: Morrow.

Tannen, Deborah. 1990. *You just don't understand.* New York: Ballantine.

Teitelbaum, Michael S., and Jay M. Winter. 1985. *Fear of population decline.* New York: Academic Press.

Terkel, Studs. 1988. *The great divide: Second thoughts on the American dream.* New York: Pantheon.

Thomas, Duncan. 1991. Gender differences in household resource allocation. Living Standards Measurement Study Working Paper No. 79. Washington, D.C.: World Bank.

Timmer, Susan Goff, Jacquelynne Eccles, and Kerth O'Brien. 1985. How children use their time. In *Time, goods, and well-being,* ed. F. Thomas Juster and Frank P. Stafford, 353–82. Ann Arbor: University of Michigan Press.

Turnbull, Colin. 1983. *The human cycle.* New York: Simon & Schuster.

Waite, Linda J., and Sue E. Berryman. 1985. *Women in nontraditional occupations.* Santa Monica, Calif.: Rand.

Wallace, Phyllis A., Linda Datcher, and Julianne Malveaux. 1980. *Black women in the labor force.* Cambridge, Mass.: MIT Press.

Weiss, Robert S. 1979. Growing up a little faster: The experience of growing up in a single-parent household. *Journal of Social Issues* 35 (4): 97–111.

Weitzman, Lenore. 1985. *The divorce revolution.* New York: Free Press.

West, Jerry, Wendy Miller, and Louis Diodato. 1985. *An analysis of course-taking patterns in secondary schools as related to student characteristics.* Washington, D.C.: National Center for Education Statistics, U.S. Department of Education.

Weston, Kath. 1991. *Families we choose: Lesbians, gays, kinship.* New York: Columbia University Press.

Whiting, J., and B. Whiting. 1975. Aloofness and intimacy of husbands and wives. *Ethos,* vol. 3, 183–207.

Wilde, Oscar. [1895] (1980). *The importance of being earnest,* ed. Russell Jackson. New York: Norton.

Williams, Edith, and Norma Radin. 1992. Predictors of adolescent academic achievement and expectations: An 11-year follow-up. Unpublished paper, School of Social Work, University of Michigan.

Williams, Edith, Norma Radin, and Theresa Allegro. 1992. Sex-role attitudes of adolescents reared primarily by their fathers: An 11-year follow-up. Unpublished manuscript, School of Social Work, University of Michigan.

Williams, Michael W. 1990. Polygamy and the declining male to female ratio in black communities. In *Black families: An interdisciplinary perspective,* ed. Harold E. Cheatham and James B. Stewart. New Brunswick, N.J.: Transaction Publishers.

Winett, Richard A., and Michael S. Neale. 1980. Results of experimental study on flexitime and family life. *Monthly Labor Bulletin* 103 (11): 29–32.

Wolf, Naomi. 1991. *The beauty myth: How images of beauty are used against women.* New York: Morrow.

Wollstonecraft, Mary. [1792] 1992. *A vindication of the rights of women.* London: Penguin.

Ybarra, Lea. 1982. When wives work: The impact on the family. *Journal of Marriage and the Family* 44: 169–77.

Yogman, Michael W. 1990. Male parental behavior in humans and nonhuman primates. In *Mammalian parenting: Biochemical, neurobiological, and behavioral determinants,* ed. Norman A. Krasnegor and Robert S. Bridges, 461–81. New York: Oxford University Press.

Yun, Kwi-Ryung. 1992. Effects of child support on remarriage of single mothers. In *Child support assurance,* ed. Irwin Garfinkel, Sara S. McLanahan, and Philip K. Robins, 315–38. Washington, D.C.: Urban Institute Press.

Zabalza, A., and Z. Tzannatos. 1985. The effect of Britain's anti-discriminatory legislation on relative pay and employment. *Economic Journal* 95 (September): 679–99.

Zeanah, Charles H. 1989. Adaptation following perinatal loss: A critical review. *Journal of the American Academy of Child and Adolescent Psychiatry* 28: 467–80.

Zeanah, Charles H., Steven Carr, and Sarah Wolk. 1990. Fetal movements and the imagined baby of pregnancy: Are they related? *Journal of Reproductive and Infant Psychology* 8: 23–36.

Zeanah, Charles H., Jacquelyn V. Dailey, Mary-Jo Rosenblatt, and Devereux N. Saller, Jr. 1993. Do women grieve after terminating pregnancies because of fetal anomalies? A controlled investigation. *Obstetrics and Gynecology* 82 (2, August): 270–75.

Zich, Janet. 1993. Ten years out: The class of '82 takes stock. *Stanford Business School Magazine,* March.

Zill, Nicholas, and Carolyn C. Rogers. 1988. Recent trends in the well-being of children in the United States and their implications for public policy. In *The changing American family and public policy,* ed. Andrew J. Cherlin, 31–115. Washington, D.C.: Urban Institute Press.

Index

Moses, 32
Mother-Infant Bonding: A Scientific Fiction (Eyer), 175
Mother Love: Myth and Reality (Badinter), 173
Mothers: and the headstart effect, 74–77, 102–4, 109, 112–14, 123–24, 195; and maternal bonding, 174–76; and maternal instinct, 173–77, 188; single, as heads of households, 116, 155–56. *See also* Birth; Pregnancy; Sex differences
Mr. Mom (film), 126
Ms. (magazine), 101
Muslims, 161. *See also* Islamic law; Koran

Nagging, 91–92, 95
Names, 151–52
National Crime Survey (NCS), 17, 18, 239*n*3
National Family Violence Resurvey, 17
National Longitudinal Surveys, 247*n*7
National Opinion Research Center, 241*n*1
National Rifle Association, 23
National Survey of Children, 230
Nation of Islam, 161
Native Americans, 161–62, 181–82
Natural selection, 173, 244*n*1
Navy SEALs, 149–50
Negotiation, 5–6; basic elements of, 9–64; definition of, 37–38; high-context, 29–32; in a nontraditional marriage, 115–29; and renegotiation, 89–100, 109–11; styles of, 31; in a traditional marriage, 67–84; in transitional marriages, 85–114; women's ability to carry out, 32–36. *See also* Bargaining power; BATNA; Commitment mechanisms; Focal points; Moral language; Possibilities frontier; Tipping; Trade-offs
Netherlands, 207

New England, 31
New Guinea, 164, 165, 180–81
New Haven (Connecticut), 67, 183
New Jersey, 212
New Mexico, 182
Newsweek, 182
New York City, 135
Ning Lao T'ai-t'ai, 140–41
Nita (battering example), 223–24
Nobel Prize in Economics, 6
Norway, 204
Nursing, 15, 70–71, 137, 138

Obesity, 20, 24
Occupational segregation, 11, 14–17
Odd Couple, The (Simon), Felix and Oscar in, 49–50, 95, 104, 111
Okin, Susan Moller, 217
Ontario (Canada), 17
On the Subjugation of Women (Mill), 153
On Women and Judaism (Greenberg), 160
Overtime, 23
Oxytocin, 176

Panel Study on Income Dynamics (PSID), 18–19, 240*n*6
Paoletti, Jo, 177
Part-time work, 210–12
Paternity leaves, 195, 204, 205
Pay equity. *See* Comparable worth
Penguins, 231–32
Pennsylvania, 229
Persuasion, 162
Phil (transitional, egalitarian marriage example), 100–114, 137, 208–9
Pilots, 15, 24, 215–16
"Pink collar ghetto," 11, 14–17
Pleistocene age, 10, 163, 166, 245*n*1
Polio, 25
Politics, 2, 12, 115; and negotiation, 30, 48; participation in, 10, 26
Polygamy, 64
Positions, vs. needs, 41